Es

Town & Country

Compiled by the Federation
of Essex Women's Institutes from notes
sent by Institutes in the County

with illustrations by Joan Bill

Published jointly by
Countryside Books, Newbury
and the FEWI, Chelmsford

First Published 1992
© Federation of Essex
Women's Institutes 1992

COUNTRYSIDE BOOKS
3 Catherine Road
Newbury, Berkshire

ISBN 1 85306 155 7

Front Cover Photograph of Thaxted
taken by Bill Meadows

Produced through MRM Associates Ltd., Reading
Typeset by Acorn Bookwork, Salisbury
Printed in England by J. W. Arrowsmith Ltd., Bristol

Acknowledgements

The Federation of Essex Women's Institutes would like to thank all Institutes whose members have worked so hard to provide material for this book. We are indebted to Joan Bill for her beautiful illustrations and finally, a special thank you to Jocelyn Need, the Co-ordinator for this project.

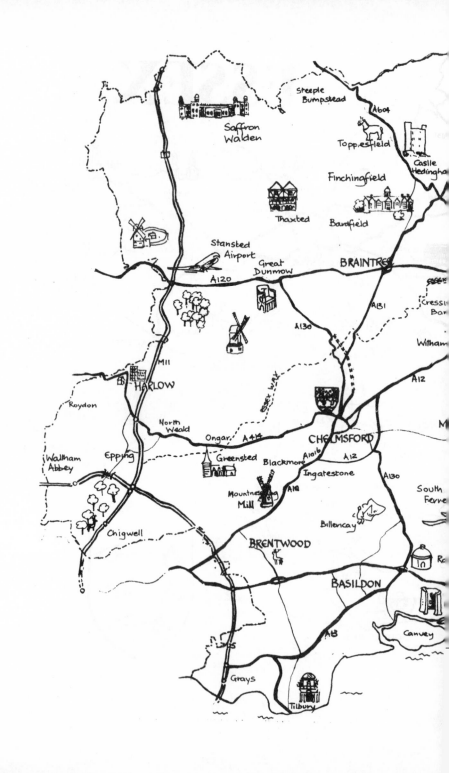

ESSEX

Dovercourt lighthouses

Abridge 🐝

Abridge is situated 20 miles from central London, between Epping and Romford, a small village before the Second World War which has spread and grown quite rapidly since.

Some think that a lot of progress has occurred, and undoubtedly it has. But in the days of the 1920s and 1930s at least we had a swimming pool! Situated on the marsh behind the White Hart, it was fed by wind pump from the river, fenced in by a close-boarded fence, and sported hutted changing rooms. It was accessible by a small bridge over the river, and was very popular with many folk in the surrounding area; it had a grand opening by the then Lord Lambourne and his lady.

The building now used for a village hall was erected towards the end of the First World War as a gymnasium, used for many years by the youth of the village, Scout groups etc. It was very well equipped and in later years it also had two full-sized billiard tables. This hall is still in constant use for functions, village groups and playgroups. There are plans for a new hall on a field in the Ongar Road. Many fundraising events and functions, and an annual Village Day, are held.

In the Market Place, where there is now a Volkswagen garage, there was a Whitbread Brewery store, and every day horse-drawn wagons took beer to Whitbread Brewery in Chiswell Street, London. The horses for this purpose were stabled adjacent to the Blue Boar, in a building which is still standing, and which was in fact used as an air raid shelter during the Second World War.

In the Market Place there was a drapery and general store, a baker's shop and bakehouse, with a daily delivery by horse and cart of bread and pastries. There was a sweet shop and tea rooms, a blacksmith and saddlery, and a butcher's shop. The post office was also called 'The Retreat', and served teas etc in the tea room at the rear, catering for many cyclists, cycle clubs and others. The shop next to the Maltsters, now used as a gun shop, sold fruit and vegetables.

St Mary's and All Saints' church, which is the parish church, is in a beautiful country setting. It dates back to 1100. The chapel of ease in the village was built in 1833. In the village Market Place there was a very old house, dating back probably to the time of Charles I, which was used as long as can be remembered as the local doctor's house and surgery. Sadly this house has now been demolished and new houses built on the site.

Roding House is a listed building and was once used as a private school, owned and run by two old Scottish ladies, the Misses Brown. The

7

house opposite named The Sycamores dates back to the mid 1500s, and was once a coffee shop. The school, now over 100 years old, has not altered a great deal. It has been extended and improved, but the main building still stands.

Lord and Lady Lambourne owned and lived at Bishops Hall. He owned most of the land for miles around, and certainly almost all the farms and several houses. Quite a few people from the village were employed on the estate as house staff, dairy maids, gardeners, gamekeepers and so on.

At the end of the Second World War, every village serviceman and woman was invited to a party held on the cricket ground in a large marquee. This was made possible by the formation of a 'Welcome Home Fund'; each was given a leather wallet or notecase and £7 in cash, a small fortune in those days! In 1953 on Coronation Day, there was a village party in the Market Square, with refreshments, dancing, a carnival and a musical procession to a bonfire and fireworks. A public television was set up in the gymnasium (village hall) and there was a service at the parish church. A programme of the event is available.

In earlier days the village had no kerbstones or marked pavements, and the road was just rolled gravel. There were cottages in Silver Street, and two cottages on what is now the Blue Boar car park. In London Road the bungalow now named Grenadine had tea rooms in the gardens, and was also used by cyclists and cycle clubs. Refreshments were served, and it was in fact named 'The Come Right Inn'.

Abridge remains a village, though few people are now employed within its borders, whereas in years gone by the village folk found employment in the shops and workshops, the brewery and stables, and at the local Squire's residence.

Aldham

The farmland of Aldham is criss-crossed with footpaths, and walking them is becoming an increasingly popular occupation. These paths were made for a more utilitarian purpose though, and are hundreds of years old. They led to and from neighbouring villages, to the church, to the school, to people's places of work. This is where Aldham's 18th century rector and historian Philip Morant wandered when visiting his parishioners.

Walk from Aldham to Chappel across the fields, past the gnarled old coppiced trees in Hoe wood and, as the land suddenly drops away, you find yourself looking across the wide and beautiful Colne valley. Scarcely a house in sight, but there, spanning the valley at Chappel, the six million bricks of the great viaduct, perhaps one of the most spectacular sights in Essex. In 1990 the Colne valley project was launched and it is hoped that people will come and enjoy the beauty the valley contains.

The path continues down to join the Essex Way, running through the water meadows beside the Colne, to emerge in Ford Street. Here are splendid timber-framed houses, including The Old House. Both the Queen's Head and the Cooper's Arms are ancient inns, timbered and dark inside. Earlier landlords were not just victuallers, but also coopers, wheelwrights, butchers and even an undertaker who put people further down than just under the table! In 1848 there were 20 artisans working in the street. Today only the blacksmith remains, working in the age old way, spending his days making exquisite wrought iron work, ornate creations for churches and public buildings, gates, staircases, weather-vanes and fences. But on Saturdays horses are brought to be shod; the metal heated until it is red hot on a calor gas forge. Proving the popularity of the horse, the discarded shoes have been carefully stacked over the years to form a pyramid over 20 ft high.

Leaving Ford Street and walking towards Colchester up the hill, you will come to the village green. Known as Gallows Green, Aldham was one of the few villages to have a gallows. They were probably taken down after 1868 when public hangings were abolished. Records in the old parchment register show that plague victims in Elizabeth I's reign were buried in an orchard nearby. The tiny weatherboarded cottage on the corner of the green was the tollgate keeper's home with the village pound beside it. A horse was tethered on the green and used, when necessary, to help to pull heavy loads up the hill. The village pond on the green has been cleared out and is now refilling with water.

When there was no transport, tradesmen travelled round the villages – 'The fish man came twice a week by donkey and cart, when he got to Aldham Hall you could hear him shouting "Yarmouth bloaters twelve for a shilling", you could rely on him. Little old Toby came with a basket on his head with pots and pans in it. Mr Creswell came from Bures with cottons and things like that and he had a bottle of sweets and we bought a halfpenny worth from him. Mr Smith came from Coggeshall with curtains, material and clothes, he brought whatever was ordered. Also the butcher, baker, coalman and oilman called and on Saturday the carrier passed through the village to Colchester and would take orders, delivering the goods that night.'

Today everyone has transport, and unless they are self employed people leave the village to work in Colchester or to commute to London. The school closed 30 years ago so even the children leave the village every morning to go to school in neighbouring villages or the town. Aldham is still an agricultural area although not an agricultural community; farming is mainly arable with one dairy farm and two fruit farms.

People talk about 'moving house' but in Aldham 80 years ago this really happened. A house was hoisted up onto rollers and dragged across the fields and through the lanes, getting stuck under the old oak tree at the crossroads. Men hung on ropes to keep the house upright while branches were cut from the tree, leaving it with a lopsided appearance. It has become a favourite meeting place for all the youngsters in the village. On high days and holidays the wide space made by the meeting of the four roads makes an ideal place for the Aldham Morris Men and the Bows and Bells clog dancers to give their cheerful and colourful displays.

Looking to the future, in 1990 a landowner planted a new wood of 2,500 native hardwood trees – oak, ash, chestnut, maple and small leaved limes. Many fine trees have been lost in the last few years from Dutch elm disease and the 1987 hurricane, so a new wood for posterity is a wonderful innovation.

Alresford 🌿

Alresford lies approximately six miles to the east of Colchester and has a population of around 2,300. The first reliable written information about the village is to be found in the Domesday Book, when there were 18 households and the manor. However, its history goes back to Roman times; Roman villas can be found marked on the OS map and it is suggested the Emperor Claudius sailed down the river Colne from Colchester into Alresford creek to visit one of the villas.

The creek, which is just over a mile from the village, used to be a busy thoroughfare for sailing barges going up to Thorrington Mill. Slates and lime were brought to Alresford and straw was shipped out to London. In more recent times sand and ballast were transported by motorised barges from quarries still to be seen along the creek. This form of transport no longer exists and the only signs of this trade remaining are the derelict quay and three gantries which supported overhead buckets employed to fill the barges. The ford which provided a shortcut to Brightlingsea is still in existence, but is not to be recommended as it is now rather muddy.

Today, the creek is a popular spot for sailing, bird-watching and picnicking. It is a pleasant walk along the riverside to the head of the creek at Thorrington Mill or in the other direction to the mouth of the creek. Here can be seen remains of saltpans from which the Romans obtained salt through evaporating sea water. The waterside footpath continues along the remains of the old railway track through to Wivenhoe, about three miles distant.

The railway arrived at Alresford in 1866. This was a single track linking Colchester and Walton. The station building on the up-track dates from this time. A branch line went from Wivenhoe to Brightlingsea via a swing bridge across Alresford creek. This bridge was demolished as a result of the closure of the branch line in the 1960s during the era of railway rationalisation.

In Alresford there are two churches. The elder, dating from 1320, is, alas, now just a shell, having been mysteriously destroyed by fire in 1971. The new church, dedicated in 1976, is a pleasant multi-purpose building sited half a mile nearer the main part of the village. The ruins of the old church can be visited and plaques are in place to assist visitors to note items of interest, including the nave and chancel from the early Norman or Anglo Saxon period.

In the floor of the old church is a stone slab marking the tomb of one of Alresford's most notable worthies, one Matthew Martin, who was a sea captain with the East India Company and rose to be Whig MP for Colchester in 1722 and Mayor of Colchester in 1726. He lived at Alresford Hall and died in 1730.

At the time of Domesday, Alresford possessed primarily rough grazing land. By the 18th and 19th centuries it had become mostly an area of arable farming; by this time there were eleven farms. Most of the farmhouses can still be found in the village, now as private homes and often surrounded by post Second World War houses. The building boom started in Alresford in the mid 1950s and has continued until quite recently.

At the junction of Ford Lane and Wivenhoe Road is a very fine horse chestnut tree which is a delight to view when the pink blossom is in flower. This was planted in 1897 on the Diamond Jubilee of the reign of Queen Victoria. The occasion was remembered by one of Alresford's older residents, Mr Knopp, when children planted trees on the village playing field to mark the Silver Jubilee of the reign of Queen Elizabeth II in 1977.

Much of the old village atmosphere has now gone from Alresford but this is inevitable in our modern world. Many people commute to Colchester, Chelmsford and London rather than work locally. Nevertheless there is still a community which enthusiastically supports organisations like the WI, and a small area of shops with a private butcher, small supermarket, greengrocer, post office and baker's shop. In addition there is a small corner shop 'open all hours'. Character remains in Alresford for those willing to seek it!

Althorne 🐚

The typically long village of Althorne lies between the banks of Bridgemarsh creek and the river Crouch to the south and Green Lane, a pleasant straight road, to the north. The parish is bordered east and west by Mayland and Latchingdon. It is on the B1010 from Maldon and about four miles north-west of Burnham-on-Crouch.

Bridgemarsh Island with its low red brick farmhouse was flooded irrecoverably in the high spring tides of 1928 and the extent of the once rich acres can now be seen only at low tide. Tides run very strongly in the narrow creek, a danger to the unwary. A brass tablet on the north wall of the church recalls the two Teasdale brothers and Leslie Macdonald, all between 15 and 18 years of age, who drowned in these treacherous currents on Easter Monday, April 1919.

A private road owned by British Rail leads to the junction with Fambridge Road and Althorne war memorial. The memorial, standing in neat lychgate style on a well kept mound of grass, was paid for by public subscription and erected on land given by the LNE Railway Company.

There are still eight or nine working farms, mostly arable but with some cattle, sheep, pigs, poultry, horses, and a small game farm. The Crouch valley is designated an area of outstanding natural beauty and three of the farms share the panoramic views. They are Stokes Hall, Andrew's Farm and Althorne Hall Farm. The last named has been in the hands of branches of the same family for over 100 years. Barns Farm with wide views over the rivers Blackwater and Crouch, is a pleasant four-square farmhouse. The Mansion House was extended and modernised and is now a residential home for elderly people. Summerhill Farmhouse, so well placed on the hill and with its lovely long south window, was demolished in 1970 to make way for the development of Highfield Rise and Austral Way.

The ancient parish church of St Andrew stands high on the ridge, looking over to the massive tower of St Nicholas, Canewdon. A church was endowed in Althorne in the 13th century and though much restored, a building in something like the present form has stood here since the late 1400s.

'Ford's of Althorne's is the sign on the red and cream luxury coaches carrying touring parties in this country and abroad, local works buses, school buses and the regular town and country bus service. The family firm was established on the site now known as Ford's Corner in the early 1920s.

It is very clear in this home owning community that most houses built before about 1970 have been 'improved' in some way and usually enlarged. There are a few easily recognised exceptions. The Essex-style houses designed by Peter Cooper ARIBA, who lived in Althorne for about 30 years from 1935, often have part mansard roofs and seem intended to defy alteration. The two weatherboarded late Victorian houses with low verandahs, built for Gilder Drake on Summerhill and Fambridge Road are still remarkably unchanged. The same Henry Gilder Drake endowed eight attractive one-storey cottages on Summerhill in 1930 for older folk from the parishes of Althorne, Mayland, Latchingdon and Southminster. The row of listed Dutch-style cottages adjoin the Black Lion in a pleasant group; the Old Forge is nicely restored and all the cottages from the late 1700s appear to be in good order. Many similar cottages have of course been demolished over the years.

The population of Althorne has more than doubled in 20 years. Houses of all shapes, ages and sizes line Burnham Road and Summerhill, with slightly less growth so far along Fambridge Road – just as well considering the frantic rush hour traffic to South Woodham, Basildon, Wickford and beyond. Plans in the late 1950s showed that main drainage pipes would be in place by 1971. River View Park for mobile homes developed rapidly in the 1960s and probably now houses 140 to 150 people on the well kept site. Summerhill Farm was sold for housing and a popular estate grew up in the 1970s with street lighting, smooth pavements and neat green verges. The Parish Council took the opportunity to buy seven acres of surplus land adjoining the estate, providing a football pitch, a small pavilion, children's play space, dog walking area and car park – all in the middle of the village. An annual Fun Day has been held here since August Bank Holiday 1981 and the popular Flower Show reestablished, to raise funds. Another estate of semi-detached and terraced houses was built opposite the Black Lion in the 1970s. Good public footpaths in Althorne are not greatly used but conscientious Parish Council members and others keep an eye on them.

Water pressure, or a lack of it, is a regular complaint today. In earlier days a burst water main was a common occurrence. The water would run very slowly, receptacles would be filled just in case, and soon the water was 'off'. An elderly Water Board employee from Latchingdon cycled round reporting any problems in his district. An enquiry would produce the response, 'The mains busted and there ain't no water nowhere'. In due course, a trickle of thick sandy water appeared and soon we were back to normal. Things certainly have improved.

Very busy roads, housing development, Dutch elm disease and the loss of so many trees in recent gales have of course changed the character of the area but the village has always been changing. You will not see otters and oyster beds in the creek, toads do not creep in Garden Close and the patches of purple cuckoo orchids have long since disappeared. But the lark still sings and Althorne really is a very nice place to live.

Ashdon ✎

Most guide books to a village or town begin with buildings of some sort – the churches, the shops, the houses, the schools etc, but when you look at a fairly large scale map you realise that it was the land itself that formed the plan of any man-made settlement. The earliest settlers needed the basic necessities – shelter, and above all, water supply. Thus the growth of Ashdon as a village in a valley, with many springs feeding small, almost ditch-like tributaries, flowing into the small river Bourne, which in its turn joins the river Cam. Growing bigger, the Cam flows into the Ouse and eventually out to sea in the Wash. With rolling low hills enclosing the whole scattered village, an area of roughly 16 square miles, a very open type of village was produced. A look at the map shows this growth clearly by the place-names of 'Ends' – Church End, Bartlow End, Rogers End etc.

With the distances between habitations it would need many walks to explore Ashdon and by car one can only glimpse the structure of the village, but there are two elements that are constant and yet have been of interest in the historical scene of Ashdon. The wind and the water. These two have been, and still are, sources of energy for the use of man. Ashdon has only low hills and a very small river, so in today's picture they seem of no practical value. This was not always so and maybe, who knows, both may in the future prove very useful again.

From the top of a hill in Ashdon can be seen a large proportion of the village. This site was evidently the major part of the community in Saxon times because here stands the church, visible from many unexpected places in the village. Yet a Roman villa stood on a much smaller rise of land, Copt Hill, between Newnham Hall and Bartlow and a Stone Age scraper was found in a garden bordering a very old sunken tributary of the Bourne; so where was 'Ashdon' then?

From the top of Church Hill the shape of the valley through which the Bourne flows can be seen and it is not difficult to imagine this as well wooded, so that in very early times, pre-Saxon, small clearings at 'Ends' were made for settlements or cultivation, always with water supply available. Then through all the hundreds of years of living, the Normans, the Middle Ages, the Civil War period, we come to the 18th century. 'The country is very open, the houses few and the roads both bad and intricate, there being scarce a direction post to be seen, or a track to be depended on; the commons over which you pass to it being more worn by the neighbouring inhabitants in passing from their grounds to their respective farmhouses than by travellers in their passage from parish to parish.' (Extract from *A New and Complete History of Essex* by 'A Gentleman' 1770).

Before you leave the church area look toward the last group of houses on the Saffron Walden road – here was a beerhouse, 'The Lamb', a welcome to Ashdon for travellers from the south. Then look west towards Ashdon Hall Farm, then south-east toward Goldstones Farm, and finally north-east toward the windmill on the horizon at Stevington End. All these four sites are roughly on the 300 ft contour line and all have been sites of windmills. The centre of the village is about 200 ft above sea level, dropping to 180 ft toward Bartlow, so the windmills would be in suitable places on the highest ground and the best trackways probably led to the mills. Home-grown corn, home-milled flour for home baking and cattle-feed; who needed 'passage from parish to parish'?

Footpaths lead from the church to Water End, to the river Bourne, and from here one of the oldest 'roads' in the village, Rock Lane, follows the course of the river back to the main area of the present village at the bottom of Church Hill. This lane passes the site of another source of energy in the past – a water mill. Nothing remains but the cottage, now greatly enlarged.

Footpaths can take you to the one remaining windmill – an obvious landmark, or it can be reached by car on clearly marked roads. From here the traveller can look back across the valley and see again the land shape that made the growth of the village of Ashdon.

Asheldham 🌿

Asheldham is situated between Southminster and Tillingham on the B1021 and can be approached via Latchingdon, Mayland to Asheldham.

It is a hamlet full of interest, with a nature reserve made out of a water-filled gravel pit, which can be reached off the B1021 on the left hand side of a row of wooden and brick houses, the best entrance being past the official entrance and over a stile which leads to a well-planned walk through a small wood, by the side of the lake.

Carrying on past the row of houses on the B1021, turn right on the road to the Dengie and Amenity site and you come to the Dengie crop driers. Their chimney emitting white smoke is a landmark for miles around. Past the crop drier on the left is Asheldham church, which has now been converted into the Asheldham youth centre, used by young people from all over the British Isles and abroad.

Carry on due east and you come to Dengie with its manor on the left and just around the corner, the church of St James made of stonework. The road will take you on to Keelings and Landwycke Farm and around the marshes to Tillingham, but access to the sea wall is not possible.

Barling & Little Wakering 🌿

Barling and Little Wakering are adjoining villages on the edge of the Essex creeks and marshes east of Southend. On the surface they may appear to a visitor as rather desolate, and sand and gravel pit workings being used as a landfill do not add to the attractions, but under the surface is much history, and walking by the creeks you can find birds, beauty and peace.

The creek from Barling runs into the river Roach, which in turn runs into the Crouch, this running into the North Sea. Following the creek eastwards it enters the Thames estuary.

In the 5th and 6th centuries the Anglo-Saxons pushed up the river valleys and founded villages where there was well drained land for wheat, rye and barley, water meadows for cattle, good water and woodlands for fuel and pigs. Some say the name Barling is Saxon for 'boar in the field' and as there have been traces of Iron Age and Bronze Age habitation, it has long been lived in.

Records in Elizabethan times show Barling as having a large fishing fleet and in the 19th century Thames barges were plentiful in the creeks, carrying hay and bricks up to London and rubbish back and building up the sea walls with it.

All Saints', Barling stands where it has solidly stood for centuries, with its medieval tower and shingle spire being a landmark in the flat surrounding countryside and no doubt to the boats coming home. At the time of the Domesday Book, Barling was held in lordship by the Bishop of Bayeux who was Odo, the half brother of William the Conqueror. The Domesday Book also mentions that St Paul's 'has always held Barling'. Edward the Confessor (1042–1066) owned the church and gave it to St Paul's and a copy of Edward's charter hangs in the church. The building is Kentish ragstone, which would have been floated across the Thames, and some of it is possibly 12th century. There are traces of flints and Roman tiles and it may have been rebuilt or extended in the 15th century. The font is 15th century and the 17th century Jacobean sounding board is quite rare in Essex. On the north wall, where the Devil's door is blocked up and can only be seen from outside, is a copy of a Stuart coat of arms taken from Ropers, an old house which was demolished.

Also in the church is an excellent model of the windmill made by Henry Manning, the last miller around the turn of the century. Barling windmill, a smock mill, was built in 1760 and ceased working in 1903 when it became unsafe. It was demolished early in the Second World War. The first reference to a mill was dated 1181.

Near the church, Scarfe Cottage is an interesting old house, recently renovated, with dates of 1480 and 1627; this was formerly an alehouse. Down an unmade road to the side of the church, standing close to the river, is Barling Hall which was rebuilt in 1822 after the earlier house was burnt down.

After Mill House, Church Road becomes Mucking Hall Road and further along stands Bannister House with its tales of tunnels and smugglers. Records of 1792–95 show F. B. Bannister paying the Hair Powder Tax. Further along still stands a typical Essex clapboard farmhouse, Bolts, with its beautiful garden, and round the corner across a field is Mucking Hall with signs of the moat which once surrounded it. Where Mucking Hall joins Barling Road is an ordinary field with an extraordinary past. Known as Gallows Field, this is reputedly where men were hanged as Barling held the right of 'furca and fossa' – to hang the men and dip the witches.

Blewhouse, overlooking the field, is a clapboard cottage. It and its adjoining house were once one, and are thought to be the oldest houses in

Barling since a stone house near Jail Farm Cottage was knocked down. Near here was the Bishop's prison. Mrs Watson's father was the last village constable and she remembers him taking men there handcuffed. More recently the prisoners from Chelmsford gaol were taken nearby to work the land where Ropers and Trumpions once stood backing on to the river.

Barling House in Barling Road was built in the early 18th century. Next door is Glebe Farm, which was the old Barling vicarage and where traces of ecclesiastical footings were found in the 1980s when building work was done.

Barling post office is now in Little Wakering and the Castle Inn has long been there. The exact date of the building of St Mary's church is not known but there is proof it was in being before 1150. On the vicars' name board in the church is recorded that of Rev Downing, an 18th century vicar and friend of Captain Cook, the circumnavigator and explorer. He officiated at the marriage ceremony of Captain Cook to Elizabeth Batts of Shadwell, which was near the village of Mile End, at St Margaret's, Barking in 1762.

Barling and Little Wakering are linked now but it was not always so. Nearly 60 years ago the vicarage at Barling was sold and St Mary's vicarage became home for the vicar of the united benefice. One hundred and fifty years ago the residents of Barling were alarmed by a light in the night. The vicar, a herbalist, was discovered sowing herbs by the light of a lantern!

Barnston ❧

The village of Barnston is situated in rural mid-Essex on the A130 road, two miles south of the small Roman town of Great Dunmow.

It is surrounded by intensively farmed arable land within attractive countryside which includes, on the boundary, Garnetts Wood, home of a small herd of fallow deer and preserved as a woodland walk and picnic area.

One of the most attractive parts of the village, especially in springtime, is Parsonage Lane where the parish church and other old houses are situated. The small church is thought to have originated from Saxon times with a timber building, rebuilt with flint walls, plastered inside and out, by the Normans, at which time the beautiful moulded main doorway was added. Two of the original Norman windows can be seen in the northern wall of the nave, although one has at some time been blocked. The most interesting survival from this early period is the rare double piscina situated in the south wall of the chancel. The church has recently been renovated and the roof retiled, and it is surrounded by a well kept graveyard.

Situated near to the church on the west side is Barnston Hall, a large house probably built in about 1540 on the site of an earlier building. The house is still in good repair and other adjacent buildings include pictures-que stables and a dovecote, as well as a large farm barn. Barnston Hall was the home of Mr H. B. Turner JP who from the late 19th century until 1945 farmed most of the land in Barnston and employed many of its residents. He was much involved in village affairs, a keen hunting and shooting man and the Hall was often the meeting place for these events. His gardener/groom planted a mass of daffodils in the green expanse in front of the house to read 'God is Love' and this can still be seen in springtime today.

Other houses in Parsonage Lane include Barnston Lodge, built in the late 18th century, and the Old Rectory dating from the 17th century. At Barnston brook by the road bridge at the junction of Parsonage Lane with the A130 Roman road, the banks of the stream have been attrac-tively planted with flowers and shrubs by the tenant of one of the nearby cottages. He was born locally and spent all his working life at Barnston Hall.

Nearby stands the village church school, closed in 1959 and converted into an attractive house by a local architect. Next to this is Brook House, a 16th century house originally a farmhouse. Close by an old bridlepath crosses the A130 to follow the brook to its junction with the river Chelmer on the northern boundary of the village. Southwards this path passes by an area near to the road which was originally allotments for the local people. It then continues through to the High Easter road where stands Albans, another original house thought to date from the 15th century. In earlier times this was a favourite place for the Hunt to meet and a special 'Hounds' room was built which can still be seen. The pathway is thought to have been used by monks and other travellers on their way from London to the priory at Little Dunmow.

Barnston includes within its boundaries an area known as Hounslow Green, where there are several attractive old houses and farms. It was here, on the site of the Taverners, that until its closure in the early 1970s stood the only public house in Barnston, known as the Onslow Tavern and owned by the local brewery.

The village shop, also an off licence, is a relatively new building which replaced a much older thatched cottage that burned down in the 1950s. Whilst the new premises were being built the business was carried on in a farm building nearby.

Prior to the early 1950s Barnston was quite small with about 150 inhabitants recorded in 1914, mostly employed in local agriculture. Since that time two housing estates have been built and the population has grown to nearly 1,000. With easy access to London, but still in a country district, Barnston has become an attractive place for commuters.

Although a small village, Barnston has always had an active community life and in addition to the parish church there is a mission Evangelical church which was started in 1901 by a few local residents in buildings owned by one of the farmers. This was subsequently purchased and modernised and is still in regular use for worship and service.

With the support of a local farmer, Mr John Salmon, who also provided the land, villagers worked hard to raise the necessary funds and to build their own village hall, which is now in constant use. Barnston now also has a small industrial site developed from the factory originally built by Mr Salmon to manufacture mechanical sugar beet harvesters, which he invented.

Basildon 🍂

Neolithic man (Stone Age) knew Basildon, leaving a stone hammer to be discovered at the bottom of a new road built in 1951. He dwelt on the marshes in Vange, which is part of the New Town. While building the first new school, gold coins were excavated dating from 750 BC, telling us that the Bronze Age people were also familiar with the area. Then came the Romans, followed by the Saxons who gave Basildon its name, 'Beorhtel's Hill' (Basil's people on the hill), and on the very same hill stands the 500 year old Holy Cross church. The first recording of a church on this site was in 1230. Today this old church is being lovingly restored to its former glory by the church members and the people of Basildon, who have responded well to the appeal for funds.

Holy Cross has its own ghost, so the early pioneers of the New Town would have us believe. Cleaners returning from Ford's new tractor plant, taking a short cut past the church in the early hours of the morning, claim to have seen a red hooded monk crossing the churchyard.

Situated in south-east Essex, earlier this century Basildon, together with the surrounding areas, was in a depressed state, its inhabitants spread widely over the land and many living in squalid conditions. During the 1930s it was designated a likely New Town, but due to the outbreak of the Second World War the plans were shelved. In 1949 these got under way again and a New Town was born.

As the town expanded there appeared to be no pattern to the buildings. They seemed to spring up in different areas with no apparent link up. Many of the old houses and bungalows together with the country lanes still remained, cornfields still produced their food in the summer sun. Children from London showing war fatigue ran freely, climbing fruit trees in forsaken smallholdings, scrumping to their hearts' delight. Too soon they were gathered into adventure playgrounds, football pitches and artificial lakes. The excitement of a muddy lane, a pond tucked round the corner, was taken from them by the bulldozer together with the wild life.

Vange, Pitsea, Laindon, Nevendon, Wickford, Billericay, together with Great and Little Burstead, soon came under the wing of Basildon Council. Pitsea has never lost its identity however much the New Town intruded with its swimming pool and leisure centre. A bustling little town, it has a colourful market each Wednesday and Saturday drawing in people from Southend and surrounding districts. Old St Michael's church stands forlornly on its mount overlooking the lovely Pitsea marshes. Thirty years ago this was a noble church indeed, standing proudly on the green hill overlooking this little market town. The march of time has taken its toll. The mount is now peppered with little private houses and the residents having no time for St Michael's watch it fade into ruins. But travel up the old A13 and you will find St Gabriel's, a new and thriving centre of worship, so all may not yet be lost.

Cross the railway lines towards the marshes and to your right find Pitsea Hall which dates from the 17th century. In the moat which has now been drained, a Cromwellian helmet was discovered. Travel on past the council tip and arrive at the treasure house of Basildon, the Wat Tyler Park, with its museum, craft shops, boating marina and a host of bird hides close to the mud flats and tidal river. So much to see and so much to do. Feast your eyes on the re-sited ancient barns and houses lovingly transferred and rebuilt in the open air museum, truly a photographer's delight. Vange – well this never was in the same class as Pitsea and soon lost its individuality to the giant Basildon, but it still has wonderful views over the little modern red houses across the marshes to the shores of Kent. This alone makes Vange worth a visit.

About 40 years ago a horse called Daisy used to pull the baker's van that delivered bread to the first residents of this brave New Town. What a thrill for the tiny toddlers, children of the cities, to feed her apples and biscuits. Jim the baker and Daisy the horse never failed to bring bread and delicious cakes to our bright new front doors. One Christmas Eve we had almost given him up as he hadn't arrived by 9pm, but sure enough he did deliver. His speech and gait were unsteady due to the kindness of his customers, but fortunately for Jim, Daisy knew her way home.

Dunton, which is safely in the Basildon grasp, was once the Eastenders' dream of owning their own home in the country air. When the railway opened up this corner of Essex parcels of land went up for sale, for as little as £5 per plot, and these folk hungry for space to breathe soon built their little boxes. There was no drainage or permanent lighting but still they travelled down at weekends, using them for retreats. Some became permanent dwellings, and when the local council could no longer deal with the influx the Government was persuaded to designate the area as a New Town. One house called 'The Haven' has been preserved complete with furniture and fittings of that era. Situated in the open fields known as Plotlands it is an ideal place to visit with its wide open spaces, walks through the woods and plenty of picnic spots.

Dunton sits at the foot of the beautiful Langdon Hills, now a Country Park with woods, ponds, coppices and nature trails. All manner of wild life can be seen there complete with magnificent views across the river to Kent. It is said that Essex is flat – not if you stay awhile to walk our country lanes close by!

If your liking is for old churches, a dear little one sits on top of a hill in Laindon. Called St Nicholas', it is a true landmark from the A127. One of its features is a 17th century school house adjoining the church where some of the poor children from the village were taught to read and write free of charge.

Basildon may not suit everyone's taste, but when you visit, pay a call to the Basildon Centre in the heart of the town, and spare a few minutes to visit St Martin's church, a gracious modern centre of worship. Since St Martin's was built in 1960 it has become a symbol 'to the Glory of God'. Stop to gaze at the uplifted sculpture of *The Basildon Christ* by T. Huxley-Jones on the porch roof. Take a walk round the precincts and see the sculptures and memorials which now are appearing, then look up and admire the magnificent stained glass windows recently completed by the artist Joseph Nuttgens. In 1984 a heartrending yet great exhibition was held in the church about the Auschwitz concentration camp. Over

17,000 people visited this in 15 days, and many lit candles. Behind the altar where a red candle perpetually burns, rests a small urn of ashes from the crematoria there.

You may understand now what lies beneath the heart of Basildon New Town. It's a good place to be born and a grand place to live.

Berden 🐚

Three miles north of Manuden is Berden, with its small, pebble and flint cruciform church dedicated to a favourite Norman saint, St Nicholas, in 1200. However, the village is much older as the Roman tiles embedded in the exterior church wall prove. These were reclaimed from a Roman villa in Dewes Green. The church tower with its four bells is 15th century, other parts being 13th and 14th century.

Berden Priory was founded in 1200 by the Rochford family and dedicated to St John the Evangelist. Of the St Augustine order, it survived until 1536 when it was dissolved. It remains as a private house. Another important village house, Berden Hall, built about 1580 on an older site, is a lovely red brick building retaining many original features. For many years it has been used for an important annual event – the village fete, which was previously held at 'The Crump' in the adjoining hamlet of Little London. There used to be two pubs, now both closed; the Raven in The Street, which boasted 300 years continuous service and sported a skittle alley, and the King's Head (now a private house) on the Dewes Green Road.

In 1901 Rev H. K. Hudson, Berden's vicar, revived the ceremony of the Boy Bishop to celebrate St Nicholas's Day on 6th December. The play performed is based on the life of the saint with the central character being taken by a child dressed in bishop's clothing. This child then holds the office of 'Bishop' for a year. The practice ended in 1937 with the departure of Rev Hudson from the village, but the staff and cross used in the ceremony are preserved in the church.

As final proof of the antiquity of this area, in 1907 workmen digging footings for the village hall, on the site of the old Wesleyan chapel, unearthed a human skeleton, armlet and beaker which archaeologists believe to have been placed in a Bronze Age burial mound. The remains of these bones and the beaker can be seen in the local museum, tangible proof that man was here 4,000 years ago.

Bicknacre 🐝

Bicknacre is situated some seven miles east of Chelmsford and five miles west of Maldon, in the parish of Woodham Ferrers. The name is derived from Bicca, a Saxon chief, and acre, a Saxon word for a clearing in a wood. As far as anyone knows, Bicknacre is the only place in the world with this name. There is no record of it in the USA or Australia or elsewhere in Great Britain. Often early settlers to the New World took the names of their villages with them but not so Bicknacre, so perhaps it is unique. (Bicknacre Grange near Mayland once belonged to Bicknacre Priory Manor).

Walking around a small village it is often possible to gain a sense of the history of the place by noting the road names: Priory Road, Priory Lane, Monks Mead, Augustine Way, Canons Close can surely only mean one thing – a very strong connection with a religious house. And there behind the hedge at Priory Farm is the one remaining tower arch of an Augustinian priory founded around 1156.

Overshot Hill on the boundary between Bicknacre and Danbury was the site of a water mill (possibly the one mentioned in the Domesday Book for Woodham Ferrers). It was an overshot mill, in other words the water drove the wheel from the top with the weight of the water pushing the wheel around. The mill has long since gone but the name remains.

White Elm Road leading to White Elm Corner is a more modern name which became popular with the story of a notorious highwayman being executed and buried at the crossroads with an elm stake through his body.

Mill Lane has an obvious meaning, being the lane leading on to Bicknacre Common or Hooe, on which stood a windmill. It is believed it was a postmill and can be traced back to at least 1686 using documents as points of reference. The last mill was destroyed by fire in 1911 after a decline in popularity for this type of small working mill.

The Old Salt Road runs behind Thriftwood (an ancient woodland) and was part of the route for the salt on its way from Saltcoats on Woodham Ferrers marshes (now South Woodham Ferrers) to markets around the country.

Some road names feature local farms; Barbrook Way, Leighams Road, Moor Hall Lane. One, Peartree Lane, features Peartree Farm and a huge old pear tree of indeterminate age.

Billericay 🖋️

The history of Billericay can be traced back to Roman times when the early settlement was known as Villerica. One of the town's famous landmarks is Norsey Woods where excavations have uncovered signs of Roman occupation. Here also, during the Peasants Revolt of 1381 the battle of Billericay was fought and 500 local inhabitants killed.

A further claim to fame is Billericay's association with the *Mayflower*. In 1620 four local Puritans set sail to America to escape religious persecution and later colonists founded the American town of Billerica in Massachussetts. The *Mayflower* is depicted on the town sign located near Mountnessing Road off London Road; one of the town's secondary schools in Stock Road also bears the name.

During the 17th century Billericay was a sleepy little village which only came to life on market days when it became the focal point for the farmers and traders of the locality. Traces of this period can be found in the old coaching inns situated in the present High Street – the Red Lion, the White Hart and the Chequers, also the Coach and Horses in Chapel Street. An important landmark of the same period was the mill standing on Bell Hill, famous for the 'Ghastly Miller', one Thomas Wood, an enormous figure weighing 60 stones who successfully initiated his own slimming diet!

The coming of the railway in 1889 brought the beginning of a change to the character of Billericay, with housing and industrial development gradually replacing the green fields and the buildings of charm. However, some of these buildings have survived to the present day. One amongst them is the Old Workhouse, now part of St Andrew's Hospital which has been much modernised and improved and houses the magnificent Burns Unit, built with funds raised by many local organisations, and opened by the Duchess of Kent in 1982.

On display in the Cater Museum situated in the High Street are many items of historical interest including prehistoric, Roman and medieval relics, and photographs and souvenirs of local trades and industries. Other old buildings which remain include The Chantry, once an ancient meeting house, and the present bakery 'Alexander's', a building of mid 16th century origin first used by Billericay Nonconformists as their meeting place. The parish church which stands at the junction of the High Street and Chapel Street is of 18th century origin, built on the site of the first chantry chapel which dated from 1342. The original 14th century bell has remained in place, except in 1890 when it was recast and rehung at a cost of £36-17-0d. The Congregational church in Chapel Street was built to replace the old meeting house which was found to be unsuitable, as the average Sunday attendance at that time was over 400. The Catholic church in Laindon Road was completed in 1926, built on ground probably used in the 19th century as the town cricket field.

Billericay today thrives and flourishes as a modern commuter town, but in spite of the inevitable changes wrought by 'the march of time', for residents and visitors alike it still retains much of its old world charm.

Blackmore 🐚

Blackmore is a very old parish steeped in history, principally because of its priory of Augustinian canons and its association with Henry VIII. It is generally accepted that its name derives from the original dark soil which has now largely disappeared, though the swampy nature of its soil is evident after heavy rain.

There were three manors in the parish, namely Blackmore, Fingreth and Copsheaves though only Fingreth was mentioned in the Domesday survey.

During the 12th century an Augustinian priory was founded by the de Sanford family and dedicated to St Laurence, who is reputed to have been martyred in Rome by being roasted on a gridiron. A detailed and interesting history of this priory exists, showing that it was dissolved in 1525 by John Alen, an agent of Cardinal Wolsey, and passed into the hands of Henry VIII in 1532. Later it was granted to John Smyth and his heirs and finally demolished in 1844.

In the spring of 1349 the terrible epidemic known as the Black Death gripped England. It is supposed that 300 out of a population of 450 died. It was probably at this time that the plague roads, Service Lane and Red Rose Lane, came into being as a means of bypassing the village. Rumour has it that Nine Ashes was so named after the cremation there of those who died of the plague.

Perhaps Blackmore's greatest claim to fame is its association with Henry VIII who was presumed to have 'Gone to Jericho' when in fact he was visiting his mistress Elizabeth Blount at the priory, where she gave birth to a son, Henry Fitzroy in 1519. Henry Fitzroy was Henry's pride and joy and he was created Earl of Nottingham at the age of six and later

Blackmore Church

Duke of Richmond and Somerset and elected Knight of the Garter. Sadly he died at the age of 17 and was buried in Norfolk.

Blackmore's church, the priory church of St Laurence has been largely unaltered for the past 400 years. The two paved aisles are of different periods; the north aisle is of the early 14th century, although it was taken down between 1895 and 1907 and re-erected with the identical material, and the south is 16th century. The timber tower, erected in 1475, is a masterpiece of joinery and has been described as the most impressive of its type in England. It contains a carillon of five bells, three of which were cast by Miles Gray, famous for his tenor bells. Many of the original church features remain, notably the tomb of Thomas Smyth who died in 1594, the cresset stone (a primitive form of oil lamp), and the mutilated effigy of a villein dating from about 1450.

Until the 20th century the population of Blackmore had remained static at about 600. It was a rural community, its inhabitants mainly concerned with the cultivation of cereal crops. Hay was sent twice weekly to London's Haymarket and charcoal burning was carried out in High Woods until 1900.

Modern development has included the building of three estates but now all expansion has stopped and the centre of the village has been made a conservation area. Blackmore today is an extremely pleasant village boasting three village greens, a modern primary school, a large village hall and a sports and social club. It is also proud of its many flourishing societies.

Bowers Gifford ❧

The parish of North Benfleet adjoins the parish of Bowers Gifford. There have always been close and friendly associations between these two parishes and during the last few years the churches have been joined by Royal Assent, so that the title is now 'Bowers Gifford with North Benfleet'.

In the reign of Edward II, 1307–1327, the population of Bowers Gifford lived down on the marshlands and worked for the owners of the farms, of which there were seven in all. They were occupied with the keeping of sheep, which in those days numbered about 18,000 and with the making of cheese from the sheep's milk for which there was a good demand. The cheese was strong in flavour and had good keeping qualities, and so was used to help stock ships with food when setting out on voyages.

The dwellings were of daub and wattle and thatched with reeds, which grew in plenty and were another source of income, for all the dwelling places needed to be thatched and many workers were employed to cut the reeds.

The largest farm was Earl's Fee. It was situated towards the Benfleet creek on the marshland. The creek was deep, for from Morant's History we read that 'vessels of good burthen may come up'. Sir John Gifford held the farm and in addition rented 500 acres from Sir John de Vere, the seventh Earl of Oxford, for which he had to pay sixpence per year and also to provide 'Silver Spurs for a Knight's Horse'.

Another large farm was Jarvis Hall, which was situated on the Benfleet side of the creek. This farm was held by Sir Roger de Mortimer who also had the custody of Hadleigh castle, which had been built in 1230. King Edward II was married to Isabella of France and the King and his Queen were quarrelling bitterly over the French connections. Sir John took sides with the Queen but Sir Roger was a great favourite of the King. Sir Roger with some 50 of his men raided Sir John's farm. On two of Sir John's own horses he mounted two of his most villainous men with orders to plunder the farm and kill Sir John. Fortunately, Sir John was not in residence at the time but on returning home and seeing the damage caused by the raid, Sir John appealed to the King for redress. The appeal was disregarded and came to naught, Sir Roger being in such high favour with the King.

Sir John Gifford, who gave his name to the parish, was in France with Edward III's army and fought at the great and victorious battle of Crecy in 1346. His brass, in his coat of armour, is still preserved in the church of St Margaret.

Boxted 🐿️

Boxted is a sprawling parish situated on the Essex/Suffolk border in Dedham Vale, to the north of Colchester. The village today consists of three hamlets, Church Street, Workhouse Hill and The Cross, the latter being much the larger both in area and population.

The parish church of St Peter, which stands on the ridge to the south of the river Stour, was started just prior to the Norman Conquest and has a magnificent Norman arch leading to the chancel. The building has been greatly altered over the centuries, the Tudors put in a dormer window and lattice windows in the south aisle, and tiles replaced the thatched roof in the 19th century, but it remains a small, compact building made from rubble and Roman brick. The immediate churchyard is kept mowed by a team of volunteers, giving easy access to the many headstones.

With Church Street being separated from The Cross by a deep valley, it would be easy to assume that the old village grew up around the church, but this certainly was not so. Various manor houses were built; the present Hall and Pond House are by the church, but Rivers Hall, a lovely partially moated dwelling, is on the eastern outskirts of the parish and its lands take in The Cross area. Rivers Hall was surveyed by John Walker in 1586 and these maps still exist today, giving minute detail of the fields and dwellings on the estate. The oldest thatched cottage of its particular method of construction in Essex, if not in Europe, was on part of the 1586 Rivers Hall estate – this is Songers, dated 1270, and can be found in Cage Lane. There are many thatched cottages and some whose thatch has been removed in this part of the village, and many would seem to be at peculiar angles to the modern road pattern.

Prior to the Enclosures Act of 1813 a large heath separated Boxted from the village of Mile End, now incorporated into the Borough of Colchester. The heath was crossed by two distinct cart tracks, one going towards the east of Colchester and the other linking up with Horkesley and on into Mile End. After the enclosure of the heath and the building of the Straight Road, some three miles in length, the character of the village changed, for Straight Road leads into Mile End, which saw much expansion with the coming of the railways into Colchester in the 1840s.

In 1906 the Salvation Army set up a 'Labour Colony' to put 'landless people on the peopleless land'. Some 67 holdings were created and at least 50 were occupied in 1910 when the settlement was visited by General Booth. There is a story about the General's visit which is very much in character. He was driven in an open carriage from North Station to Boxted, passing Severall's Hospital. On being told what the institution was used for, General Booth promptly stopped the procession, rose to his feet and pronounced loudly against the demon drink, opium and the Devil, much to the embarrassment of the dignitaries who accompanied him. Unfortunately General Booth's visit did not do much for the land settlement, for discontent with administration led to eviction of some tenants in 1910 and by 1916 the scheme was wound up and sold. Several holdings were bought by Essex County Council to resettle servicemen returning from the First World War.

What General Booth thought of the older parts of Boxted is not recorded, a pity perhaps seeing that there were at least seven public houses or houses licensed to sell liquor in the village. Of the licensed houses, only two remain open. The oldest, the Cross Inn, has recently been refurbished after four years of dereliction and now offers an excellent restaurant as well as a bar area. Whilst restoring the building the owners found what appears to be a priesthole in the roof-rafters, not surprising as Boxted lies on the backroads to the port of Harwich. What better place to hide an escapee from the tyrannies of religious bigotry and the Civil War. The Cross Inn has a mention in John Walker's 1586 survey and the builders found evidence of a 15th century building. The other inn still open for refreshment probably grew from a kitchen alehouse, and is situated at the northern end of the Straight Road where the old cart tracks divided to cross the heath. This is the Wig and Fidget, a unique pub name, which has a fine reputation for hospitality.

At present Boxted still has its own private bus service, run by the son of the founder and his wife. The village also boasts one of the few remaining Methodist Silver Bands, which is much in demand at fete times and for charity fund-raising events. The band is attached to the Methodist church, which has flourished, in true East Anglian Nonconformist style, since the days of Charles Wesley. Next to the chapel is a small school-room which, prior to the 1944 Education Act, was Boxted Junior School, where all the village children went before finishing their education at the Church of England school in Church Street. Long before modern ecumenicalism, Boxted's churches were sharing in the education of the young and religious tolerance is still important to the population. The present primary school is controlled by the County Council, but continues its links with the Church and occupies the Church of England buildings, opened in 1836.

The third hamlet is Workhouse Hill, which takes its name from the use put to an old cottage at the bottom of the hill. It seems that people, particularly men, walking from Suffolk to the port of Harwich could usually find succour and a bed here, and, probably because these walkers were shabby in appearance, the cottage became known as the workhouse or dosshouse. At the top of the hill the bridleway across farmland is known as Harwich Lane and goes across Boxted into Langham, where it becomes a metalled roadway.

The King George V Jubilee Trust enabled the villagers to create a sports field in Cage Lane, which today boasts football and cricket pitches, a social club and an excellent children's playground with a hut for playgroups and youth clubs. Alongside the sports field is the village hall, which runs carpet bowls as well as other leisure activities. Along with the defined footpaths all this gives the people of Boxted plenty of leisure facilities, but sadly the shops are becoming a memory with only the small post office stores and hairdresser's remaining open.

Bradfield 🐚

Wander along by the old main road through Ardleigh and Mistley, where it becomes the B1352, and keeping close to the river Stour go towards Harwich. After leaving the last houses in Mistley you will cross a brickbuilt bridge, erected to carry the road over a railway line that was never completed. As the road turns right, pull your car into a little unofficial parking space where you can have a panoramic view of the estuary of the Stour and standing high up on your right is the old part of the village of Bradfield clustered about its 13th century parish church. You can see the church tower, not built until the 16th century, showing quite a lot of red bricks and standing up in a most commanding position; the top of the tower would have been a good place from which to have looked out for sailing vessels coming up the river or distinguished visitors approaching by horse-drawn coach or even the approach of the press-gang!

Not far from the church is an inn, the Stranger's Home, kept by a delightful couple with a most appropriate name, Mr and Mrs Tankard! Actually the inn was rebuilt some years ago and is not on its original site, but why the Stranger's Home? It is said that like the French word étranger it means foreigner, and refers to the Huguenot weavers. On the same corner is a shop, formerly a typical village general store although now an antiques shop. Near to the shop is a fine specimen of magnolia grandiflora, grown as it should be with the protection of a wall and producing its lovely large cream coloured blooms at least from July until September and, if the autumn is mild, even until November. Almost adjacent is a cast-iron mile-post.

Continuing your walk through Bradfield, you will see behind the inn called the Village Maid a well preserved cottage which was originally two cottages built in the local style. Further on, on your right, is the Methodist church; the present building is 140 years old and is on the site of an earlier building erected more than 200 years ago.

Unless you are local countryfolk you may wonder at the name of the next public house, the Ram and Hogget. Ram you will know as the male sheep, but the hogget is a yearling female sheep. There are still quite a lot of sheep kept in the district and even within the Bradfield parish boundaries; come at the right time and you see lambs in the fields and hear the bleating of mothers and lambs.

Barrack Street contains typical modern bungalows but also has some of the old traditional cottages. The name arises because it contained a building in which soldiers were once housed ready to defend this part of the country from Napoleon. The road to the right at the crossroads is called Windmill Road and photographs still exist showing a windmill in full sails in that road. The village post office and stores is adjacent to the corner and is a good example of a well run village store that makes a tremendous contribution to the community; in a sense it is the hub of the village and central to its life.

Bradfield had two windmills but it also had a steam driven mill and the next stretch of the road is called Steam Mill Road. At the next road junction and on the left is the large farm belonging to Bradfield Hall; look over the hedge at the right time and you will see the modern version of the peasants working in the fields! These are the people who come on 'pick-your-own' expeditions to gather strawberries and other soft fruits. If you take advantage of the opportunity to pick first class fruit then, as like as not you will have it weighed and paid for in a building which once housed the steam mill.

Within living memory the old manorial house, a moated farmhouse, Bradfield Hall, still existed, but age took its toll and it has been replaced by a modern house. Its most famous occupant was Sir Harbottle Grimston, born in the house in 1603. He was a distinguished judge, Member of Parliament and Speaker of the House of Commons. He managed to continue to serve the country both under the monarchy and under Cromwell. John Evelyn, the 17th century diarist, records that Sir Harbottle had a small acorn nursery at Bradfield and that having raised little oak trees, he planted them out in his fields in uniform rows about 100 ft from the hedges and so '... did wonderfully improve both the beauty and the value of his Demeasnes'. It could be that some of the oaks still on the estate are derived from Sir Harbottle's planting.

Brentwood 🐿️

Brentwood is situated on the Roman road from London which passes through Essex via Chelmsford to Colchester. The town is unfortunate in that virtually all its buildings which were of any antiquarian interest have been destroyed over the past 30 years, including Warley Barracks, on the site of which there now stands the head office of Ford Europe. Local industry includes a Thermos factory. The 'great house' – Thorndon Hall, completed about 1770 and designed by Leoni – has been preserved as flats behind its imposing facade. Too little left and too late, one might think, to contemplate setting up a museum. Yet in 1976 the Brentwood Museum Society was formed and in 1989, in a little Victorian cottage called Cemetery Lodge, off Warley Hill, once the home of the sexton, Brentwood Museum was opened.

Brentwood remained a hamlet until 1873, when it became legally a parish. It was first mentioned in 1176, when it was known as Burntwood. The parish church is uninspired Victorian, but the Thomas a Becket chapel, ruins of which still remain, was built in 1221. William Hunt was burnt here at the stake in 1555 for refusing to recant his Protestant beliefs.

Brentwood was for centuries a coaching stage on the main route out of London. In 1662 complaints were made that heavy traffic was ruining the roads! The White Hart, still standing, was a coaching inn. A postal halt was made there from 1637 and in 1892 a postman, 'old Bill Porter', was appointed to deliver letters to Brentwood, Shenfield, Warley and Herongate for twelve shillings weekly.

Where Sainsbury's now is there used to be a draper's store, sold to the Palace Cinema in 1912 where silent black and white films of Charlie Chaplin, Harold Lloyd etc were played. Seats fivepence, ninepence and one shilling and sixpence! A pianist played during the show and one lady who played, now in her nineties, is an old member of the WI.

In Hart Street, where the car park is, was a row of cottages owned by a Miss Betts, and a house called the 'dosshouse' where tramps spent the night for sixpence, having walked from the workhouse at Romford on

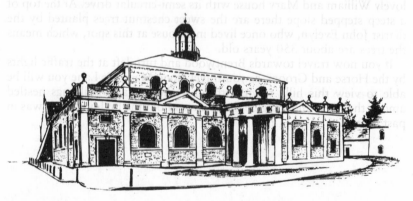

Brentwood Cathedral

their way to the workhouse at Billericay. In the High Street a Miss Twinn, nicknamed 'Sweetie', had a little sweet shop, terribly muddled, with two stone models, 'Gog and Magog', by the door. It used to be possible to buy a farthing's worth of sweets there.

Brentwood is a town built among trees, many of them hundreds of years old, and now on the edge of the future forest of Thames Chase. At Thorndon Country Park, on the south side of Brentwood, on certain Sundays throughout the year, you will be able to take a leisurely walk with a Park Ranger. You will marvel at the ancient oaks, not felled as were many others during the war years and post war, because their deformities rendered them unsuitable for the timber trade. There is a most enormous one by the road which bears a large 'carbuncle', the cause of which has several explanations; possibly when the tree was younger, the deer rubbed their horns on it, or it may be caused by a virus. Another specimen in the parkland appears to wear a skirt and another is like an oddly-shaped bottle.

As you leave the park, by the Lion Lodge gates travelling west towards South Weald Country Park, divert for a visit to Great Warley. Here beside the Thatcher's Arms public house you will find the white barred gate, entrance to Warley Place, once owned by the famous horticulturist Miss Ellen Willmott, but now managed by the Essex Wildlife Trust for the present owner. Providing you are a member of the Trust or that it is an open day, you can spend a very pleasant hour or so strolling around this reserve. There is a ha-ha, a deep straight-sided ditch to prevent cattle getting into a cultivated area, right opposite the spot where stood the lovely William and Mary house with its semi-circular drive. At the top of a steep stepped slope there are the sweet chestnut trees planted by the diarist John Evelyn, who once lived in a house at this spot, which means the trees are about 350 years old.

If you now travel towards Brentwood and turn left at the traffic lights by the Horse and Groom, as you travel along Mascall's Lane you will be able to view this hilly town with all its houses and buildings nestled among the trees, and imagine the scene without the buildings as it was in past centuries.

Broomfield 🌿

Broomfield hospital is gradually being expanded to serve a huge area of Essex around Chelmsford. In the grounds of the hospital was found a Roman coin dating back to AD 287. In a curious way, the coin and the hospital represent the two ends of Broomfield's known history.

In a field not far from the hospital are traces of Broomfield's prosperous 4th century Roman villa. It once commanded an extensive area of arable land near to a prehistoric trackway which runs through this part of Essex, but when the Roman army left Britain in AD 410, the villa farm gradually fell into decay.

Once the Roman garrisons had gone, eastern Britain was open to invasion by the Saxons. First came the raiders and then came the settlers. One settler, following the ancient trackway, found the overgrown and abandoned Roman fields. He called the place 'Scrub lands', or 'Brom Feld' in his own tongue. Another Saxon settler called Paecc set up his wooden hall about one mile to the south where the track forded a small stream. Today the area is still called Patching Hall. Yet another Saxon settlement was on the other side of the river at a place we now call Belstead Hall.

To begin with, these East Saxon settlers were independent farmers who only temporarily banded together for defence but in due course they would elect one of their number to be a permanent king of Essex. One of these kings was buried beside the old track about halfway between Brom Feld and Paecc's Hall. The grave goods of this pagan burial and their layout are reminiscent of those at Sutton Hoo although not quite on such a lavish scale. Like Sutton Hoo there is no sign of a body. Was it cremated at Belstead which according to some linguists means 'the place of fire'? The pagan regalia was found by Victorian gravel diggers and is now in the British Museum.

After 1066 the manor farms were shared out among William's followers. The de Mandeville family had many manor farms in Essex including Broomfield and one of the Patching manors. About this time, Broomfield church was built next to the manor house. It consisted of a nave and a short chancel with corners built almost entirely from Roman building tiles. The walls contain pieces of hypocaust and tiles, some with the Roman mortar still attached. A local legend tells of a dragon moving the stones there at night. The field where the Roman villa stood is still called Dragon's Foot Field!

Walter de Mandeville, younger brother of the infamous Geoffrey, first Earl of Essex, held Bromfeild at the time when all the Barons were building themselves stone castles. Not to be outdone, Walter had a strong tower built onto his church. It is one of only six round towers in Essex. Many of the great timber-framed houses for which Essex is so renowned were built in the 14th and 15th centuries. Broomfield's two pubs, the Kings Arms and the Angel were built about 1450, although the first was a private house for many years. At this time also, the church had a tall timber spire built on top of its circular flint tower. The huge timber beams forming the frame are still there. Two timber-framed houses near the church, Vineries and Well House, were built soon afterwards.

In 1541 at the dissolution of the Aldgate monastery, Broomfield's parsonage and the great tithes were acquired by Lord Rich. The parsonage was let out to tenants but Broomfield's great tithes were used to help fund Lord Rich's charities in Felsted. There is still a field in Broomfield, Felsted Field, which belongs to Felsted school. Broomfield also had a number of charities, the most famous being that of Thomas Woollard who in 1700 gave three cottages 'for the use of the poor'. They are still there, facing the green, although they are now in private hands.

Broomfield appears occasionally in the Quarter Sessions records. In 1573 three Broomfield men confessed to stealing and were branded. In 1802 a soldier held up a Broomfield inhabitant and stole his silver watch. The soldier was caught in Chelmsford and sentenced to hang.

Philip Morant, the famous Essex historian, was vicar of Broomfield from 1734 to 1738 and we depend on his work for much of the early history of the parish. His neat writing appears in the church records of that time.

By 1851 there were 180 dwellings in Broomfield, housing a population of 851. A school had been provided by one of the local landowners but many villagers wanted a National school. The whole village voted on it and a National school was built in 1873. The boys school is now the church hall and the girls school is still there, tucked away behind the Old Bakehouse. Chelmer Valley High School was opened in 1975 as a comprehensive school to serve children from villages north and east of Chelmsford.

In 1943 a bomb damaged the parish church and blew out all the windows. Four windows were reglazed in the 1950s with stained glass designed and made by the artist Rosemary Rutherford, daughter of a previous vicar.

Broomfield Court and grounds, constructed in 1904 by Mr Christy the owner of Brooklands for his daughter Mrs Nash, was bought in the 1930s in order to build a hospital for the treatment of tuberculosis. Later it became a general hospital and now it is being expanded to treat patients from a wide area.

During its long history, life was not all hard work in Broomfield. The cricket team has been playing matches for over 200 years and the football team is nearing its centenary. The Cottage Gardeners' Society was founded in 1879 and still has a large membership. Broomfield's Women's Institute is therefore relatively young, having been founded in 1917.

Buckhurst Hill 🏫

In 1852 the sale of King's Place Farm estate of 157 acres took place to the British Land Corporation for £10,546, and this sale marked the turning point for Buckhurst Hill from rural to suburban.

The major event of this period was the coming of the railway in 1856. The Eastern Counties Railway from Bishopsgate (now Liverpool Street) to Stratford was then extending its line to Loughton and named its new station 'Buckhurst Hill'. Planning of the railway speeded up the growth of the population considerably. Workmen's cottages 'below the line' in Albert Road and Alfred Road, together with those of Bridge Terrace and Albert Terrace date from this period. The railway line cut Queen's Road in two with a level crossing, making the bottom part (which originally appears to have been designed to run down to the Roding) into Lower Queen's Road.

The clay at the bottom of the road was ideal for making bricks to build homes 'above the line' and Ephraim Butler (the landlord of the Bald Faced Stag) who owned this patch of land, developed brick production on site, bringing the limestone and coal via the new railway to the railway yard adjacent to the Railway Tavern in Queen's Road. Brick production, which had depended on Chigwell for many years, was now firmly established in Buckhurst Hill (and was to continue through to the late 1940s).

The lane running down from the Bald Faced Stag, 'Back Lane', was extended beyond King's Place over a new railway bridge down to Alfred Road, from which the footpath still ran across the field to the White Bridge and to Chigwell. At the top of the hill, the High Road was realigned in 1858 taking it close to the church and giving Buckhurst Hill a straight road from Woodford through to the cricket field before the

38

steep descent to Loughton. The winding section by Lord's Bushes became first 'Hospital Lane' and then later 'Knighton Lane', from which Monkhams Lane ran through the Forest to Monkhams Farm and on to Woodford Bridge.

Buckhurst Hill continued to grow apace. The 1881 census shows a population of 3,421 – having practically doubled over the previous decade. By 1891 it had grown to 4,130 living in some 755 dwellings. The pressure of numbers raised the need for more school places and in 1872 St John's School ceased to take boys in the junior department. All boys were then educated in the new board school in Princes Road, St John's School being reserved entirely for girls and infants.

However, the biggest change in local life that took place in this period was the sudden expansion of the 'Sunday Population'. Railway records show that Buckhurst Hill station saw in excess of 20,000 visitors each Sunday, carried by the railway from London to enjoy the delights of the Forest. These day-trippers were poor Eastenders and their needs were catered for by the local inns and tea-gardens and by three 'retreats' – Guys near to the present Roebuck, Riggs in Brook Road, and one in Queen's Road. The old Roebuck Inn had been demolished in 1875 and the name taken over by John Green, who opened a 'tea garden' in Epping New Road which used the name and had a hall in which 500 persons could dine and over 20 acres of pleasure ground. These establishments served thousands of teas every Sunday and gave entertainment with swing boats and donkey rides. In 1896 there was on Connaught Waters a coal-fired clinker-built paddle steamer 90 ft long capable of carrying 250 passengers! Buckhurst Hill and the Forest was the Victorian equivalent of the more modern Southend 'Kiss me quick' hats and candy floss!

Bulphan 🐑

Tracing social history through house-names in Bulphan can provide an interesting theme for anyone walking round this south Essex village.

Noke Hall, Garlesters and Appletons were the first three farms established by freemen in the early 14th century. Garlesters, on Brentwood Road, was first known as Galysty; Appletons is now known as The Plough House and is a well known motel and restaurant. The original owner, Sir Henry Appleton of South Benfleet, engaged the Dutch engineers who built up the Thames seawalls over 300 years ago. Noke Hall was first recorded in 1319, when the land was granted to Thomas atte Noke. Noke here probably refers to oak.

Another name that goes back many generations is Wick Place (Brentwood Road). In the 14th century there were in Bulphan large numbers of sheep whose milk was made into large, thick cheeses, prepared at the Wick.

Unfortunately, some of the more picturesque names have been changed or ceased to exist. Lower Coal Carters is now Fen Farm, Fen Lane; Hunger Hill is now Ongar Hall; Tapslaps is now Elm Farm, Church Lane; and Stringcock Fen and Sweet Briar Lane are now part of Church Lane and Parkers Farm Road.

Some house names make it clear what their function once was; for example, Old Forge, China Lane. With the laying of the railway tracks in the late 19th century, Londoners were able to 'escape' to plots in the country for weekends and holidays. Many of the holiday homes became their permanent homes during the Second World War, and some Londoners who came to Bulphan during the war as children still live in these same houses. Jusootus and Avarest in Albert Road and Welivere in Victoria Road are fine examples of the typical style of home and house-name that became popular then.

Many of the houses in Bulphan have been self-built, and both the owners of these and other houses built by developers often like to incorporate their own name into the house-name. In Stanley Road, for instance, you can find Jaysbee (the initials of the Christian names of the original owners were J, J, J and B). Other appropriate names of self-built homes include Abinitio, which means from the beginning and is in Stanley Road; Old Stocks and Touch Wood (Albert Road); and Little Acorns, Stanley Road, which was built in the grounds of Oakford. During the building of Tantivy in Albert Road, the hunt passed the site and the hounds chased the fox through the partly-completed house, causing some damage (Tantivy is a huntsman's cry for full gallop).

Many house-names have sentimental origins. Arley House is named after the small village near Coventry where the original occupants spent their childhood; Dhekelia (Albert Road) is the Forces base in Cyprus where the first residents met. Milford Cottage is a tribute to the occupant's grandfather, who was Captain Jimmy Gale ('Captain Tempest'), skipper of Milford Haven. Lanesra (read it backwards!) and Highbury are football-supporter's homes, both standing in Victoria Road.

Finally, people from all over the world spend farm holidays in the delightful surroundings of Bonnydowns Farm, Doesgate Lane. How

40

many of them realise that the farm was named after the notorious Bonnydown Road in East Ham where the farmer spent his tough childhood?

Burnham-on-Crouch 🦪

Once a centre of the oyster, cockle and whelk trade, Burnham is now called the 'Cowes of the East Coast' because of its popularity with the thousands of yachtsmen who visit it each year.

The elegant Georgian High Street, which runs parallel to the river, has an octagonal clock tower built in Victorian times, and many delightful old wooden cottages. The equally elegant quayside has recently undergone reconstruction by the NRA and all the improvements to the sea defences have now been completed. Maldon council in conjunction with the NRA have almost completed a red tiled and cobbled walkway along the whole length of the quay from the Royal Corinthian Yacht Club to the Royal Burnham Yacht Club, so walkers can enjoy the views of river and boats in comfort.

There are many old wooden buildings in the town. 'The Long Row' consists of 24 houses under one slate roof. It was built in 1891 for John Smith, an oyster merchant, and rented out to his crews originally for two shillings and sixpence a week. Much of the original roof suffered in the 1980s hurricanes and there are not many of the original slates left. A similar row was planned from Witney Road, running parallel to Granville Terrace, but John Smith was bankrupted by the sinking of three uninsured ships before this second row on the Chapel Road site could be built, hence the very long narrow gardens of the terrace. Granville and Witney were John Smith's sons.

'Sweetings' is another old wooden building which was enlarged as the owner's family grew. A new room was added as each addition to the family arrived. The original fishmonger's sign still stands above the entrance to the old wet fish shop. The end room is now a souvenir shop. There is a museum in Providence Road, open on Wednesdays and at weekends. There are now several cafes serving afternoon tea, morning coffee etc for the visitors to the town. There is a new snack bar in the High Street as well as many shops, pubs and restaurants.

Burnham Week, one of the great events of the yachtsman's year, is held the last week of August. There is also an annual well-lit night carnival every year at the end of September.

With a new sports hall and an excellent library, old and new blend well together in this little town which is a very good place to visit, especially in the summertime.

Buttsbury ✒

A flourishing Women's Institute, and at least two churches, St Mary's and Christ Church. All are in Buttsbury parish, but where is Buttsbury village?

Sometimes one thinks that the various local authorities in Essex – to say nothing of the map-makers – combine deliberately to try and mislead any innocent traveller who may be searching for Buttsbury. Should such a traveller be coming northwards from the direction of Billericay, going towards Chelmsford, he will come first to the village of Stock. Right in the centre of the village is a signpost directing him to keep straight on for Chelmsford, or to turn right for Wickford or left for Margaretting. This, as I say, is right in the middle of Stock village, but should he glance up to the top of the signpost he will see a circular plate telling him he is not in Stock but in the parish of Buttsbury!

Now, if he should retrace his steps and go southwards again, he will see a turning on the right directing him to Ingatestone – nowhere else. Let him proceed along this road, with the charming name of Honeypot Lane, and about midway between Stock and Ingatestone, right in open farm country with no houses in close proximity, he will find the ancient and charming little church of St Mary, Buttsbury! But where is the village?

Historians have put forward various theories as to the disappearance of any dwelling houses in the area around the church. One theory is that the village may have been decimated by the Black Death in about 1348, and another is that there never were any houses, but that the church was built near the junction of two or three roads or tracks to make it more easily accessible from all quarters. If that were so, one might expect the church to be dedicated to St Giles, patron saint of travellers, but the church is dedicated to St Mary. The whole area might well repay archaeological investigation to establish the truth.

Undaunted, the traveller may retrace his steps, or turn his car, and proceed again towards Billericay. Some half a mile along the B1007 road he will see a turning on the right named Orchard Avenue, which will lead him into Perry Street, a well built up area now with many pleasing modern houses. Here he will come across a modern church, Christ

Church, the full title of which is 'Christ Church, Buttsbury'.

A little further along the road is another new church, describing itself as Billericay Baptist church, and of course the postal addresses for all the residents in and around Perry Street, is 'Billericay' – though historically they are in Buttsbury. If he continues on towards Billericay station he will come eventually to the only signpost telling him he has just left Buttsbury! So where *is* this elusive place?

To give the true answer one must go back into ecclesiastical and manorial history, when Buttsbury, by reason of its many manors, was a very important place – in fact some of its manorial lands covered nearly all of what is now the village of Stock, and extended southwards to join the ancient parish of Burstead – now modern Billericay. Some of the farmhouses still existing hereabouts bear the ancient names of illustrious manorial families – Tyrells, Blunts etc, whose stories feature in many volumes on Essex history. Since the early 16th century much of the land has formed part of the vast estates of the Petre family, and even today Lord Petre is lord of the manor of much of Stock and parts of But' ;bury.

The countryside is pleasantly undulating, with wide views, especially around St Mary's church. Queens Park is now a place of 'most desirable' modern residences, always described as 'sought after' by estate agents. If anyone was brave (or foolhardy!) enough to beat the bounds of this ancient parish, he would 'touch the fringe' of every period of local history, from the Iron Age, through Roman, Saxon, Norman and medieval to modern.

Canewdon

Canewdon is bounded on the north by the river Crouch, which takes its rise from two springs at Little Bursted and Laindon. The river meanders through fields and meadows and joins the sea just below Burnham on Crouch. To the south, but at a distance of two or three miles, the river Roche is navigable to Stambridge Mills.

It is said that from Canewdon church tower you can see seven hundred churches; a bit misleading this, as the areas around here have always been known as 'Hundreds' – Rochford Hundred, Dengie Hundred and so on. Even so, the view from the unusual church tower is well worth the climb, with the rivers below like silver ribbons, the green meadows, and in season, the fields ablaze with the brilliant yellow of rape flowers.

Some reminders of the long history of the village are to be found near the church. The famous lock-up and stocks, originally erected in the early 1800s near to the village pond, were moved to this site during November 1938.

The new village community hall, erected in 1979, is the hub of village life, and is in constant use for all village events. A village fete is held in and around the hall every year and is well attended, even offering all and sundry the opportunity to plough a straight furrow with horse-drawn plough, in the adjoining field, courtesy of the local farmer.

The start of the Second World War saw Canewdon as the base of one of the first of the new RADAR installations around the coast. Radar was then a closely guarded secret and the rumours abounded as to exactly what the 'pylons' were to be used for. Young airmen were billeted around the area bringing the glamour of their uniform, to the delight of the local girls. The radar installations stood until September 1973 when they were demolished, but instead of taking a few hours work it took nearly two days to dismantle the structures. Some folks said it was the six witches, who are a part of Canewdon folklore. Having accepted the pylons, they would not have them destroyed. Legend has it that as long as Canewdon church tower stands, there will be six witches in Canewdon, three in satin and three in rags.

Let us now take a walk through the village, starting at the church, which is on the western boundary. On the right hand side is the 'new' model village, with its large village green, bordered by houses, and on the left hand side pleasant bungalows. Passing the Congregational chapel on the left and the Chequers, one of the two village inns, on the right, we are now in the part of the street with some of the oldest dwellings in the village, mostly renovated, but retaining much of their original cottagey charm.

At the end of the street is the other inn, the Anchor. Both of these hostelries now serve excellent meals and are well favoured by folks from near and far.

At the village pond, if you are lucky you may be able to count some 17 ducks swimming around hopefully waiting for tit-bits from anyone passing. These ducks alternate their time between this pond and another further down the road, and can often be seen winging their way between their two homes. Another few yards on are more delightful old cottages on the right and on the left the village hall.

The community has recently lost, through retirement, its much respected village 'bobby', who served Canewdon and the adjoining villages for 27 years. Tony Blake achieved very successfully the fine balance that is required in enforcing the law, being friendly, but commanding respect from all who crossed his path. When he joined us he was not allowed the comfort of a car, but pedalled around his beat on his trusty bike.

Thinking of local characters, one who will be remembered for many years to come, but now sadly deceased, was 'Rosie' Fox, the landlady for many years at the Anchor inn. Rosie was indeed a character, but all agreed that Rosie knew how to run a pub. A stickler for keeping an orderly house, you abided by the rules if you visited the Anchor. No crisp or nut packets were allowed on the tables, but the beer was always well looked after. On the wall in the Anchor hangs a portrait of another character, 'Frizzles', painted by a local insurance roundsman. This painting depicts Frizzles resplendent in hunting pink. He was an ardent follower of the hunt, but no four-footed friend for him, he followed the hunt on his bike, sleeping rough wherever the fancy took him.

The parish boundaries of Canewdon stretch roughly a mile in each direction from the village, encompassing several farms and smallholdings, and many dwelling places. The natural hub of the village, as in most villages, is the church and chapel, the community hall, the village stores and post office and the inns.

Castle Hedingham ✒️

The village of Castle Hedingham is a picturesque assortment of old cottages, large houses and inns, with narrow lanes connecting its ancient streets, and surrounded by centuries-old farms and woods. It is divided from its neighbouring village of Sible Hedingham by the river Colne, and nestles in the sheltered Colne valley. It dates back to Saxon days, when it was owned by a wealthy Saxon thane named Ulwin but was granted to Aubrey De Vere in the Norman Conquest of 1066 by William the Conqueror.

Since then it has seen many changes and the variety of architecture to be seen as a result of the differing styles from each century only adds to its charm. Small medieval cottages stand alongside imposing Queen Anne, Georgian and Victorian houses (although the elegant facades of these often conceal Tudor or Elizabethan interiors).

It is fortunate to have several shops and businesses, and historically it was always referred to as a town as it was granted the right to hold a weekly market in its wide main street in the time of King John, Monday being market day. The Moot House (now a restaurant) is a lovely old timbered building which stands at the widest end of St James's Street (called the High Street in a map of 1592). Another equally picturesque building is The Falcon in Falcon Square, the very heart of the village. This was once an inn, the valuable hawks and falcons used for falconry at the castle being kept at the back. The oldest of the present inns is the Bell, situated in St James's Street, and was a well-known stopping place for coaches.

The parish church of St Nicholas is situated in the centre of the village, surrounded by a beautifully kept churchyard. This is reputedly one of the finest Norman churches in Essex, being built by the De Veres in about 1180, replacing an earlier, smaller Saxon church dedicated to St James. It has a magnificent Norman nave and pillars, a rood-screen and a wheel window, which according to experts is one of only five in the country. The tower is of brick, rebuilt in the 17th century. Guide books are available in the church. There is also a United Reformed church in Queen Street, built in 1842.

At the end of the street alongside the church, behind the row of houses facing it, once existed some small ponds, in which the water collected from the higher slopes. This locality is still known as Church Ponds, although the water is now drained away to the river, and the sites of the ponds are now gardens. On the side of Falcon Square, opposite the church gate stands the Youth Hostel, with its magnificent old chimney, and from the entrance to the little lane beside it (Castle Lane) can be seen a wonderful view of the building from which the village derives its name, and for which it is most renowned – Hedingham Castle.

It was built and owned by the De Veres (later to become the Earls of Oxford) in 1140, and is one of the most important ancient monuments in Essex. Its high position overlooking the village and surrounding country-side commands wide views from the top floor windows, and it contains the widest Norman arch in Western Europe in the Banqueting Hall. It is still privately owned by a descendant of the De Veres.

To the residents of Castle Hedingham it remains very much part of their lives today. Coming home from a holiday or trip out for the day it can be seen several miles away, just a glimpse over the tops of the trees welcoming you home. And so it must have done to others for over 800 years.

In the 19th century the village was one of many in North Essex where straw plaiting took place. Wages were poor so women and children took up this skill as a means of bringing extra money into the home. The straw was split lengthwise by the means of a small instrument called an 'engine'

46

made of bone and wood. Four to six strips were made then the nimble fingers would plait the strips together and pretty designs were produced. A dealer would go round the villages collecting the measured lengths, paying by the amount of work each woman had done. This was then made up into hats. In the 1851 census records 188 women and children were employed, and old men no longer fit for labouring lent a hand and helped earn a few shillings. Women could be seen leaning against their garden gates chatting, with their nimble fingers busy plaiting away. The industry died out by the turn of the century, then young girls would walk or take wagons to the local mill in Halstead, the silk mill owned by Sam Courtauld.

Today things are very different with one or two pubs, a post office, the village shop, the garage for your petrol, and one or two lovely places to eat. The main street is often quiet, sounds of tennis ball on racquet, a lawn mower chugging away.

The Castle Hedingham sign erected to commemorate the Silver Jubilee was a complete village venture, beneath the castle. Bingham's pottery is depicted, also the De Vere star. The girl is Poll Miles, who today would have been considered a keen bird and animal expert but in the 1800s was thought to be a witch and after drowning in the castle lake was buried outside the village at a crossroads. Even to this day a fresh bunch of flowers is seen every Christmas on the spot, laid by whom nobody seems to know.

It's still got the community spirit, this modern Castle Hedingham. If you're not well you find what kindness there is. A village wedding brings out the hats and summer frocks. The church bells ring out for evensong each Sunday calling the people of Castle Hedingham to church as they have done for nearly 800 years.

And so dusk falls and the castle disappears into the darkness with only the bats flitting in and out of the turret windows.

Chappel & Wakes Colne 🌿

The combined villages of Chappel & Wakes Colne ramble in all directions and even the oldest inhabitants are not quite sure where one ends and the other begins. Even so, it is one of the prettiest villages in Essex, with lovely views of the surrounding countryside and woods.

Like most villages it has its share of tales, such as Butchers Corner where two butchers are said to have fought to their deaths, and a story about a horse and cart that was driven into a bottomless pond when rounding a sharp corner one dark night and was never seen again. A certain part of the village is reputed to be haunted as it is rumoured that many innocent people were hanged there.

There are several organisations in the village, amongst the oldest being the WI. The cricket club is also an old organisation and in recent years has changed its ground. The present one, plus a smart clubhouse and bar, was created from a badly flooded field by the hard work and determination of the members. Many people go to watch the cricket in the summer and enjoy a pleasant afternoon.

Prominent features of the village are its viaducts, the subject of many an artist's drawing and a local landmark. Several pill-boxes were built during the Second World War under these viaducts and are a source of forbidden joy to many a youngster, and the cause of many a broken leg or ankle through jumping off the top. This is not the only place for children to play, however, as they have a well-equipped playground on the land which used to be called the common, where an annual fair known as Chappel Fair used to call but long since has been discontinued.

Many people are also attracted to the village because of the Railway Preservation Society, which has part of the railway line which serves passengers travelling between Sudbury and London. The society run steam trains in the summer and at Christmas, when Father Christmas comes!

The village sign is situated at the crossroads and has Chappel on one side and Wakes Colne on the other. This sign was dedicated to the memory of a local landowner and the dedication service was attended by a descendant of Hereward the Wake. Chappel was formerly called Pontisbright but its name was changed when a chapel was built halfway between Colchester and Great Tey. There are still some cottages called Pontisbright. The mill in Wakes Colne is very old and was the subject of an Albert Campian story by Margery Allingham. It was set in and outside the mill and fields around and the old name of Pontisbright was used.

Also in the village is a monetary fund called The Loves Gift. This was left in trust by an old man named Arthur Love who used to tramp the villages. When he died he left a sum of money to be given out at New Year to the widows, poor and needy etc in the villages he had travelled in.

There are no vicarages left in the village as both were old and are now private houses; the vicar lives in Great Tey. There have been many vicars over the years but perhaps the most memorable was the Rev Jackson Hodgins who revived the age old custom of Rogationtide, when the fields, crops and animals were blessed together with the river water. Two choir boys were bounced on the river bank as a reminder to them never to forget where the boundaries were.

There are two seats in the village, the one in Wakes Colne provided for the use of the village people and the other in Chappel erected in memory of a local St John's Ambulance man.

There are two churches, two parochial councils, two parish councils, one village hall, one school (the other was closed down several years ago), and only the sub-post office in Wakes Colne is left. There is also only one public house, the Swan Inn in Chappel, although not so long ago there were four. The Railway Tavern is now a private house, the Gardeners Arms likewise and the Rose and Crown, which was used as a cafe, is now private houses. The popular butcher's shop and the four shops in the village are now also in private hands. There is also a motor racing track in Wakes Colne.

A lot of building has gone on recently including houses on the old petrol dump, which was a source of great concern during the war, but all in all nothing has really spoilt the village which is still one of the prettiest in Essex.

Chelmsford 🌿

Chelmsford has changed almost beyond recognition since the Second World War, but many residents have cherished memories of what it used to be like.

Most of the shops were small in the 1930s, nearly all owned by the shopkeeper himself. Each one seemed to have an atmosphere and a smell all of its own! There was Warren's the chemist's, for instance, owned by Mr Plattin, where the Co-op now stands. It was very small, not very light, but had a distinctive smell of cough mixture and liniment and the walls were lined with interesting green bottles and brown tins.

There were eight grocery shops, including Lipton's and the Maypole. Luckin-Smith's grocer's shop had a very narrow frontage and ran from the High Street towards London Road parallel to Wenley's. You entered by climbing several steps and opening double doors made of wood with little windows. Inside the shop was very long and not very light as there were no windows. The floor was made of wooden planks and on either side ran a long polished wooden counter stretching from the front to the back of the shop. As you entered you were greeted by the men behind the counters, all of whom probably knew you by name and stood ready to serve. They all wore black suits, white shirts and long white aprons. On the customer's side of the counter were ranged large square tins with glass lids which contained all varieties of biscuits – including a very popular line, broken biscuits, which were a mixture of every type in the shop. For the benefit of customers, chairs were placed at regular intervals, usually round wooden seats with curved wooden backs.

The other Luckin-Smith's was a hardware shop. Both were owned by Mr Luckin-Smith who lived at Springfield on the main Springfield Road, in a really beautiful house with wide sweeping lawns. Sadly it is no longer there, having given way to more houses – the story of the disappearing Chelmsford.

The Springfield Road corner with the High Street, the main road to Colchester, was a very busy road and there was always a policeman on point duty on that corner. Behind him stood the Conduit which now stands in Tower Gardens. It was of course the original source of water for the town when water was piped through the High Street in wooden pipes from Burgess Well Road (now hidden under the ring road behind the Civic Centre).

Spalding's was a shop never seen these days, a photographer and fancy goods shop. He had the reputation of the best known photographer in the town as well as being a well known civic dignitary and landowner. The 'fancy goods' consisted of expensive items of silver, inkwells, photograph frames, brush and comb sets and small glassware items, all beautifully displayed on polished tables. The whole place had an aura of peace and quiet.

The Corn Exchange, busy with farmers on Friday market day, has long since disappeared. The market place has occupied various sites too. Originally the cattle, sheep and pigs were in pens on one side of Market Road, and all the little animals and birds, such as rabbits, ducks, chickens and guinea pigs, were in hutches on the opposite side of the road. Farm implements of all descriptions were displayed in front of the old fire station, and the stalls were in Threadneedle Street, and later in the Bell car park. The next move was to Victoria Road, cattle and car auction on one side of the road and stalls opposite at the side of the car park backing onto Victoria Road school. Now the cattle and car auction are at Boreham, and the stalls have the coldest, draughtiest spot ever – beneath the town's multi-storey car park.

Chelmsford was a boom town during the Second World War, with its many factories playing a vital part in the war effort. Hoffmann's ball-

Chelmsford Cathedral

bearing factory was essentially for munitions and women were brought to Chelmsford from many miles away to take the place of men conscripted into the Forces. There were many casualties during the war, especially at night. The marshalling yard for both Hoffmann and Marconi was situated where Rowntree Mackintosh stands today.

Hoffmann's unfortunately no longer stands and its workers have been made redundant. Marconi's was once just the part now visible from New Street and looked very much as it does now. It had another building in Hall Street, which was the original factory. Crompton Parkinson's, which was then where Marconi Radar stands, was a factory producing electric machinery and was responsible for Chelmsford being the first town in the country to have its street lighting by electricity instead of gas lamps.

It was once virtually impossible to cross the High Street between twelve noon and twelve-fifteen or five o'clock and five-thirty when the factories closed for lunch or for the day. The only means of transport was the bicycle and when they all 'left off' it was one solid mass of bicycles. They advanced into the High Street five abreast and stretched from Springfield Road to New Street in one solid mass.

51

There were country walks through the Baddow Meads and Brook End, and swimming in the pool at Barnes Mill and the river Chelmer. Horse-drawn barges were towed from Maldon, through the many locks, to Brown's timber yard off Springfield Road – now owned by Travis Perkins. A humped back bridge crossed a small stream running through the meadowland opposite the timber yard. This land was owned by Hugh-Wright, the butcher, and his cattle grazed where Tesco's stands today.

Tea dances were held on Saturday afternoons in the ballroom of the Odeon cinema, and annual balls (with evening dress) were enjoyed in the Shire Hall, where court sessions are held today. Chelmsford had five cinemas, and only one of these, the Select, is still in use today. The old Empire cinema in Springfield Road was destroyed by fire long ago and the Pavilion in Duke Street has recently closed. The Regent is now a bingo hall, but was once also a live theatre. There is now the Civic Theatre in Duke Street, and the old Springfield parish hall, opposite Chelmsford Prison, has been extended and modernised and is used by the Theatre Workshop for their performances.

There was a racecourse on Galleywood Common, and rowing boats, skiffs or canoes could be hired by the hour from Hunts at the Stone Bridge in the centre of town, or at Barnes Mill. Afternoon teas, with platefuls of delicious cream cakes, were very competitive, and Chelmsford had several good restaurants. The Blue Bird was opposite the bus station. The Wimpy is there now, and Cannon's Restaurant and Ballroom is now the Anglia Nationwide Building Society. There was a choice of ballrooms and dance halls on Saturday nights – and in many respects there was far more pleasurable entertainment in the Chelmsford of the past than there is today.

Chigwell ✖️

'Chigwell, my dear fellow' wrote Dickens, 'is the greatest place in the world. Such a delicious old inn opposite the churchyard, such a lovely ride, such beautiful forest scenery, such an out of the way rural place.' Today this is still partly true. Mentioned in the Domesday Book, situated ten miles from Aldgate Pump, and bordered by both Epping and Hainault forests and open farmland, remnants of Chigwell's rural past still remain.

Take a walk from the station. This building has had the facade modernized but still retains much of the old architecture from the time it was built in 1903, when the steam train ran from Chigwell to Ilford and in 1939 the fare was sixpence. In due course it was electrified and now reaches to central London and beyond. Of course, with the railway came much desirable development and today Chigwell is a commuter's paradise. The small parade of shops nearby caters for most requirements, but this unfortunately causes much traffic congestion.

Happily we still keep our green, enhanced in spring by the crocus bulbs planted by the WI. Nearby Dolphin Court, a large new block of flats – far too large for the area, stands on the site of the old forge and some residents can still remember the ring of hammer on anvil. The mineral spring which caused many problems during the building construction is now covered over and largely forgotten.

Further along the High Road is the original Chigwell village, which has changed very little over the centuries. The centre of most villages being the pub, the King's Head is no exception, and is famous as the 'Maypole' in *Barnaby Rudge* as well as for its pigeon pie. From 1730 and possibly earlier it was used for meetings of the Waltham Forest Court of Attachments. Sir Winston Churchill is named among the many appreciative diners there. Over the years there have been many alterations to the building, but the Chester Room on the first floor still retains its original 17th century panelling and is said to be the room where Queen Elizabeth I slept when visiting the forest. The pub is of course, a 'must' for visitors, particularly Americans.

Chigwell is well known for its school built in 1629 and founded by Samuel Harsnett, vicar of Chigwell from 1597 to 1605, who became Bishop of Chichester then Bishop of Norwich and finally Archbishop of York. Many have been educated there, one well known 'old boy' being William Penn, founder of the state of Pennsylvania in the USA. Two schools were built and endowed at the same time and the indenture of 13th April 1629 states that one school should instruct the Latin and Greek tongues, and in the other school children should be taught to Read, Write, Cypher and Cast Accounts and to learn their Accidence. This school became the village school and later a library, but was burnt down some years ago and new houses built on the site. The stone arch over the doorway which stated 'Fear of the Lord is the beginning of Wisdom' was sold and regrettably lost to the community. A new primary school now serves the area and recently a famous Jewish school, the Beth Shamai, has moved from its original London home to a new school here.

The jewel in the crown is undoubtedly the parish church of St Mary, of

Kings Head Inn, Chigwell

Norman origin, where people have worshipped for over 800 years. The church plate is some of the finest in Essex, but unfortunately in this vandal plagued age has to be kept in bank vaults. Archbishop Harsnett, who died in 1631, is commemorated in a stained glass window in the London Guildhall listing England's archbishops and is remembered in the church by a magnificent brass in the chancel. This brass is considered to be the best of its kind in the country, and bears a Latin inscription, composed by the Archbishop, which reads 'Here lies Samuel Harsnett, formerly Vicar of this Church, first the unworthy Bishop of Chichester, next the more unworthy Bishop of Norwich, and finally the most unworthy Archbishop of York, who died the 25th day of May AD 1631.' Samuel Harsnett could not be accused of 'blowing his own trumpet'! Another interesting plaque, in bronze, is to the memory of George Shillibeer, whose grave is in the churchyard. He was the inventor of London's omnibus. His horse-drawn bus carried 22 passengers and made its first journey on 4th July 1829 from Marylebone Road to the City. The church also possesses the finest collection of hatchments or funeral escutcheons in Essex. The lozenge-shaped panels were formerly hung in front of a house as a sign of mourning.

A few wooden cottages still remain near the church. Hadyns, formerly the village bakery, has now become a bistro, but still retains its external appearance and name. The village shop and dressmaker's have now become desirable residences.

Many 18th century houses in the area are still lived in by local residents. One of these, Rolls, was owned by Admiral Eliab Harvey who commanded the *Temeraire* at Trafalgar. His brother, Sir John Harvey, who discovered the principle of the circulation of blood in the human body, was a frequent visitor to Rolls. Another house built between 1723–56 and called Bowling Green has now become a Roman Catholic convent. Yet another, Little West Hatch, was for many years a small mental hospital, but now houses a unit of the Peto Institute treating children with cerebral palsy.

The beautiful Georgian house named Chigwell Court was purchased in 1948 by Old Chigwellians as a memorial to those boys from the school who gave their lives in the Second World War. The house and grounds of Chigwell Hall have for many years been owned by the Metropolitan Police, providing them with sports and recreational facilities, as well as maintaining one of Chigwell's old and beautiful houses. Each year a Grand Fete is held there with many and varied attractions, and always very well attended by Chigwell residents.

The old almshouses are still in use – the rent being 25 shillings per week. It is becoming increasingly difficult to find those who qualify for the 'poor widows' legacy. Four hundred years ago one, Joan Simpson, left money for the upkeep of the footpath from Abridge to Stratford. This is now interpreted a little more locally, and some of the money used to maintain and create local footpaths.

Woolston Hall estate dating from the 17th century is now a leisure centre. It borders the old Roman road that runs through Chigwell to Abridge, and some years ago a very well preserved Roman well was uncovered there with human bones at the bottom. It is not known whether these were the result of Roman 'dark and dirty' deeds, but the bones now rest in the Passmore Edwards museum in London E15.

A bequest was left for the benefit of the people of Chigwell by J. Lewis, in the form of the Lewis Trust. This included the building of the local hall, named the Victory Hall and in memory of Chigwell men and women killed in the Second World War. The hall is of great benefit to the community and is regularly used by many local clubs and societies including the WI.

As yet the Green Belt is holding off the rapaciousness of developers around the area, but changes in farming will undoubtedly result in alterations of land usage in future years – hopefully the surrounding fields will survive this.

Chipping Ongar

Ongar gets its name from the Ongar Hundreds, which date back to William the Conqueror's time and covered a great part of south-east and south-west Essex.

Sir Richard Lucy, Justiciar, lived in the castle (when Ongar had one!) in the 12th century. The mound of the motte and bailey is still visible behind one of the car parks, at the north side of which are the earthworks of one of the fine moats around Ongar castle and outbuildings and dwellings. Part of a moat still exists attached to a farm.

Castle House, now the Manor House in Manor Square, and the White House are the two oldest secular buildings in the town but there are rows of listed buildings used as shops and a timbered Elizabethan cottage. There are also two coaching hostelries with coach arches attached.

Ongar bridge over the Cripsey brook at the south end of the town must have been very important in days gone by because it was the only way towards London. Sir Peter Siggilswyk's will was proved in 1503 in which he 'left ten shillings to be spent on the upkeep of the bridge'. In 1628 it still needed repairing. A county rate had to be set and repairs were finally carried out in 1715!

The town was a popular staging centre for carriers, passenger coaches and waggons, of which there were many in the early 19th century. The very first postmaster was paid £25 a year in 1717.

St Nicholas' church is nearly 1,000 years old. The brickwork is probably Roman, and it was built before the 11th century. The late proprietor of Boodles Club, London, one Mr Boodles, is buried in St Nicholas' churchyard.

The Nonconformist church owns six small cottages, in one of which lived Jane Taylor, who wrote 'Twinkle, twinkle little star'. She was the daughter of Isaac Taylor, a Nonconformist minister and who also wrote several books for children. It was also in one of these same cottages that David Livingstone, the explorer, once lived for a time.

The second oldest Saxon church in England is situated in the environs of Ongar. Greensted church has tree trunks for its remaining walls, a

Tudor brick walkway to the door, and a shute in the wall for alms to be passed to lepers who came to collect them.

The name Ongar means 'grassland' and it is only a matter of a very short walk in any direction before one finds oneself in fields and farmland. The famous Epping Forest is nearby and borders on one of the Ongar Hundreds – North Weald. The Ongar Hundreds is mentioned in the Domesday Book and consisted of many surrounding villages and estates, most of which were broken up by about 1860. The 19th century also saw the demise of many watermills along the river Roding and quite a few windmills too. When the Domesday Rodinges were divided, two were allotted to Ongar – High Ongar and Chipping Ongar.

There were several schools in the town, some of which have closed, sadly. Two doctors' surgeries take care of the health of the residents. There is a sports club, Guides and Scouts, two clubs for retired folk, a club for the disabled, a very active musical society and amateur theatricals. Budworth Hall houses many clubs and activities, as does the church hall.

Ongar War Memorial Hospital was built in 1932 to commemorate the lost lives in the First World War. Friends of the hospital work very hard to keep it going, mainly for elderly people.

There is a train connection to Epping and so to London – not as regular as would be preferred but handy for schools and business people.

The Essex Way from Bury St Edmunds to Canterbury, for pilgrims doing the long walk, runs through Ongar, an historical and interesting town.

Coggeshall 🐝

Coggeshall lies in the path of the old Roman road, Stane Street, and parts of Roman dwellings, coins, bricks and tiles have been found throughout the years. Part of a Roman aqueduct can be seen inside the Clockshop on Market Hill.

Close by is the Clock Tower, a prominent feature of the town. The clock was purchased in honour of the 1887 Jubilee of Queen Victoria and started in 1888.

On the opposite side of Stoneham Street is the Old House, which in the 1840s was a public house called the Black Horse, where the notorious Coggeshall Gang had their headquarters.

Walking south into Bridge Street, the visitor will come to a bridge over the river Blackwater. This is called the Long Bridge and is claimed to be the oldest brick bridge in the country. It contains bricks made in the 13th century when Coggeshall Abbey was in existence. In the past, horses and carts could cross the river by a ford alongside the bridge.

From this point, but farther up Grange Hill, the Grange Barn can be seen. This was built in the 15th century as a tithe barn for the abbey. Older inhabitants remember it as the scene of plays, pageants, flower shows and other public events, but it was allowed to fall into a delapidated state until 1984 when a complete restoration took place. It is now owned by the National Trust.

Opposite the Barn is Abbey Lane, where St Nicholas' chapel is situated. This was built in 1220 and was originally the gatehouse chapel for the abbey and it is said that it only escaped demolition during the Reformation through being used as a cowshed. In 1863 it was restored and later endowed by the Gardner family, and is now regularly used as a place of worship.

Little remains of the abbey, which was founded in 1140 by King Stephen and then taken over by Cistercian monks, who learned the art of brickmaking from sister houses on the Continent and established the industry in Coggeshall. Many handmade bricks can be seen around the windows inside St Nicholas' chapel. The monks also introduced the rearing of sheep, which may have led to the wool trade on which the town's prosperity was later founded. In 1538 the abbey was dissolved and almost totally destroyed. Some buildings survived, however, and these can be seen near the Abbey House, which is an Elizabethan building.

Also nearby stands the picturesque Abbey Mill, which is a watermill in working order. The present owner has it in operation on several days during the summer, when the public are admitted and a miller is present to grind corn. Stoneground wholemeal flour is usually on sale on these days.

Paycocke's House, another National Trust property, is situated in West Street and was built in the 16th century by John Paycocke and left to his son Thomas, a successful wool merchant and clothier, who employed many of the local people in carding and weaving. Several rooms in the house are open to the public on specified days and there is also a garden leading to the river. In 1584 Paycocke's no longer belonged to the family and was allowed to deteriorate over three centuries. However, in 1904 it was bought by Mr Noel Buxton, later Lord Buxton, and restored to plans approved by Sir Edwyn Lutyens.

Memorial brasses to the Paycocke family can be seen in the parish church, which was rebuilt in the 15th century largely as a result of the prosperous wool trade. During an air raid in 1940 it received a direct hit and the tower and much of the nave had to be demolished but were later restored and the church was rehallowed in 1956. It has a resident colony of bats (not in the belfry – it's too cold in there, according to the vicar) which are counted regularly.

The manufacture of wool cloth declined from 1800 and was replaced by the making of silk thread. Several silk factories were established. In 1820, Drago, a Frenchman, arrived in Coggeshall with his two daughters and introduced lace making to the town. It proved a successful business, giving employment to many local women and girls. Today, quite a number of examples of old Coggeshall lace are owned by the townspeople, and tuition is available to anyone wishing to learn the craft.

Past industries included straw plaiting, tanneries, breweries (a well-known one being Gardner's of Bridge Street) and an iron foundry at the Gravel, owned by Mr Kirkham. Seed growing has for many years been a very important industry in the area, the names E. W. King and J. K. King being well-known as suppliers of flower, vegetable and agricultural seeds.

A path leads to Markshall Estate, situated about two miles to the north of the town. Markshall mansion, now demolished, was the home of the Honywood family in the 17th century, and Colonel Honywood, an active supporter of Cromwell, led a contingent from Coggeshall at the siege of Colchester in 1648. The estate is now in the hands of the Thomas Philips Price Trust and an arboretum is being planted, with many trees obtained from Kew Gardens and other important collectons. An area has been set aside as a memorial to the RAF and USAAF.

During the 1970s there was a big increase in the amount of heavy traffic passing through Coggeshall, which was causing considerable inconvenience in the town and damage to the old buildings. After a great deal of effort on the part of the Council and citizens, a bypass was suggested and a Public Enquiry followed. Permission was finally given for a new road to be built and in 1983 the Coggeshall bypass was opened.

Another successful venture has been the Community Bus, a 16-seater which, since 1982, has provided a twice-weekly town service, makes regular journeys to and from Kelvedon station, and can be hired for private functions. It was provided by the Parish Council with the help of Essex County Council and the service is operated by a splendid band of volunteer drivers. It is much appreciated, especially by older members of the community.

In 1986 a piece of land was given by the Parish Council to become a nature reserve for the benefit of the local people and children's groups. Mr B. Tebbutt acts as volunteer warden and has planted 28 trees including rowan, oak, alder, willow, holly, crabapple and hawthorn. Nesting boxes and a bat box have been erected and there is a marsh area and pond inhabited by frogs and other varieties of pond life. In 1990 the reserve won the Braintree Council Heritage Award Certificate, also a grant and certificate from the Shell Better Britain Campaign.

Colchester

Colchester has existed for about 2,000 years. It lies at the highest navigable point of the river Colne, eight miles from the sea, and is built on top of a small hill which in early times made it ideal for trade and for defence.

There are traces of Bronze and Iron Age culture, but not until the Romans came in 54 BC did it have any long term stable identity. Its name then was Camulodunum and this first appears in about 10 BC. By AD 25 Cunobelin (Shakespeare's Cymbeline) was ruling the whole area, which extended north to Stowmarket, west as far as Reading and probably included Kent. Colchester became his capital in south-eastern Britain.

The Romans built an elegant, thriving town with all their usual amenities of public baths, a theatre, and of course the temple to the Emperor Claudius. Julius Caesar garrisoned his troops in the town and Colchester has been a military town ever since.

Unfortunately, in AD 61 while most of the Roman garrison was away fighting in Wales, the Iceni tribes from Norfolk and Suffolk, under Queen Boadicea, swept through and sacked the town killing everyone in sight. Traces of those fires still remain.

The Temple of Claudius was rebuilt and probably ended its days as a Christian church, since a Bishop of Colchester led the delegation to the Council of Arles in AD 314.

The Romans withdrew in the early 5th century and, although suffering invasions from Saxons and others, the town continued to survive and be a centre for trade.

The Saxons renamed the town Colchester, 'the fortress on the Colne'. This is the period of the legend of St Helena who is supposed to have discovered the true Cross. She was the daughter of King Coel of Colchester (that 'merry old soul'). The legend ties Helena with the Emperor

Constantine and reaches back to the days of the great Cunobelin. All very comforting to people living in those uncertain and hazardous times. Her statue, bravely holding aloft the cross, stands on top of the town hall.

The Saxons moved their capital to London but Colchester was still a town of importance when the Normans invaded in 1066. Using the remains of the Roman buildings and on top of the foundations of the Temple of Claudius (which are still there), they built their massive castle, commanding a fine defensive position over the whole area.

Times moved on through the Dissolution of the Monasteries, which we see from the remains of St Botolph's Priory and the St John's Abbey gatehouse. Next came the rise of the cloth and wool trade and the establishment of wider education through the Colchester Royal Grammar School.

In 1648 the siege of Colchester saw the Cavaliers defending the town against the Roundheads. The citizens suffered greatly. It is said that the nursery rhyme 'Humpty Dumpty' originated at this time. Humpty was a defending sharpshooter on top of the 'wall' of St Mary's church tower on the western edge of the town. He wreaked havoc among the attacking Roundheads, but ultimately was killed – hence the line 'all the King's

Colchester Castle

horses and all the King's men couldn't put Humpty together again' – and the town fell. Bullet holes from the siege are still visible in the timbers of Siege House at East Gates, beside the river.

From that time the cloth and wool trade diminished, but the surrounding area had rich farming lands and the market continued to bring prosperity. Gradually manufacturing became the mainstay of the town and by Victorian times there were engineering works, iron foundries, clothing factories and corn and oil mills. Cants began growing roses, which are now world famous, as are the Colchester oysters. Many are the celebrities who have attended the Colchester Oyster Feast over the years.

At the present time the town centre boasts two new shopping precincts, many new shops, cafes, museums and interesting boutiques and specialist shops. Unlike so many other towns parking is relatively plentiful and includes six multi-storey car parks all within a few minutes walk of the High Street.

The castle still dominates the eastern end of the town. It has the largest central keep of any castle in Britain. It has a lovely setting of extensive parkland and sports fields. Here the Cants roses make a lovely display every year. Inside the castle is a truly excellent museum and conducted tours will show the visitor the 'dungeons', which are in fact the foundation arches of the Roman Temple of Claudius.

South of Colchester, extending from Rowhedge on the river Colne westward through East and West Donyland, was the estate of Berechurch. It was part of the lands belonging to St John's Abbey.

It has no village, being just part of the road to Mersea Island, south of Colchester. But Berechurch Hall, the manor of West Donyland, is first mentioned as being acquired by Sir Thomas Audley, Lord Chancellor to King Henry VIII and Speaker of the House of Commons, after St John's Abbey was dissolved. He settled the property on his younger brother, but he himself lived at Saffron Walden where he had also been given the Abbey of Walden. It was Sir Thomas' grandson who built Audley End.

Members of the family continued to live at Berechurch Hall. They built the little family church where many of them are buried. In 1800 it was owned by Sir George Smyth, who built a lovely grotto in a natural hollow, fed by a spring, for his daughter Charlotte. She died in 1845, age 33, and the grotto was kept as a memorial to her. The church is now derelict and vandalised and is expected to be soon demolished. The grotto is no more, just a hollow in the ground.

In the Second World War the Hall was taken over by the Military and used as a POW camp. After the war the Hall was demolished and the grounds developed by the Military as a prison, or 'glasshouse' as it was popularly known. Today it has developed into the Military Corrective Training Centre and is the depot and HQ of the Military Provost Staff Corps.

Berechurch is surrounded by land belonging to the Military. These large, wild, open spaces ensure the preservation of many species of plants, animals and birds which thrive in land which would otherwise have been submerged under concrete and houses.

Copford 🐝

Copford has a link with Roman Britain in its largest road – to the Saxons it was Stane Street, now we call it London Road – and this road crosses the Roman river in Copford, just short of Colchester.

Present day Copford is situated just off the A12 in north-east Essex approximately four miles from Colchester and a mile from Marks Tey. Copford used to be a far larger village than it is now (in 1815 there were eleven miles of road in the village) with parts of the original Copford now incorporated into the surrounding areas of Stanway, Lexden, Aldham and Eight Ash Green.

The village is roughly T-shaped, with London Road (the old A12) representing the 'cross-bar' of the T and the stem or vertical branch of the T leading southwards away from the main road to the more rural area of the village. Because of its former usage as the main road from London to the East Anglian coast and beyond, the present London Road consists of a mixture of both commercial and residential properties. A considerable number of new houses are being built in the northern part of Copford on land between this and the new A12.

In addition to these, the charity Help the Aged has recently built an extremely attractive set of flats and houses for the independent elderly nearby, partly on newly acquired land and partly by converting the well established dwelling known as Copford Place, set amidst large and very scenic grounds. Another feature on London Road is the police sub-station, which we are most fortunate to have in our midst and which is manned by two sergeants and four constables part-time. The stem of the T is represented by School Road, Copford, which wends its way southwards, passing en route the fruit farm and the village shop.

School Road continues past the village hall, behind which lies the children's playground and the area known as Pits Wood and then leads on past the village school, built in 1851, at the bend in the road. The original headmaster's house, which stands alongside the main school building, was sold a few years ago for private use and there is no longer a schoolmaster's residence on the site.

Immediately beyond the school is the area of Copford known as Copford Green. The entrance to the green is a most attractive one, being marked by two listed buildings, both of them barns. The village green itself is triangular in shape and in the centre of this there stands a beautiful oak tree which was planted by the village residents to commemorate the Coronation of Edward VII in 1902. Around the base of the oak tree there is a circular, wrought iron bench – painted dark green and originally built to celebrate the Silver Jubilee of King George V in 1936. Some houses built in Copford in the 15th century of local sand and clay were very strongly built and one of these, Pink Cottage on the green, still stands today.

Alongside the green there is the Alma public house which, although originally having been named both the Lion and the George, was renamed following the battle of Alma in 1854, during the Crimean War. Around this time the building itself also encompassed a brewery, but the only part of this remaining today is the current cellar. Today the Alma is a popular rendezvous with both local residents and visitors alike.

Leading away from the village green there are three roads – one of which, after passing a residential home for the elderly, leads to the small village of Easthorpe, which combines with our village to form Copford with Easthorpe Parish Council. Another road leads to another neighbouring village, Birch, passing on the way both the chocolate factory, where delicious home made chocolates are produced and also the road to Hill Farm. Church Road leads around to the south-eastern corner of Copford.

Copford Hall, which remains in the ownership of descendants of the Harrison family even today, is surrounded by beautiful grounds, covered with magnificent oaks, cedars and other trees amidst attractively landscaped grounds. This old red-brick mansion which, during the First World War was used as a military school of divisional instruction, is currently being leased for private commercial purposes.

Copford church, now called St Michael and All Angels, was formerly dedicated to Our Lady the Mother of Jesus. This church was built soon after 1125 and the earliest murals were painted as soon as the church was completed, but it is thought that there was an earlier place of worship on the site. The present roof dates from 1400 and the bell turret was added a short time after that. In all medieval ironwork placed on timber it was usual to insert leather or cloth between, to prevent sweating timber from rusting metal and, in the case of the ironwork on this door the leather was found, centuries later, to be human skin, possibly that of a Dane.

Copford Cricket Club, the ground of which adjoins both the Hall and the church, was originally formed in the mid 1960s. A notable feature of the club ground is the presence in its midst of a beautiful oak tree which, under certain circumstances, is considered to be a 'fielder', and about which special local playing rules have been written. As with Copford church, a visit to this lovely cricket ground is a must, particularly at weekends during the cricket season, when you should be fortunate enough to see village cricket still being played at its best – either before or after the players have participated in one of Copford Cricket Club's afternoon teas, for which the ladies producing them are justly renowned.

All local groups undertake their activities in Copford village hall, outside which there is a beautifully carved and decorated village sign. In the recent past the Parish Council bought some land behind the village hall and converted it into a children's playground containing swings and other play equipment for younger children, whilst the more green areas of land are very popular with the older children for playing football and cricket.

Immediately behind the playground is the area known as Pits Wood. This wood was bought by the Parish Council several years ago both in order to prevent it from falling into the hands of property developers and also to preserve it as an area of nature conservation and relaxation for village residents to enjoy for posterity.

Crays Hill 🐑

Crays Hill is in the parish of Ramsden Crays and is situated two miles east of Billericay. Ancient records date the village from the 13th century.

Called Ramesdana in 1086 and Rammesden in 1262, Ramsden is a compound of the two Saxon words Ram and den, signifying Ram's valley. Adjoining the Bursteads, on the north-east, are two parishes of this name, known at the time of the Norman Domesday survey only by the general appellation of Ramsden, but distinguished afterwards by the surname of their ancient possessors, the families of Crey and Belhus.

In Edward the Confessor's reign, part of it belonged to two freemen. There were two manors in this parish; the manor of Ramsden Crays and that of Tyled-hall, or Thill-hall. The first named rector of Ramsden Crays is in the rolls as William, described as 'Persona Ecclie of Crey'. He was accused in 1257 of helping Simon and Ralph de Creye eject Andrew de Blund from the manor of Rammesden Creye by force of arms.

The parish church of St Mary stands near the middle of the parish. In 1870 the church was entirely rebuilt at a cost of £1,120, but incorporates some old work. The nave has a 15th century roof with moulded plates and three tie-beams, with king posts having four way struts. The bell-turret at the west end stands on four 15th century posts, with heavy braces forming two centred arches and square framing above to support the turret. There are two inaccessible bells, said to be by Thomas Bartlet, 1617. The font has been entirely retooled and is of doubtful date. The church is nestled in countryside and in a popular area for walkers and horse-riders.

Like many other villages, Crays Hill is a mixture of old and modern properties. A new development stands at the top of the hill, but at the foot of the hill by the village store is a pair of cottages which are known to be well over 300 years old. Whilst renovating his cottage a few years ago, the present owner of one of the cottages found coins dated 1663 and 1691.

Pump Cottage at the foot of Crays Hill was built around 1860, about ten years after the village well was built. Villagers who had not contributed towards the cost paid one shilling a quarter for use of the well. The well still exists in the garden of Pump Cottage and is believed to run under the road near the bus stop. A blacksmith's shop stood between Pump Cottage and Manor Cottage but this was demolished in 1933.

Crays Hill National school built in 1863 for 100 pupils stood in the church hall grounds, but was demolished 50 years later and another school was built on land which was part of Great Barns Farm.

The Shepherd and Dog public house which stands at the top of the hill was originally built about 300 years ago and, although it has been rebuilt and modernised over the years, retains some original charm inside.

Plans at the beginning of the 19th century for the Islington to Wallasea railway to run through Crays Hill never came to fruition; neither did plans for the village to be linked by canal from Battlesbridge to Purfleet.

There is a story of a phantom boy dressed in white (of course!) who haunts the spot at Crays Hill where, according to rumour, the gallows used to stand.

Danbury 🦢

Until recently, it was thought that the Danes had settled here and given the place its name. Now we know that it was probably Dengiebury, because it was in the Dengie Hundred. No doubt the Danes looked at the hill – a foot above sea level for every day of the year – and decided to go round it. Much earlier, Stone Age man had left mounds of discarded arrow heads in Lingwood.

On the common can be seen the trenches which soldiers dug when they were expecting Napoleon to invade England. Later, during the First World War, soldiers who were billeted here carved some unique pew ends in the church. These depict mythical birds and animals, and managed to survive the bomb in the Second World War which left the church without any stained glass windows. Luckily, the three effigies of 14th century knights, carved in wood and resting peacefully on top of their tombs, are still there.

The church on top of the hill has a glorious spire, and a lovely tale about the Devil visiting it in a rage and throwing the bell down the hill. It came to rest in Bell Wood, where the hollow it made can be seen to this day. The locals, perhaps to commemorate this event, still quench their thirst at the Bell public house.

Some winters the village can be snowed up, when the snow is so deep that pavements are impassable and cars are imprisoned in garages. The birds are duly fed, and left over food happily eaten by the foxes. Candles are at the ready, but hopefully are not needed. Then the hill becomes like the Swiss Alps. The schools are closed and hundreds of children slide and toboggan down the hillside. For once the 'Public Open Space', usually just a steep grassy slope, becomes noisy, crowded and the centre of village life.

Spring is a time of awakening. Are the snowdrops waiting under the snow, to appear when it melts? Soon after come the golden daffodils, in gardens, on the roadside verges and wild in the woods. The trees become green and the woodland paths are bordered with a succession of wild flowers. Foxes and badgers make paths through them, and can be seen at dusk, wandering along them in search of food.

Summer is a time for picnics, and admiring the heather which still clings to the hillsides, or you may be lucky to find some stone arrow heads, hidden in the stony ground. On Sundays gardens are opened for charity and one can wander around them, drink tea, and wonder why the garden at home is not quite so lovely.

On Guy Fawkes Night the village plays host to at least 20,000 people, who come to see the Boy Scouts' firework and bonfire display on the playing fields. The police arrive in force, and line the roads with 'no parking' bollards. Later they are to be seen trying to make order out of chaos, as hundreds of cars slowly ascend the hill and are directed to find parking space in the dark surrounding lanes. For one evening the Queen's Firework Maker turns the village into fairyland. It is an unforgettable night of noise, flashes and bangs, and it lights up a very happy crowd of parents and children, who have come under the spell of its enchantment.

Christmas is perhaps best of all. The house gardens have lighted Christmas trees in them, and we all sing carols round the tree, near the village pond. The Salvation Army band and the bell ringers fill the village with the sound of carols, and it is happily contented and isolated on its hill.

Debden & Debden Green

Approaching Debden from the local market town of Saffron Walden, the major landmark on entering the village is the massive radar tower used to guide aeroplanes to the new airport of Stansted. Behind the tower is the old Second World War Debden airfield, now an army barracks.

The road from Walden drops down to a crossroads. To the left in its own parkland is Debden Manor. An imposing building of white brick with a stone extension, it was built in 1796 as the rectory. Proving too large for the rector as long ago as 1908, it was subsequently known as Harleyfield House and used as the quarters for the commanding officer of the adjacent Debden airfield during the war. Charles Bland acquired the house and the manorial rights between the wars and was responsible for planting many of the trees around the house. He also planted the avenue of horse chestnuts on either side of the main road into the village.

On the opposite side of the crossroads is a fine thatched cottage. Formerly the Fox public house, it was one of five refreshment houses in the village, of which only two survive.

The Memorial Hall, erected in memory of those who gave their lives in the First World War, and the community shop are adjacent to the village pond, the playing field, the White Hart pub and the school. The Memorial Hall is the focal point of many village activities, including the WI. The adjacent community shop, believed to be the first in Essex, was established by a team of volunteers and is still run largely with voluntary labour. The shop provides most foodstuffs including fresh produce and the post office is located within the shop.

The fine red-brick school, with headmaster's house attached, was built in 1852 with funds provided by the then rector Henry Hodgson. When the airfield was converted into a barracks in 1979, the doubling of the school population with children from the army families meant the old building was too small. An extension was built in sympathy with the old building, but a portable classroom is still needed to meet present demand.

A wooded road to the right of the school leads down to the church. Built in the 13th century, the building today looks much as it must have done following an extensive restoration in the late 18th century. At the same time the Chiswells, lords of the manor, built themselves a private chapel of white brick. Almost octagonal in shape, the chapel forms the east end of the church and the Coade stone coat of arms on the exterior still looks new today. The present small tower and spire at the west end was built in 1930 by the Blands of Debden Manor, to replace a steeple erected in the 1786 restoration.

The Chiswell family and their descendants lived in Debden for 150 years. Richard Chiswell, a London merchant purchased the Debden Hall estate in 1715. Although there had been a house on the site of Debden Hall since the 14th century, major improvements were made to the house in 1750. Towards the end of the 18th century the park with a substantial lake was laid out. Debden Hall was demolished in 1935. Today's visitor, who follows the footpath downhill past the church, can still view the boating lakes, now somewhat overgrown. In the field adjacent to the church are some red-brick buildings and a high brick wall. Now three private houses, these are the old Debden Hall gardens.

Opposite the White Hart, the village pump marks the centre of the village. Deynes Road leads off to the left to Deynes Farm and Rowney Wood and the High Street continues straight ahead. The large number of modern houses in the centre of the village replace the wooden cottages destroyed in the great fire of Debden in 1907. A Mrs Bunting poured paraffin on her boiler fire and set her chimney alight. Although Mrs Bunting's cottage was unharmed, 20 buildings were affected by the fire and twelve completely destroyed.

The High Street extends past what was once the Ship pub and a former chapel, built in 1829, to the Plough, the second working pub in the village. The Plough once marked the end of the village, but, since the Second World War, the village has extended down the hill to Smiths Green. The 1960s bungalows and council houses are separated by the concrete Pentecostal chapel, which also serves as a doctor's surgery. A small estate was erected at Highfields, on the right of the road, in the 1980s.

About a mile along the road to Thaxted from the centre of the village is Debden Green, the second major centre of population in the parish. Until the 1950s Debden Green consisted of several small farms, each independently run, and a row of cottages. Today most of the farmhouses are separated from their surrounding land, which is farmed by two or three larger farmers. Some modern bungalows, adjacent to the Debden Green post office and garage, have increased the population.

Debden Green merges into Hamperden End, where old cottages and farmhouses mix with more modern dwellings. The Three Horseshoes thatched cottage was once the fifth pub in the village.

Until the Second World War Debden was a largely self contained village growing its own food and milling and baking its own bread, with most of the local population working on smaller farms of 100 acres or much less. As farms have been amalgamated and hedges removed, the former farmhouses and cottages have been occupied by those who commute from the village to find work.

However, some local enterprises now replace the employment once offered by the farms. Ducks are reared in large numbers at Telmara Farm for the restaurants of the neighbourhood and the London trade. A European pay and benefits consultancy operates from a converted barn at Monks. Computer hardware is designed and sold by an electronics company based in the village and, more controversially, motorbodies are built in the barns at Roothers Farm.

Doddinghurst

Doddinghurst lies about four miles between Brentwood and Ongar.

In 1876 it had a recorded population of 426, consisting of a few cottages and some outlying farms, no pub but a Georgian three storey mansion for the priest and a large gabled brick house known as Doddinghurst Hall with farm buildings surrounding it. The old rectory was pulled down and sold for housing at Bakers Meadow. It has been replaced by a modern rectory. Doddinghurst Hall has also disappeared and the Moat House pub built on the site.

Mr Wooltorton who owned the Hall in 1934 sold off small plots of land to London Eastenders for weekend cottages which proved a boon to owners for a respite from the intensive bombing of the East End during the Second World War. Some of these still remain in Doddinghurst Road and Wyatts Green.

Main gas was piped to the village before the Second World War, electricity immediately afterwards. The early 1960s saw the laying of a main sewerage system. Now with all 'mod-cons' available, an explosion of very desirable houses were built situated in cul-de-sacs with such delightful names as Apple Tree Crescent, Beehive Chase, Bakers Meadow and Plovers Mead.

During the 1880s the then rector carried out extensive rebuilding of the chancel of All Saints church. Out of his own pocket he also built a school next to the church. A few years ago this was converted to a modern house – the school population having outgrown the little building. Children were having to be 'bussed' to Blackmore (the next village along) to school before the county council bought glebe land and built a modern infants and junior school next to the village hall. M. Wainwright of Emblems House was responsible for bringing a second hand entertainments hut to use as a village hall. The beautiful building of All Saints church, typical of a small Essex church spans history from the 13th century door to the recently refurbished spire covered in cedar wood shingles.

On the left of the path up to the church is the grave of an Indian princess who it is said married an Englishman and died of a broken heart and lack of sun. One notable parson Nehemiah Rogers buried here in 1660 is remembered for his writings on the parables. West of the church stands Priest House, an Essex boarded cottage dating from Elizabethan times and lived in until very recently. Now it makes a welcome meeting place for coffee after morning Sunday services.

Earls Colne 🐝

Earls Colne is situated on the A604 between Colchester and the small market town of Halstead. It is the largest of the four villages receiving their name from the river Colne. At the time of King Edward the Confessor it belonged to a Saxon named Ulwin. Ulwin's whole estate was given by William the Conqueror to Alberic De Vere, who later became the Earl of Oxford, thus the name Earls Colne.

A priory was founded in 1100 on the bank of the river by Alberic De Vere; it was surrendered to Henry VIII on 3rd July 1534 by Robert Abel, the prior. A large house now stands near the site and is still known as the 'Priory'.

There is a very fine church dedicated to St Andrew, in a prominent position looking over the Colne valley. The tower has ornamental stone carvings depicting the coat of arms of John De Vere, the 16th Earl of Oxford, dated 1532. A notable vicar of the parish from 1641 until 1683 was the Rev Ralph Josselin MA who kept a unique diary, an edition of which has been published. The village architecture is most interesting and has been featured in a BBC documentary. Standing in the High Street are a number of 16th century houses still with their Tudor interiors, but alas they now have Georgian or Victorian facades.

R. Hunt & Co Ltd, makers of agricultural machinery, has been of importance to the village during its short but prosperous history. It provided jobs for the villagers, and many amenities were given by the Hunt family. The factory closed down in June 1988. When William Hunt of Colne Place died, he left a trust fund to Earls Colne to be used for the benefit of the residents. A sports centre has been erected, a building was bought and is now the William Hunt Library in the centre of the village, and a large meadow known as Long Meadow and Brickfields Meadow was purchased for villagers to use for recreation. A piece of land in Station Road has been purchased, and a hall is to be erected on the site for the use of the Scouts and Guides of Earls Colne, while the village hall in York Road originally given to the village by Sir Reuben Hunt, is to be refurbished with money from the trust fund.

In recent times two golf courses have been designed, one near the river in the picturesque Colne valley, and the other on the Earls Colne airfield. This airfield was home to the 455 Bomber Squadron of the American Air Force in 1943. The roof of the public house in Coggleshall Road had to be removed to accommodate the bombers taking off. A flying club now carries on the flying tradition. Also on the site is an expanding business park providing jobs for local people.

The village is a minor shopping centre and serves the surrounding smaller villages. As a central village, Earls Colne also has four doctors in the modern surgery in Queens Road. There have been doctors serving the village since at least 1730.

A school with instruction in grammar as the chief subject was founded in Earls Colne in 1520 by Christopher Swallow, vicar of Messing. In 1673 the last Earl of Oxford sold the school estates to the Cressener family, who became patrons of the school. By the mid 18th century the school had achieved a high reputation, but it was closed in 1837. It reopened in 1843 under a new scheme as a Free grammar school. However in the reorganisation on comprehensive lines the grammar school closed in July 1975.

The village Church school was started on the 18th August 1813 and in 1843 Vicar Watkinson built a school in Park Lane, enlarged in 1875. In 1938 a new wooden building was put up in Park Lane opposite the church. The Earls Colne primary school is now a new building on the site of the old wooden one.

In addition to the Anglican parish church there are two other denominations in the village. The Baptist church was founded in 1786 in two converted cottages on the village green. A Major Gooday Pudney was its pastor from 1788 to 1832. He was one of the old class preachers, and on a hot Sunday afternoon when the congregation were rather sleepy he would call out 'Don't sleep Copsey', or 'Brother Adam, wake up Brother Smith by your side'. A chapel was built on the site of the cottages in 1818, and with the increase in the congregation a larger chapel was built and opened in 1860. The Quakers set up a meeting house in 1674. It is the oldest meeting house still in use in Essex.

Earls Colne village green is divided by the A604. It is little used now, but it has a village sign that is a memorial to Police Constable Jeff Perry, our very much respected village policeman who died at the early age of 35 in 1981.

On Pound Green there is a water pump donated by Mrs Gee in 1853, 'In Thankful Commemoration for the absence of Cholera' in the village.

Eight Ash Green 🐿️

As parishes go in Essex, Eight Ash Green is a virtual newcomer, having been created as a new civil parish in the rural district of Laxden and Wilstree in January 1947. Land was acquired from the neighbouring parishes of Aldham (four acres), Stanway (125 acres), Copford (641 acres) and Fordham (844 acres). Lying five miles to the west of Colchester, the parish straddles the main A604 road to Cambridge, extending northwards from the main railway line and A12 road across undulating gravel and boulder-clay slopes towards the wide valley of the river Colne.

In 1949 the total population was 660, most of whom were involved in agriculture or local trades. They lived in scattered farms and cottages with two main hamlets – around Fordham Heath and at the old cross-roads by the Brick and Tile, where an ancient road from Copford to West

Bergholt crossed the main road from Colchester. Smaller groups of cottages stood beside Seven Star and Daisy Greens.

Today the population has grown enormously to over 2,000, reflecting the increasing popularity of this part of Essex as improved road and rail links attract both new industries and commuters. As a result, where 40 years ago there was prime agricultural land, there are now modern housing estates.

Because of the manner of its creation, Eight Ash Green, unlike most Essex villages, has no ancient centre. There are some scattered timber-framed houses of considerable interest, dating mainly from the late 16th century, such as Martells, Chippetts, Lampitts, Kemps, Abbots Hall, Greenacres and Fiddlers Farm, while Gatehouse Farm on Fordham Heath is actually mentioned in a document of 1291. Fordham Heath itself may well have been the site of an early manufacturing industry; in 1968 a particularly fine example of a Neolithic polished flint axe was found in a field behind the Cricketers, where there were many other flints of a similar honey colour.

The church of All Saints was built of locally made brick beside the main road in 1898 to serve this northern outpost of the parish of Copford, whilst the nearby Methodist chapel was opened in 1936 to replace a little one which stood in Huxtables Lane at the edge of the heath. Here, it is said, in fine weather services were often conducted from a farm wagon open to all the winds blowing across a treeless heath where cattle grazed and birds sang.

In one respect Eight Ash Green is blessed above almost all other Essex villages. It is a village of greens. The original green which gave its name in 1777 to the little hamlet of cottages clustered at the end of Blind Lane, has been gradually eaten away until only a pathetic remnant remains, looking for all the world like a rather wide roadside verge. Even the old village pond has been filled in. But there are others.

Daisy Green and Seven Star Green, lying south of the main road, together account for almost nine acres of open land. Both had small clusters of cottages on their edges. Daisy Green has one 18th century farmhouse and a series of modernised cottages which were originally built in the mid 19th century to accommodate workers on the new railway line. The name given to one of them perpetuates the old country name for an animal no longer seen hereabouts – the sally is a hare, and a hare-catcher once lived there.

Seven Star Green also has one 18th century house, the Maltings, whose name reflects one of the most important rural industries of an agricultural area. A few old cottages remain, but the inter-war years saw the beginning of development along the edges of the green as the need for grazing decreased. Today, these two small greens are being returned to their original state of ancient grazing common land and at least 125 species of wild flowers have been recorded growing there. The name Seven Star is curious and has nothing to do with stars. In 1438 it is recorded as 'S(t)ethenho(o) grove or grene' and may possibly be derived from the name of a Saxon landholder. Both these greens were given to Eight Ash Green Parish Council in 1974, by deed of gift, by the lord of the manor of Copford, Mr Brian Harrison.

Fordham Heath is another matter entirely. An ancient heathland with rights of common grazing, and reputed to be the second largest village green (of some 36 acres) in Essex, it was granted by Act of Parliament to the parish of Eight Ash Green in 1965, the rights of common grazing being confirmed in 1980. Older villagers remember a very different heath from that which exists today. Apart from the military lands at Berechurch and Donyland, it is the last surviving remnant of the seven great heathlands which surrounded Colchester in the past, but which have succumbed to the sprawl of housing or to the extraction of the gravel which gave them their being. Until the Second World War and the disappearance of working horses from the land, the heath was well grazed; cattle, horses, donkeys, sheep and goats kept it an open area of heather, bracken and gorse, the annual burning of which ensured the growth of sweet hay grasses.

The old well at the top of the northern slope provided a constant supply of pure sweet soft water for all the villagers who lived round the heath. They collected it in two-gallon buckets which had to be supported on a rectangular yoke, although sometimes a barrel on wheels and drawn by a donkey was used instead. Piped water came to the heath in the late 1930s, and now the old well is difficult to find being overgrown by brambles and tangled undergrowth, but tapping a deep source, it never dries up.

The old tithe map of 1839 shows the outline of the heath much as it is today with two areas marked as 'for the poor of the parish'. These were used as allotments. One of them, on the upper heath, is still used in this way although some of the allotments are now privately owned. The other, the Parish Field, is rented out to a local farmer.

Today the upper heath is a valuable recreational amenity for the village, and is the home of the cricket and football clubs originating in the immediate post-war period. Changing agricultural practices and the demise of the heavy horse have led to the abandonment of grazing although there is just one commoner left who is entitled to enjoy the rights of turbary, and the grazing of one horse and one cow if he should so desire.

In addition to the greens, the village is fortunate to contain a nature reserve at Iron Latch managed by the Essex Wildlife Trust where an orchid-rich meadow is being recreated. The adjacent woodland, full of large hollows, was once the source of gravel ballast for the nearby railway line.

Elmstead Market 🦐

Elmstead is situated 4 miles east of Colchester, bounded by a small brook. In the centre of the village is the village green which years ago was used for a market and fair. In the year 1253, in the reign of Henry III, Sir Richard de Tany obtained a licence to keep a Market and Fair at Elmstead whence it is called Elmstead Market to this day. The market soon died out, but the fair was held annually every May until 1914. Modern revivals have taken place from time to time.

Elmstead Market is 1 mile south of Elmstead Church and Hall on main road from Colchester to Harwich and to Thorpe and Walton. Many houses date back to 17th century, including Momples Hall Hunting Lodge, which was used as a workhouse for the poor. Later it became the village bakehouse and has now reverted to a private dwelling.

The village sign erected in 1983 depicts the elms and the working life of the village with three heraldic shields.

The Parish Church – there is evidence of a Saxon church on the site. Much of the building is 13th century. North doorway (uncovered 1931) is Norman. Over the doorway is an arch of Roman bricks, above which is a Saxon arch discovered in 1988. The original door preserved in church, replaced by a replica by Mabbett's wood carvers, Colchester.

The Wesleyan Methodist Chapel built in 1816–1817 was restored in 1863. The Wesleyan Schoolroom for Infants was built in 1872.

The Church of England School, built in 1846 was enlarged several times and vacated in 1973 and converted into a thriving Community Centre in May 1976.

The original village school is still standing in Old School Lane. Built circa 1830, the thatched and boarded building is now used as a private dwelling.

Two public houses, the King's Arms on the south side, dating back to the 17th century at least, and the Bowling Green facing north of the main road. The original part of the house, among the oldest buildings in Elmstead has been altered and refurbished on several occasions. The unique pub sign of a bowling green was chosen because there was a games pitch at the rear of the long back garden which extended to Chapel Lane. The inn eventually became a hostelry where passengers and mail coaches from London to Harwich stayed to rest, often overnight, and exchange horses.

James Noah Paxman, famous founder of the worldwide engineering works known as Davey Paxman & Co of Colchester 1865, was the son of James Paxman, 'wheelwright and machine maker' and was born at Elmstead where his father had a forge and engineering works in the village and made traction engines.

Elsenham

Elsenham is a typical country village, situated between Stansted Mountfitchet and Thaxted and adjacent to the recently constructed 'Third London Airport'. It has an ancient background, being mentioned in the Domesday Book.

A Baron De Abrince owned a manor here in the time of William the Conqueror. A later knight, Sir William Say, forfeited the manor for supporting Perkin Warbeck, who claimed to be Richard Duke of York and led an insurrection against Henry VII in the year 1497. The rising failed and Warbeck was hanged. Sir William was eventually pardoned by the King and his estates were restored to him in 1500. He died in 1520 and with his wife Elizabeth lies buried in the chancel of the Norman church.

The last lord of the manor was Sir Walter Gilbey 1875–1914. Sir Walter was a friend of the Prince of Wales (later Edward VII) who visited the Hall on many occasions. Once he was on a visit to Lord and Lady Brooke at Eastern Lodge with several members of the nobility, when they drove over to inspect the Gilbey Stud of thoroughbred horses. A parade of horses was arranged and they later lunched at the Hall. We are informed that the Prince was well pleased with the visit.

Sir Walter is well remembered because in 1900, in memory of his wife, he had a pump erected in the village street. It has round brick sides, from the top of which oak posts support a gilded dome. This pump supplied water for the villagers until the main water pipes were laid in about 1936. For some reason the metal pump was removed and the well covered.

He also started the jam factory employing many villagers and to this day one can see Elsenham jam on sale in many countries. Another sideline of Sir Walter's were the lavender fields which were planted and yielded the flowers from which was made the delightful Elsenham Lavender Perfume.

The Norman church of St Mary is built on the site of an earlier Saxon church. The feature of this beautiful church is the arch with its star and chevron decorations. In the chancel, coloured metal panels with portraits of saints were brought from France by Sir Walter Gilbey.

The Great Eastern Railway came through Elsenham in 1843 and Queen Victoria and Prince Albert travelled from Tottenham passing through Elsenham on the way to Cambridge; this must have been a very exciting journey at that time of railway travel. The original station was sited at Fullers End, but subsequently moved to its present site in 1850. A horse-drawn omnibus ran from Elsenham to Thaxted until a branch railway service commenced in 1913. This line was closed in September 1952, coming under the Beeching railway axe. Once again an omnibus, motorised this time, made the connection.

The Hon Dorothy Paget bought Elsenham Hall and paddocks in 1936 and was the owner of *Golden Miller*, the greatest steeplechaser of all time. He was the winner of five Gold Cups 1932 to 1936 and of the Grand National in 1934. He is buried at the paddocks with a stone marking his resting place.

In 1933 the population was 500, and in 1990 approximately 3,000. Many housing estates have been built, but one may still find a few beautifully thatched cottages, and lovely gardens. There is a new village hall, attached to the junior school, which caters for most social activities, and a Memorial Hall in the playing field with adjacent sports field and children's playground. There is one public house, the Crown, for the benefit of locals and visitors alike.

The countryside around the village is very beautiful and many wild flowers can be enjoyed. If one is lucky there are deer and foxes to be seen, and maybe peacocks perching on the roof of a lovely old house called Elsenham Place.

Epping 🐾

Despite its proximity to London, Epping has preserved its identity as an attractive market town.

In 1878 all the forest rights were vested in the Corporation of London. Queen Victoria officially opened the forest to the public in 1882. The Crown continue to appoint a Ranger, the present one being the Duke of Gloucester. The forest sustained considerable damage in the hurricanes of October 1987 and January 1990 since when some restorative work has been undertaken.

Newmarket race course was formed during the reign of King James I and there is evidence that the road through Epping soon became an important route to Newmarket and the eastern counties. By the early 19th century 25 coaches a day passed through Epping where the horses were changed and travellers could obtain refreshment. In 1800 there were 26 inns in the town although the population was under 2,000.

In 1253 King Henry III granted a charter so that a market could be held in Epping on Mondays. For centuries hundreds of bullocks were walked through the town on their way to Smithfield Market in London. Epping became renowned for its butter, cream and sausages.

The sale of livestock in the market ceased in 1961 after an outbreak of foot and mouth disease. The flourishing market still encourages visitors from all around the area. The centre of the town is covered now by a Conservation Order to preserve the character of the High Street.

The tower of St John's church is one of the four landmarks in Epping which are visible from several miles away. The present church was built in 1889/1890 and the tower was added in 1909. The organ, renovated in 1976, is one of the finest parish church organs in the country.

In order to celebrate the Silver Jubilee of Queen Elizabeth II, 20 members of the Epping Women's Institute made a collage which depicts the buildings on the eastern side of the High Street. It was made to scale and is 22 ft in length. A few years later the same number of ladies made a collage, 30 ft long, to portray the buildings on the opposite side of the High Street. Both collages are on permanent display in Epping Hall.

Many of the buildings are of architectural interest. Aberdeen House, a butcher's shop, is reputed to be the oldest building in Epping. Batchelor's, the saddler's and shoe shop, has a weatherboarded front, small dormer windows and an interesting profile. Savory and Moore, the chemist's, was formerly the White Hart public house and has Victorian

View of Epping from Epping Upland

windows. In complete contrast, at the far end of the High Street, is the council office complex built at an estimated cost of £13.9 million and opened in 1990. The winning design, which was chosen from 51 entries, was by Richard Reid Associates. It has come in for a lot of criticism from local residents, who dislike the mixture of architectural styles. The tower is the most recent of the four conspicuous landmarks in Epping. The other landmarks are a 90 ft high water tower built in 1872 and the chimney of a laundry at St Margaret's Hospital.

Just beyond the council offices, on Church Hill, is the Roman Catholic church. The presbytery is one of the oldest houses in Epping. It was built in the Stuart period and the alcove of the parish priest's study was originally a gunpowder room.

Around the corner, in Lindsey Street, are some 17th century timber-framed cottages facing a small green. Just beyond these is the United Reformed church. It started as a meeting house in the early 17th century and is one of the oldest free churches in the country. The present building was erected in 1774. It was restored and the handsome front added in 1887.

Epping was one of the first small towns to boast its own sports centre. This is in Hemnall Street and the building was formerly a Territorial Army drill hall. The conversion was completed in 1970. There are now four squash courts, a rifle range and a large activity hall. The town has

four recreation grounds, the largest of which, Stonard's Hill, has tennis courts, football pitches and a children's playground. The famous wartime airfield at North Weald is also used for recreational activities. The Essex Way, an important long distance footpath, starts at Epping station.

Epping Forest Band was originally formed in 1894 and was re-formed in 1935 after a break of a few years. They have played at Westminster Abbey, in the London parks, in national contests and at concerts in many towns and villages. It was as a result of a visit by a band member to Eppingen in Germany that the first links were made between the two towns. Later this developed into a formal twinning of the towns in 1981. Members of the Epping–Eppingen Association pay frequent visits to the German town which, like Epping, is very close to a famous forest. In the case of Eppingen it is the Black Forest.

Farnham

In the early 1930s village life was bound up with farming, and many of the men worked on the land as farmworkers or estate workers. Others walked or bicycled into Bishops Stortford to work in industries such as Millars works and the match factory, both of which have disappeared. At busy times in the farming calendar many of the wives came out onto the farms to help, especially with weeding crops in the springtime, and harvesting in the summer and autumn. Children from the school also helped with the harvesting; it gave them an insight into working life, and as most of them left school at the age of 14 they knew what was expected of them when they did start to earn their living.

Many of the girls went into service as maids, or into the town as shop girls. There was also a laundry and a Snap factory where they could work in the town. Most of them married locally.

Little changed until the outbreak of the Second World War in 1939, when the way of life changed. Many of the men were called into the Armed Forces, and the women were expected to fill the gaps they left behind them. Landgirls came from towns and quite long distances away, they and men home on leave from the war brought a new look to life in the village. There were also evacuees from London at the beginning of the war.

In the early 1930s village social life revolved around the church, the pub and the village hall, known then as the parish room. There was a Mothers Union and a Temperance Society; this latter used to have Lantern Lectures, using a gas light to show the pictures, on the evils of drink. Whist drives and dances were held in the hall and occasionally some plays would be put on. The football team used it as their dressing room.

There was no mains water until about 1936, and all water was drawn from various wells scattered around the village, the men and sometimes the women carrying it in two buckets on a yoke, or they would use a hoop to keep the buckets from touching their legs and making their feet wet. There were no more than about ten motor cars in the village, but there was a bus of sorts – some said it was used for carrying animals for the rest of the week. The postman cycled round, and you could set your watch by him, so accurate was his timekeeping. He would also bring people's medicines for them. The bread was delivered on a motorcycle and sidecar, later a motor tricycle was used.

Various tradesmen came round with vans and sold groceries and fuel, as there was no electricity supply until 1939, and then only in some houses. Paraffin was used for lighting and heating, and some people used it for cooking as well. A Mr Bishop came with a pony and high wheeled cart selling fruit and fish, and sometimes in the summer, custard ice cream. Mr Warwick, who lived in the village, travelled around two or three other parishes as well as his own selling sweets, cottons, clothes and other things. He rode a bicycle with his goods in cases on carriers front and back and baskets on the handlebars, and because the cases were attache cases he was known as 'Tachy' Warwick. He joined the RAF for the war.

The school had a headmistress, Miss Senior, and in the early days she used to ride a motorcycle and sidecar, and lived in the school house. The children spent all of their school life at the school, which is a Church of England school, and much emphasis was placed on religious education. Everyone marched down to the church on Ascension Day for a service, also on Empire Day, when the Union flag would be run up the flagpole. Other social occasions at the school were May Day, when a May Queen was chosen and a maypole erected and danced around, and at the end of the summer term there was Feast Day, held in the parish room, followed by games in the rectory garden.

The rector of the village was Canon Geare, who served for over 50 years. He drove a Clyno motorcar and was one of the few car owners in the village, while his wife rode a large upright bicycle. They descended on the school most days of the week to take religious instruction and prayers, and to make sure that discipline was maintained – the fear of God was wrought in us all!

There was not a lot of leisure for adults, who mostly worked a five and a half day week. There was both a football team, with the pitch under the rectory windows in Walkers Field, and a cricket team, pitch at Hazel End, and in those days the bulk of the teams were local men and boys. Sometimes junior teams were got up and went to Manuden or Albury to play a game, but mainly youngsters whipped tops, bowled hoops, threw marbles, played hopscotch and conkers, and in the spring collected birds eggs.

The pace of life seems much faster now, there is no time to stand and stare. Many of the old village cottages have been renovated and are lived in by people working well outside the village; for much of the year they leave for work in the dark and arrive home in the dark. Perhaps there are some who would welcome back the allotments and the flower shows, and no mowers or chainsaws on Sunday.

Felsted ⚜

Evidence of Roman occupation of Felsted is now in Colchester museum; artefacts revealed as the Dunmow-to-Braintree railway was being built in 1868. Digs revealed the foundations of dwellings with timber frames and wattle and daub walls. This style of construction continued, with modifications, for many centuries. More recent buildings, of a similar structure, are still standing in the village. An old survey, by the Royal Commission of Historical Monuments in 1921, listed 108 timber-framed houses (most of which are still extant) largely dating from Tudor times.

Wooden-framed houses, in the Essex vernacular, are easy to identify in the village centre. Notably, one by George Boote, churchwarden and builder, still proudly proclaims on one of its external beams, 'George Boote made this: 1596'. This house faces the church and guildhall. The guildhall probably dates from soon after 1500, according to carbon-dating tests. Built for the Trinity guild, it was converted to use as a school by a foundation deed in 1564. It was intended to provide 'lernyng of Grammar and other vertues and godly lernyng' to male children born in Essex. Preference was given to boys born on Lord Rich's manors and farms, parts of his widespread and prosperous estates.

Some poor people were well provided for by Lord Rich, who built a set of five thatched houses, with attached meadow for six cows, a barn, a brewhouse and an orchard. On the site of these tenements, one can see the modern almshouses, next to a pub, east of the guildhall. These were erected in 1879 after a destructive fire, which started in the cowshed. However, the really poor – destitute, tramps – were catered for more reluctantly. In 1597 an Act of Parliament levied a compulsory Poor Rate in each parish and Felsted housed some 20 inmates, at subsistence level, and ensured work for seven and eight year olds. They worked all day, seven days each week. When the law was amended in 1834, the workhouse was closed and sold. It became two private houses, now known as Nunty's and Little Garnetts at the end of Workhouse Lane.

At the time when 'baize' cloth was exported to the Continent, returning boats brought back bricks as ballast. These Flemish bricks tended to be used merely for chimneys, until local brickworks began to produce a cheaper product. At that time (Causeway brickfields began working in the early 19th century, for example), fashion moved towards brick, rather than timber-framed houses. It is believed that the first house in Felsted made of brick was the New School House. This was designed by John Johnson, the architect who built the Shire Hall and the Stone Bridge in Chelmsford, along with part of Chelmsford Cathedral. Dating from 1800, this is still used by the school but called Ingrams Close. It stands east of the churchyard wall, beyond the guildhall.

Although the original church must have been Saxon and wooden, the oldest standing structure is the Norman tower. One can see pieces of Roman brick and tile, incorporated in the flint-rubble dressed with stone, from which it is built. The present church was built in stages, between the end of the 12th and the early 14th centuries. Amongst its treasures is the tomb of Lord Rich.

Along the road, next to the Victorian almshouses, is the other place of worship. The chapel, in pale brick, was built in 1833 at a time of decline of Anglican vigour and growing nonconformist power in the village. Sadly, it no longer serves as a church. Its congregation has moved to compact premises at its rear and the refurbished chapel has been put to commercial use. There is a private chapel, consecrated in 1873, attached to the school.

The independent school dominates the road eastwards out of the village centre. Many of the buildings facing the road and a triangle to its north, belong to the school.

Beyond the heart, around its clutch of shops, restaurants, pubs, church and school, one can find other interesting and handsome buildings. Felsted parish extends to nine so-called 'greens'. Some still show their commonland or pasture spaces, as at Bannister Green. There, the Three Horseshoes pub adjoins the erstwhile smithy. On the road out of Bannister Green, towards Leighs, stands the thatched cottage, with pargetted walls, called Quakers' Mount. In its garden one can glimpse the burial mound used for plague victims. Continuing towards Leighs, the gatehouse of Leez Priory stands up amongst the trees. The Elizabethan brick building can be better viewed from the lane which passes over the neck of the river Ter and then turns in front of the priory. The grounds are occasionally open to the public.

The use of places changes, of course. Recently, the sugar beet factory on the road to Dunmow fell into disuse, its towers now idle next to the dismantled railway bridge and the sidings given over to housing caravans. Nevertheless the continuing prosperity of the area, through the siting of its independent school and popularity with commuters to London and other nearby towns, means that most buildings are nurtured. They continue to add a charm which can be enjoyed by residents and visitors.

Fordham 🐾

The parish of Fordham is separated from the parish of Aldham by the river Colne. The name of Fordham is thought to have originated from the ford across the river at Ford Street. Fordham is about six miles from Colchester, which is the main shopping town. However, about two and half miles away, at Stanway, a new business park has been built, with several large stores, so Colchester has literally come out towards us!

All Saints' church is a 14th century building, consisting of a nave, two aisles and a chancel with a square tower containing three bells. It is constructed from flint, pebble rubble and Roman brick. The tiled roof was originally lead, but was stripped of this during the Civil War for ammunition.

Close by the church stands Fordham Hall, part of it as it was in medieval days. The house is of lath and plaster construction with a tiled roof. During the early 1990s extensive repairs were carried out and interesting finds made. Some old plaster was removed from the walls of what had been the communal hall, uncovering the original wall of oak frames and 'daub' surfaces painted with decorative designs – flowers and foliage – undoubtedly of the Tudor period, perhaps as early as Henry VII. A small part of this was removed and is now displayed in Colchester Museum. Fordham Hall is now the home of local farmer, John Jinks, and his family, who has done much for the village in the planting of hundreds of trees and has undertaken conservation work in the area, as well as farming the surrounding land.

Oak House was formerly known as Church Cottages and comprised four cottages. The cottages were thought to have been used as the village lock-up at one time and as the poor house in the 17th century and housed 13 men and 13 women. In 1924 the cottages were converted into two dwellings, and it is now one cottage.

Fordham Mill was referred to as Tower Mill on old maps. Fordham appears to have had a mill during pre-Domesday times and is certainly listed as having one in the Domesday census, but the actual mill itself was demolished in 1903. It was thought to have dated from 1780. The mill was primarily a grain mill but in 1653 records show that it held fulling stock for the woollen trade (teazles still abound in the surrounding fields – another link with the cloth trade). The Mill House as it is now called, is a private dwelling house.

Fordham has three public houses, one in Moat Road called the Vulcan Inn. The Three Horseshoes in Church Road was first mentioned in Kelly's Directory in 1855 but is thought to have its origins somewhat earlier than this. It is of timber framework, lath and plaster construction. The name is probably derived from the blacksmith's that used to be housed at the rear – in 1861 a miller/blacksmith is listed as the occupier and in 1874 it was listed as a pub and blacksmith's. The Shoulder of Mutton at Ford Street is a 15th century building almost unchanged from its original structure. It was first mentioned as a pub in 1859. All three pubs are thriving businesses and each one has its own character.

Fossetts & Chancers Lane is situated opposite the church and the Three Horseshoes public house. 'Fosse' is a Middle English word, derived from old French, meaning ditch or moat; and Chancers means doing something risky whilst hoping to avoid discovery! Poaching, maybe! Part of the lane has been included in the Essex Way, and is frequently used by hikers and walkers during the summer.

There are now six houses and two farms in the lane; Fossetts is a very picturesque thatched cottage worthy of any chocolate box. In the 1980s, just behind these houses, a lead coffin was found in a shallow grave, inside which were the skeletons of a woman and a child. Surrounding the coffin were pots, pans and kitchen utensils. The archaeologist's opinion was that it was probably a mother and child dating back to the Roman period, obviously from a rich family, and that if excavated the site would probably reveal a Roman villa of some importance.

Travelling down the lane, we come to a pond which is purported to contain a ghost. This is the only remaining evidence of Bretts Farm, demolished well over a century ago. The lane continues downhill with twists and bends and the sound of running water from the ditch which never runs dry, and eventually comes to the first farm, Watercress Hall, so-called because of the abundance of wild watercress which grows profusely there.

Watercress Hall was built in 1777. It was originally two houses. In 1953 it was without electricity, mains water and telephone. The garden was a profusion of self-sown greengage trees and old-fashioned apple trees, pheasant-eyed narcissus, and horse-radish. The animals on the farm were free to wander where they pleased. The little pigs went for long walks up the lane in groups of 20 or so, jumping off the banks and rooting in the hedges, turning and running home fast if a car came down the lane. The chickens also roamed everywhere, so the foxes were well-nourished.

At the bottom of the hill lies the 'Artist's' field. This was an acre of land alongside the brook. It was swampy and full of trees, bushes, daffodils and primroses, and in the middle of all this was an old railway wagon which could not be seen from the road. This was the home of the 'Artist'. He was a conscientious objector and more-or-less hid there during the course of the Second World War.

Just opposite the 'Artist's' field, which is now a lake and wild duck sanctuary, is Lovers Lane. This is a cart track and public footpath which ends down at the river Colne. There used to be a footbridge to continue the path to Eight Ash Green. The name Lovers Lane speaks for itself; it is lonely! Down this track was a cottage, where today, over the hedge, cows graze happily down to the river edge. Yet this was the scene of a tragedy some hundred years ago. A mother, father and retarded son lived in the cottage. One day the son lost his head and killed his parents with a spade, and he ran up to Watercress Hall brandishing the spade. The woman who lived there saw him coming and, running out of the back door, she fled towards the village. Half-way up the hill she turned and looked back, to see him crazily beating her apron which she had dropped. She ran on, calling for help. Beside the Three Horseshoes was the old blacksmith's shop. The men came running out and caught the enraged man, and locked him in the forge until the police came. No-one would live at the cottage again. It became derelict and was eventually demolished. The nature of the place has been changed recently, but one can still feel a strange quietness whilst walking down there.

Frinton-on-Sea

Frinton-on-Sea is unique. One turns off the main road across rail tracks into the little seaside town. If the rail gates are shut, that's it. No-one can enter until the train has rumbled past. Once upon a time the cachet of living 'inside the Gates' separated the sheep from the goats and the term is still used in estate agents' blurbs. Between the wars it was almost a private enclave with beautiful, large houses built by the wealthy, the famous, the notorious and all their entourages for use as summer residences. Winston Churchill's house stands on a corner of the Esplanade not far from the sprawling white establishment of Douglas Fairbanks Junior, now two large residences, one of which is still called Hollywood. The beautiful greensward that stretches the length of the Esplanade was thronged with after dinner strollers in full evening dress, among them Edward VIII, then Prince of Wales, and Mrs Simpson. Titled gentlemen were not always accompanied by their wives, as one very old local resident said. She had 'helped out' at the big houses to supplement the staff brought down from London. 'We called her Lady Blank', she said darkly, 'but we knew she warn't for all her jewels and her three children. She war his *fancywoman*!'

All this pomp and circumstance had to be looked after and Frinton boasted its own police station then. It was an arduous task! In those days the Essex police had a rule that bicycles (no cars for rural forces in those days) could not be used for distances under four miles. A retired police inspector remembered that one unfortunate colleague was bidden to meet his inspector at a rendezvous just under the four mile limit. Mutinously, the policeman rode his bike to the meeting place and hid the machine behind a barn. The inspector arrived in a pony and trap. 'Good man', says the inspector, 'jump in and I'll give you a lift back to the station.' The unfortunate bobby had to walk three and a half miles in the rain after duty to retrieve his bike! There is a simple but moving memorial on the greensward to PC Brian Bishop, shot near this spot while attempting to arrest a young man carrying drugs. The crazed youngster threw a satchel of drugs into the bushes near Pedlars Wood before drawing a gun.

The Frinton and Walton Heritage Trust, formed in 1985, made it one of their first projects to tidy up the approach to Frinton station. When in 1987 it was known that Liverpool Street station was being rebuilt, the Trust felt that as the line to Frinton started from that terminus it should have some reminders of the old station. British Rail generously sent two massive cast iron capitals from supporting pillars, one weighing over half a ton, and some other girders, all over 100 years old. These have been incorporated in the area overplanted with shrubs. A mural depicting Frinton's Edwardian seafront was painted under the canopy of the now unused down platform by local artists.

Ernest Luff, probably the best known evangelist of his day, was a Frinton resident all his life. In 1902 he was the lamplighter and 20 years later opened the Bible Shop in Connaught Avenue. At the age of 75 he opened a home for the elderly, long before anybody else had considered such places. Now there is a purpose-built residential home on the new Triangle estate, his memorial, where he is remembered with love and affection.

The essence of Frinton is still contained 'within the Gates'. There is an apocryphal story of the elderly lady driver embroiled in a slight accident in a Connaught Avenue rather busier than she was accustomed to coping with. Asked, apologetically, by a young policeman for her driving licence and insurance certificate, she snapped 'Young man, I have been driving for over 50 years within the Gates and', her voice quivered with outrage, 'I do not need a licence or insurance for that!'

Crime, passion, comedy, violence – Frinton has been home to it all. Don't be fooled by the decorous, staid exterior presented to the world. Underneath, it gives the lie to that hoary old joke 'Harwich for the Continent, Frinton for the incontinent'. The wit who thought that up probably wouldn't be able to stand the pace of life in Frinton-on-Sea.

Fryerning 🪶

Fryerning, one of the loveliest villages in Essex, is situated on a hill three quarters of a mile from Ingatestone. The church of St Mary the Virgin was built in Norman times. The tower is a landmark for miles and is surrounded by a large churchyard and cemetery. Three huge yew trees grow near the building, though one was badly damaged by the October 1987 gale.

The public house, the Woolpack, is at the top of Fryerning Lane. Before the boundaries were altered some years ago, part was in Fryerning parish and part in Ingatestone. The windmill, privately owned, is in good order but has been out of work for years. At one time it was the habitat of the white owl.

Standing as high as the village does, the main stretch of road is almost, if not quite, level with the top of Ingatestone church tower. Strange though it may be, there are still three large ponds left. There were a few more but these have been filled in. The largest one left, always known as the Bob Pond, was full of carp and roach until it dried up in the warm summers of 1989–90. Fishing always began on Whit Monday and finished when the cold weather set in. Dates and seasons were not thought of in those times. Hard winters and frosts made skating possible. On moonlight nights all the village turned up with their skates.

The horse pond, a few yards along the road, was open at both ends for the horse drawn carts, hunters and other horses to go through and drink. The herd of cows from Fryerning Hall Farm were driven twice a day to be watered, also the mules belonging to the army of the First World War that were stabled at the farm.

At one time, again before the boundaries were altered, a bride-to-be wishing to be married at Fryerning church had to pack a suitcase for the rector to have at the rectory for the three weeks her banns were published in church. They also had to be called in Ingatestone, making three sets of banns if the bridegroom-to-be lived out of either parish.

The highlight of the year was the fair on the green, always on the Wednesday after Whit Monday. The fair folk with their horse-drawn caravans and equipment would arrive at daybreak and leave the morning after. No one ever saw their comings or goings. The whole village, rich and poor, turned out for the great event. The roundabout was only for children and was worked by a man turning a handle. The swing boats, hoop-la, coconut shies and rock-making stall all added to the fun. Sad to say it only came once after the First World War as the menfolk did not come back from the war.

There were other interesting events before 1914. One afternoon a large balloon landed in the field at the back of the parish room. All the village gathered round it and the crew were entertained by Colonel and Mrs Hilder at Huskards.

Building has been kept to the limit as Fryerning is in the Green Belt. Huskards' large garden was sold off in plots, the house itself being converted into an old folks residence by the Essex County Council. Now it is flats, as are Delamars and Lightoaks. Fryerning Hall, Adkins, Murcocks and Jack's Croft are four of the oldest houses, all being marked on Walker's 1601 map.

Other interesting buildings and houses still stand. Two are pubs at Mill Green. The Cricketers was known by the old inhabitants as the Bat and Ball and cricket was played on the common in years gone by. Further along the road is the Viper, or the Snake as some people call it, said to be the only pub of that name in the world. Between the two pubs is the common which was a network of trenches during the First World War. There locally billeted regiments practised hand grenade throwing.

Another landmark is the water tower built to supplement the water supply for Fryerning and Ingatestone. Some years later Fryerning residents came down one morning to no mains water. The tower was empty. Hence the building of the reservoir along Beggar Hill Road. At one time the waterworks was halfway down Fryerning Lane, now new houses have been built on the site.

Beggar Hill is supposed to have got its name from the 'men of the road' who used it on their way to St Leonards where they would be given a meal and a night's lodging. Blanket Hall, for years known as Fryerning Grange, was so named because these men would call there for a blanket.

The large oak on Fryerning Hall lawn is said to be over 1,000 years old. The oak on Fryerning Green was planted to commemorate King George V and Queen Mary's Jubilee, the maple on the greensward in front of the parish room was planted when Fryerning won the Best Kept Village award, and the silver birches on Huskards Green were given by the WI for Plant A Tree Year.

Eventually the Eastern National ran buses on Fridays and Saturdays from Chelmsford to the Viper and back. Cars came into their own and the buses were taken off the road. 'Mod cons' were the next thing. Telephones were installed, the sewer laid on, then gas and electricity. Hopefully the district will not alter too much now, as it has been declared a conservation area.

91

Goldhanger 🐚

There is much to be seen on a visit to the village of Goldhanger. At the top of Church Street, stand on the larger grass triangle and, looking up the drive to Follifaunts, imagine how it looked when the manor was given to help found Beeleigh Abbey, close to Maldon, in 1180. Then cross to the smaller triangle and glance up the drive to the big red brick house, built in 1851/2 by a well-to-do clerical family to be the rectory. They had good parties there, and entertained Lewis Carroll. Walk down Church Street and you will see on your right a row of red brick cottages, neatly built to the edge of the road to house four Coastguards and their families. On the other side is the school building which served us well from 1875 to 1977; today the children go by bus to a school in Tolleshunt D'Arcy. The Goldhanger building has been developed as a Field Study Centre by a school in Romford.

Now you are in the centre of the old village, with the 11th century church, the Chequers pub, very old and of uncertain origin, and the Square. The inside of the church has been altered over the centuries, but the two small Norman windows in the north wall give it the 11th century date. Outside, the stonework shows clearly how in the 15th century they built the tower a few feet away from the church, and when it was complete knocked down the church's west wall and joined the church to the tower.

Back by the churchyard gate, one finds that the road takes only half of the old Square, the other half, with a brick wall making the division, being the Chequers car park (and previously a vegetable garden). On the north side only the first house shows how the buildings used to face on to the Square; the next three have taken a piece for their front gardens, this again defined by the brick walls that marked out the village, probably in the latter part of the first half of the 19th century.

All this would have mattered more over 640 years ago, for they needed a big square with the pump in the middle, not on the pavement as it is today. In 1348 the lord of the manor got royal permission for a market every Thursday, and at the same time for an annual fair which included for sale ribbons, gingerbread and knick-knacks, held in the 18th century on 14th May and later on Whit Monday. Nowadays we block off that stretch of road and so use half the old Square for the May Fair on the first Bank Holiday in May.

Leaving the Square by Fish Street, you pass the place where, until earlier this century, a mill was still working. The Mill House, rather reduced in size, still stands in a commanding position with the main mill building converted into a pair of cottages. The mill was powered by both wind and steam, and its chimney is said to have been taller than the church tower. Walking down past these buildings you will find you are close to the wide tidal estuary of the river Blackwater, on the old road that led down to the head of the creek where fishing smacks unloaded their catch. The water has receded, and today the road ends at a large playing field edged by a footpath that is a tunnel of trimmed hawthorn bushes and leads to the creek and the sea-wall.

You can walk for miles on the sea-wall, upstream to Maldon and downstream to Tollesbury, and as you go you can see where the tracks come down from the farms to small coves and beaches. Here the sailing barges used to pull in and load goods for London, sometimes mounting a whole hay-stack on the deck and giving the barges the name of 'stackies'. They returned laden with manure from the horse-drawn traffic of the London streets, which was good for the land but inconvenient if crops were growing. This difficulty was met by driving the carts used for unloading (some 20 carts for one barge's hold) up the lanes until they found a grass verge to dump it on until it could be used.

On either side of the creek, in stretches of saltings that have now been turned into arable fields, there were Iron Age salt workings. Salt continued to be extracted in various ways over the centuries, but now the sea salt of the Blackwater is extracted only by the Maldon Salt Company in the town.

Good Easter

Not only is Good Easter isolated by the River Can, but even its name is shrouded in mystery. A monk claimed that a lady called Godgyfu had left her Eowestras (Sheepfolds) to Ely Abbey in her will. Ultimately the lands seem to have been restricted to High Easter, higher up the valley of the river Can, and the name left to Good Easter (Godgyfu's Eowestras).

Just before the Conquest in 1066 Engelric an Anglo Saxon Nobleman is in possession of Estre.

The Domesday Books tells us that Ailmer held Good Easter, consisting of some five hundred and twenty acres of rich boulder clay, ideal for corn, barley and other arable crops.

Today as nearly a thousand years ago the parish is devoted to arable farming. Commuters, the young affluent and the retired occupy the cottages and old smallholding farms. Good Easter is a very pleasant place to live. Often described as a sleepy village, here is the record of one day when it woke up:

On March 2nd 1885, coming out of Sunday School, Emily Tyrell saw the steeple of St Andrews on fire. Running to the mill she raised the men who hastened to the site. The fire was first seen by the Rev E. J. Bicknell. His diary records that a man was sent to Chelmsford by horse to get the Fire Brigade, only seven miles away. It was 9.20 am. Arriving at Chelmsford an hour later the man called out two Fire Brigades. Meanwhile at Good Easter as the spire became ungulfed in flames, Mott the carpenter and his men removed the pews, furniture, desks and organ, as the inferno blazed above. These were transferred to Falconers Barn (the second oldest barn in the country to have been in continuous agricultural use). In Chelmsford the Board of Health Fire Brigade under Mr Gripper Chairman and Captain Johnson got off to a cracking start. The other brigade, on hearing that the Board of Health Fire Brigade had a twenty minute lead, gave up, turned round and went home, not wishing to share the Insurance cover money. By 11.30 am the sweat-lathered horses had pulled up the hill and the fire engine had arrived. But it was too hot to do anything with the pump.

Christopher Matthews of Newarks and his men were dragging blazing baulks of timber into the water-filled ditches and ponds, and did so until 12.30 pm. Now that the fire was dying down the Fire Brigade was able to get close in to put it out. This took until 4 pm in the afternoon, solely by manual pumping.

By July 20th 1886 the money was raised and repairs to the steeple completed. The Bishop of Colchester took the Thanksgiving Service and then all repaired to the vicarage meadow for tea. Asking the assembled company to raise their glasses the Archdeacon proposed a toast to the village which was

'Seven miles from everywhere,
On the way to Nowhere'

It still is. But it has the distinction of holding the World Daisychain Record. This happened in May 1985 when a team made a daisychain 6,980 ft 7 inches between 10.30 am and 5 pm beating the previous record by a team from the Derbyshire Museum of Childhood and earning a place in the Guiness Book of Records.

Grays 🐚

In the 1930s and 1940s South Ockendon was a small country village on the outskirts of Grays, which itself was a small country town. All this changed when after the Second World War South Ockendon and the Aveley area was used to build houses for the homeless from the London County Council area. Unfortunately no attempt was made to maintain the beauty of the countryside – just rows and rows of identical houses.

At one time there were 11,000 schoolchildren on the estate. As these children grew up and married they were not allowed to have a house on the estate, with the result that they moved to places like Basildon, and Ockendon became an estate of elderly people. Today they are demolishing some of the good schools built in the 1950s as there are no children to fill them.

Meanwhile on the outskirts of Grays, on the opposite side of the A13, another large estate is being developed called the Chafford Hundred, with new homes, five new schools, a church, community centres and a railway station. This estate stretches from Grays to less than a mile from the new Thurrock Lakeside shopping centre. This was opened on 25th October 1990 by HRH Princess Alexandra, with parking space for 9,000 cars and 250 coaches. It has all the favourite department stores and familiar names, and a good few European stores have chosen the centre for their British debut.

Great Baddow 🐚

Great Baddow lies on the south-eastern side of Chelmsford and grew up around the river crossing the Maldon and Southend routes. Historically it appears the village grew from two parts, the larger being concentrated round the church. Many names currently used for roads and buildings have their origins in the 15th century, such as Noakes, Rothmans, Skinners and Dines. Visitors today approaching the village from Chelmsford would be excused for finding it difficult to establish where the demarcation boundary exists.

The accepted commencement of the village from this direction is the junction of the Maldon Road and High Street. There is a convenient car park here at the side of the Blue Lion public house. Opposite the Blue Lion is Ebernezer Terrace comprising a group of small cottages, once condemned, but now attractively restored in a period style.

Going up the hill of the Maldon Road, the grassed area on the right once formed the gardens of the Vineyards, a large 18th century house, a victim of postwar development after years of neglect. The splendid trees partially screen the rather out of place office block which bears the old name. On the left of the road is a mixture of period buildings, Valley Cottages, Manor Place and Beech House which with its massive 17th century brick chimney stack, dominates this part of the road.

At the brow of the hill turn right into the Causeway. This leads past the front of the modern shopping area to a minor junction with Pump Hill. There are a couple of quaint restored cottages on the left of the road going straight on, which is called Bell Street and leads to the church and Church Street. On the right of the junction at the top of Pump Hill, is another pair of old cottages, again restored in period style.

About halfway along Bell Street on the right is a long wooden building currently housing the local library. This building at one time was used as a British Restaurant, a wartime innovation much used all over the country.

The end of Bell Street will bring into view the junction of the High Street, Galleywood Road and Church Street with the small village green. Until a few years ago this area had a medley of small shops of varying trades. The White Horse public house, in old photographs, used to display a large sign advertising the local Baddow Brewery beer, now long since gone.

Carrying on up the slope to the left leads to the porch and pathway to the entrance of St Mary's church. The church first appears on record in 1172 and had quite a chequered history until the 17th century. The present church was erected on the site of a former building, probably made of wood and plaster and thatched. This was then superseded by a simple form of Norman construction of rectangular plan. The main walls are of flint-rubble with fragments of Roman brick and tile. Opposite the church, is the vicarage. Built in the early 18th century it has still many of its original features.

From the church the road runs southerly to the village boundary with Sandon. Along this stretch of road will be found several large houses such as Baddow Place. The original Baddow Brewery buildings, with huge windows, built in 1868 has been renovated and is now a thriving antiques centre with small craft workshops.

Although not possessing a highly dramatic history there is still much of interest in Great Baddow's past. An example of one of the fragments to be gleaned is the fact that Great Baddow was one of the major assembly points for the Peasants Revolt in 1381 led by Jack Straw!

Despite its lack of physical separation from Chelmsford, the village has nurtured its independent social associations and activities. There is a strongly supported Women's Institute, Flower Club, table tennis and tennis club, bowling, cricket and football clubs and many more. Despite progress, the village seems determined to survive!

Great Bardfield 🐝

In spite of invasion by the motor car, Great Bardfield still retains a goodly measure of the peaceful atmosphere of a country village which was such a feature when it was almost entirely agricultural and occupied only by farm workers or traders and craftsmen serving the farming community. Change is always going on, of course, and even in living memory there have been considerable developments and yet somehow the village retains its atmosphere. If a 15th century inhabitant could return he would at least find familiar landmarks in the church, the White Hart and Gobions, which still retain much of their 15th century appearance.

We know from the Domesday Book that there was a thriving Anglo-Saxon settlement here before the Conquest, the land being held at that time by Wisgar and Felaga, the lord being Earl Aelfgar.

Throughout its known history the village seems to have led a peaceful and probably humdrum existence with only the occasional village excitement to liven things up. There was, for instance, the story of the 'bloodsticks'. Great Bardfield Fair was held on 22nd June each year and in early days was a great occasion, especially for horse trading. Drovers came long distances bringing horses for sale and on one occasion in 1790 two Welsh drovers, John Jones and Robert Ellis, having sold their stock and celebrated suitably, set out for Braintree at the start of their journey back to Wales. On the way they called at the White Hart at Great Saling and while there, quarrelled violently over John Jones having too close a relationship with Mrs Ellis. The landlord quietened them down and sent them on their way. At a quiet spot along the road the quarrel broke out again and this time turned to a fight in which Robert Ellis was killed. Jones hid the body in a deep ditch and having plenty of money from the fair soon found himself a horse and got back to Wales. He went to see Mrs Ellis and told her her husband had been taken ill and had died and would she marry him. Incredibly she agreed but shortly afterwards a police constable from Essex appeared and asked her to return with him to identify a body that had been found. Jones was found guilty of murder at Chelmsford Assizes and hanged. Such is the story and it is still believed that if the spot where the body was found is visited in the early spring, the dogwood shoots growing there come up blood red.

The village has many reminders of other former inhabitants. One of these was Henry Smith who was born at Great Bardfield Hall in 1804, his family having farmed there for several generations. In his turn he took over the farm and in 1859 built the Town Hall, allowing it to be used for various village functions. It remained in the ownership of the Smith family until 1947 when Mr Thomas Smith, the last miller in Great Bardfield, sold it to the parish. Standing in front of the Town Hall one can see on the right hand side a small extension or outshot which is now used as a ladies cloakroom. This extension was built to house the village fire engine – another of the Smith family benefactions. The engine, a horsedrawn manual, was bought by Henry Smith in 1860 for his own use and was presented to the village by his son Henry Junior in about 1871. It remained in its Town Hall lodgings until the 1930s.

Another reminder of Henry Smith can be seen by the side of the brook in Brook Street in the shape of the fountain which Henry installed in 1861 to bring water from a spring in the Hall Meadows. Many Great Bardfield inhabitants can remember having to fetch the day's supply of water from the fountain before they went to school since mains water did not arrive in the village until the 1930s.

William Bendelow, Serjeant at Law in the time of Queen Elizabeth I, is another worthy who must be remembered. Although he practised in London and was a prominent member of Lincoln's Inn, his home was the house now known as Place Farm, and he was probably the greatest benefactor the village has ever had. The list is too long to give here but one of his gifts, a small almshouse, is now the Great Bardfield Museum and is well worth a visit. A very fine copy of his portrait can be seen in St Mary's church.

Also in the church is a funerary helm believed to be of the Lumley family who came into the village in 1623 when Sir Martin Lumley, a well known London personage, bought the manor. A cloth merchant by trade he became Master of the Drapers Company, an Alderman of the City of London, Sheriff of London and Master of Christ's Hospital, and no doubt now wanted to set himself up as a country gentleman. The old manor house, now Great Bardfield Hall farm, did not suit his purpose and he built a grand mansion in the centre of the Great Park calling it Great Lodge. The estate was sold in 1725 and soon after that the mansion was pulled down and the remaining barns and stables converted into a house. The old drive leading to Great Lodge, now called Lovers' Walk, can still be seen opposite the churchyard.

Great Bentley 🌿

Great Bentley has the largest village green in England, 43 acres; the very name means 'large green' for in Anglo-Saxon times it was a wide, flat marshy area covered in 'bent', or coarse grass, surrounded by forest, and gradually brought into use for grazing, hence 'ley' a pasture.

There has been no 'great' house attached to Great Bentley since Ulwin the Saxon was dispossessed after 1066 in favour of Alberic De Vere, Earl of Oxford, whose family were lords of the manor for the next 600 years. The De Veres were always absentee landlords, and Great Bentley never had a local Squire to run the community.

St Mary's church, on the north corner of the green, dates from about 1135, and the font which was presented by Robert De Vere, Earl of Oxford, dates from 1221. The church has undergone much internal alteration, but the stone spiral staircase which once led up to the rood screen gallery remains. There has been a peal of bells in the tower since the 17th century; most have been replaced or recast and two were added in the 19th century. There has been a long tradition of bell ringing in the village and the bells are still rung regularly.

During the reign of Mary Tudor (1553–58) the vicar was deprived of his office because he had married, and his successor promptly denounced five villagers as Protestants. They were arrested, taken to Colchester, condemned, and burned at the stake. A memorial tablet marks the site of the cottage from which they were taken.

Subsequently an unusual degree of religious tolerance developed in the village. By 1718 there was a Quaker meeting house, now a private residence, and by 1819 a Methodist chapel, later rebuilt and enlarged and still flourishing, but worshippers in both these places still kept in touch with the church. There was a Quaker churchwarden, records of the baptism of Quaker children in the church, and both Quakers and Methodists were buried in the churchyard. In the 1840s the church and chapel Sunday schools appear to have been combined, owing to lack of space in the church! In 1878 the chapel minister and congregation took part in the church Harvest Festival. This close association has continued ever since, and during the last ten years the Roman Catholics have celebrated a weekly mass in the church.

The green is, and always has been, a common, and has never been enclosed and very rarely encroached upon. The absence of a local Squire has meant that the villagers were always, to a certain degree, independent, and have guarded their rights very vigorously. In 1812 a faction, mostly farmers, wanted to enclose part of the green but villagers led by Mr Thompson (who owned a coalyard at the wharf) opposed the scheme and eventually obtained a private Act of Parliament declaring the green a common for the use and enjoyment of the villagers. Again in the 1890s a faction wanted to restrict grazing rights, but the Act was invoked by Mr Wright, a grocer (whose descendants owned the shop until it closed in the 1970s) and the green was declared inviolate. The only buildings on the green were those which the villagers wanted – a windmill from 1755 until the 1890s, and then a steam mill, which lasted until 1925. There is now little trace of these, or of a carpenter's and coffinmaker's shed, but a disused forge still stands and the chapel which is still very much in use. About 30 years ago the village was again rent asunder by a proposal to build a new village hall on the green. After much heated argument and many meetings the Parish Council organised a vote, and the motion was defeated. The village had to wait for its new hall, now built on council land opposite the railway station.

Cricket has been played on the green since the 18th century and football probably since a much earlier date, and still the teams flourish, but maypole dancing and fairs have rather fallen into abeyance, with fetes, carnivals and gymkhanas taking their place.

The southern boundary includes the tidal creek which flows, eventually, into the river Colne and from medieval times until the coming of the railway the Bentley wharfs were an important trade centre for shallow-draft vessels plying between here and London. The old wharfs are now silted up and returning to salt marsh, but one still remains reasonably clear and until the recent water pollution scares was a pleasant swimming place at high tide – if one did not mind the occasional eel slithering across!

There was an exciting incident during the Second World War when an American Airforce ambulance, on its way to a crashed plane, was held up by the crossing gates; the stationmaster refused to open them and the young officer produced his gun to shoot off the lock. It was pointed out that this would probably only cause the heavy old Victorian mechanism to jam so that a blacksmith would have to come and free it. The officer shouted 'There are eight American boys dying out there' and the stationmaster retorted 'And there'll be a train load of passengers dying here if I open the gates!' The officer was actually turning the gun on the station-master when the train – a fast express – came in sight.

During the first half of the 20th century, Great Bentley had a fairly static population of about 1,000 inhabitants. The village, since 1866, has been served by the London–Clacton railway but it is a mile or so from any main road. There have always been several shops here although the numbers have dwindled in the last decade or so. Before and during the Second World War there were three bakeries, two butchers, three grocers, a hardware store, post office and newsagent's, a dairy, two cobblers as well as a garage which sold petrol and undertook repairs to cars and agricultural machinery. After the war there was also a drapery and a dress shop, and a hairdressing salon. All these businesses were run by the families who started them, often a generation or two back. Today we have only a butcher-cum-grocer, a post office, hairdresser, newsagent – and a video shop! The last bakery closed late in 1989. However, to compensate this loss of village trade there is a small, modern and flourishing light industrial estate with workshops accommodating small firms. Another recent loss has been the Victory Inn, first listed in records in 1848. However, the Plough and the Red Lion (also listed in that year) are still popular and friendly pubs, along with the Fusilier (1866) just up the road in the hamlet of Aingers Green.

Great Canfield 🐝

Great Canfield, situated south and well away from the A120 as it runs between Bishop's Stortford and Great Dunmow, is a most unusual village. Eight miles of road link its four 'Ends': Bacon End, Church End, Hope End and Hayden End which is better known as Helmans Cross, but there are only 131 houses and 274 adults on the electoral roll.

Remains of Roman settlement have been found around the village.

The whipping post survives at Helmans Cross close to the notice board. An oak tree was planted near the whipping post to celebrate the end of the First World War by Hubert (Billy) Maryon Wilson, later the 13th and last Baronet. Mementoes were buried with it such as coins, photographs and newspapers. At one time the village shop was also situated here but closed in the 1930s and there was a sub post office until the late 1970s. Great Canfield lost its pub and school in the early 1900s. The Griffin Inn became a private house (The Grange) and the school building is now used as the village hall. There is also a most attractive cricket ground, with club house, at the junction of Green Street and Fitz Johns Lane, where it is possible to score a very short boundary when the wicket moves close to the lane.

Great Canfield used to form part of the Fitz Johns estate belonging to the Maryon Wilson family and their mansion was situated near the lake at the end of Fitz Johns Lane. All that now remains is a tumbledown stable block and the kitchens which have been converted into a cottage, and this still has the bell on its roof which told the workers when it was time to break for lunch. The clock which used to be part of the stables is now the church clock. The present house called Fitz Johns was formerly the rectory and was added to considerably in Victorian times to accommodate the large family of the Rev George Maryon Wilson, who was rector of the parish from 1872 to 1906. His son, the Rev John Maryon Wilson was also rector for over 30 years until the 1950s. Fitz Johns Farm, comprising 250 acres, remained in the Maryon Wilson family until the 1980s and the death of the last member of the family to bear that name. Their coat of arms is commemorated in a stained glass window in the church and by tiles bearing the Maryon Wilson wolf crest on many of the cottages. A splendid avenue of horse chestnut trees also acts as a memorial and is particularly spectacular when in full flower in May. It is said that there is so much comfrey in Canfield as the Maryon Wilson coachman used to plant it everywhere 'to keep the horses right'.

Great Canfield boasts a host of charming houses and cottages, many most lovingly restored. By day it is very quiet with little traffic and many inhabitants commute as it is convenient for London, Cambridge, Chelmsford and Bishop's Stortford.

Great & Little Leighs 🌿

The parishes of Great and Little Leighs are a combination of two villages, but are one community. The villages are nestled between Chelmsford to the south, Braintree to the north, Boreham to the east, and Felsted to the west.

The church of St Mary the Virgin stands in the middle of the parish on rising ground above the river Ter, which gives its name to the next village, Terling. A hundred yards from the church is the manor house of Lyons Hall, called in the Domesday Book, Laghen Beria. Until 1726 the patrons of the church were the lords of the manor of Great Leighs (Lyons Hall), but since then the patrons have been the College of the Blessed

Virgin Mary and All Saints, Lincoln, commonly called Lincoln College, Oxford, and the rectors of the church have been members of the college. The church tower is one of six round towers in Essex. The tower was probably a place of defence against North Sea pirates coming up the Chelmer and Blackwater. In the third storey of the tower are five bells, each one inscribed 'Miles Graye made me, 1634'. There are several old cottages close to the church, also the lovely old rectory, which is now privately owned. Further up the road is an old flint and stone cottage which was once the church school.

Most of the land around the villages was farmland, either arable or grazing land. With the population growing, the villages were now beginning to expand further towards the High Road, which is now the A131. A new government school was built for all village children to attend. After 132 years, this also had to close in 1977, owing to further expansion to the two villages. A new modern school was built on another site which connected up with the building of a private housing estate during the early 1970s. To make way for this, a beautiful old 16th century house was pulled down which was known as The Cheese House. This house was originally a farmhouse situated on Cheese Hill, just outside Boreham, and was used during the Civil War by Oliver Cromwell as his headquarters. The house was aptly named, as cheese was made there continuously through the centuries. In 1937 Henry Ford of the Ford Motor Company bought the Cheese House, and numbering every beam as it was dismantled, was going to ship it out to America, but as the Second World War approached, this project was abandoned. The house was eventually bought by a gentleman from Little Waltham who bought eight acres of land at Great Leighs, near to the High Road, and resurrected it, including the beautiful Carolean staircase. The house remained until 1977 when 68 houses were built on the site.

Another larger estate of houses was built behind the first one, and this was where Mr J. S. Wright had first started and built up a willow merchant business, employing many men since 1894. The main product of the business is cricket bats, which are exported worldwide. This company is still in business in Great Leighs.

A good landmark for visitors is the St Anne's Castle public house. This is right on the crossroads of the A131. St Anne's Castle appears on the Greenwood's map of Essex, published as long ago as 1824. It is also said to be the oldest public house in England, and to be haunted.

St John's church, Little Leighs, stands just off the A131 turning into Church Lane, from Blacksmith's Corner. The church was erected by the

Normans after the conquest. Today's building gives an initial impression of being Victorian as a major restoration was carried out at the end of the 19th century, but it retains much of its original work and many interesting features. It is said there is a passageway underground which goes through to Leez Priory. The priory and Warrocks was founded in 1229 by Sir Ralph Gernon for Augustinian friars (Black Friars or Canons). The patronage and advowson remained in that family until Henry VIII's time in 1537. He granted it to Sir Richard Rich (afterwards Lord Rich), who was that year elected Speaker of the House of Commons, and in 1548 became Lord Chancellor. He founded Felsted School in 1546. In 1550 Leez Priory was one of the most important private residences in Essex. It was described as a worldly paradise. There are some beautiful old buildings around this area of Little Leighs, including Leighs Hall Farm, also known as Seabrooks the fruit farmers.

As you come from the church back on to the A131 the old forge stood, hence Blacksmith's Corner. This no longer operates, but was of course very much a working forge in years past, with horses being shod and iron tyres made for the farm carts.

Great Leighs is widely known as the venue of the Essex County Show. This became the permanent site about 30 years ago and was opened by the Queen Mother, who was driven from the show ground through the villages en route back to Chelmsford station. The school children lined the roads with their flags waving and everyone who could be at the roadside enjoyed the event. Over the years many other Royals have visited the show ground.

Great Totham 🦌

The village of Great Totham is in four parts. Beacon Hill, which closely adjoins Wickham Bishops, is quite half a mile from either North or South Totham, and Broad Street Green consists of several ancient farms and many houses along the roadside. It was included in Great Totham parish only in the 1930s, under the provisions of the Divided Parishes Act. The area in question apparently included the Bull Inn, but this seems very mysterious as the 17th century Bull Inn is miles from Heybridge, the parish which used to take in Broad Street Green. Perhaps the present day Crown Inn used to be called the Bull. Part of Totham Hill was at the same time transferred from Little Totham to Great Totham.

Hill Farm is a listed building, parts of which probably date back to

Henry II's reign, when it is believed to have been a hunting lodge at a time when the area was thickly wooded. There is a fine carved 15th century ceiling in the main room. Close by, Fabians and Paynes Farm are both buildings with a long history, as are Croft Cottage and the pair of cottages, Bean and Walnut, at nearby Totham Hill Green.

There are many more listed buildings of architectural interest. Mountains, part of which dated to the 15th century, contains features brought from Braxted Park by Lady Du Cane, who also had laid out some Japanese gardens.

Attractive and unusual almshouses built in 1855 by William and Louisa Gooday, and known as the Willie Almshouses, are grouped around a courtyard and have their own tiny chapel with a bellcote and clock on its small tower. These houses, which are near the old school building, are still occupied today.

Lofts and Poplar Grove farms, both several hundred years old, lie within Broad Street Green. Sains, or on old maps, Saints, farm and the Sheepcoates, not far from the church both date from the 16th century and Sun Farm which in days gone by used to be the Shoulder of Mutton Inn, is a 15th century building. Whilst on the subject of pubs, a bill of sale was found from 1828 when the Compasses was offered for auction. It was described as being 'contiguous to the race ground' at that time, but no trace of this interesting feature is now apparent.

The Prince of Wales in Totham South, was completely gutted by fire in 1990, so many historic features have been lost for ever, but it has been rebuilt and was recently reopened, the first pint pulled by Ted Newton, who was born there over 80 years ago.

Another recent change in the village is the completion of a new extension to the Norman church of St Peter, well blended in with the old building and very well used.

Great Totham has changed a great deal over the centuries, some of the crafts and trades having died out or been brought up to date. There are no longer any walking-stick makers, brickworks or saddlers, but there is a coachbuilder's and a thriving haulage business. The old gravel pits have become recreation areas for children or fishing lakes.

Great Wakering ✒

Great Wakering has water on three sides and is situated in a very flat landscape of extremely fertile land. Large areas of the locality have been excavated for brick earth and the brickfields have been a main source of employment for generations. At one time some 600 men, women and children were employed making bricks by hand. Today the workforce is in single figures but, with modern machinery and techniques, this number can produce as many bricks.

Until recent years the village was a typical linear one. The High Street, approximately one mile long, runs directly east and west with the parish church at the eastern end. Many of the wooden cottages have been demolished to make way for modern developments, resulting in a virtual doubling of the population.

Approaching the village from Southend you pass Oldbury Farm, one of the largest and most up to date farms in the district. At the junction of the High Street and Little Wakering Road stands a recently enlarged building, built before 1838 as the National school at which 70 pupils attended. Paton's Pit, a pond, was situated on the south side of the High Street (now No 319) and was the remaining part of the moat to the manor house. The house had been demolished before the 15th century and the pond was filled in during the mid 20th century.

The Exhibition Inn was named after the 1851 Great Exhibition. Nearby is the Methodist church, the second on the site, the first being erected in 1867.

Little Wakering Hall Lane runs past the village allotments to the 15th century manor house of Wakering Hall, alleged to be haunted by the ghost of Betty Bury, a serving maid. Close to the Hall stands a large 17th century barn. Near to the lane stands the Evangelical church, formerly the Peculiar People's church. This religious sect was started in this district.

Opposite the school is Lee Lotts estate, built on farmland of the same name. There were two meadows here used in the past for fetes and Sunday school treats. One of the blacksmith's forges remains, although now used for car repairs, at 125 High Street. 'Bell House' provides sheltered accommodation for elderly folk, and is built on the site of a former public house of the same name. Another similar establishment is at 'Goodmans', a quarter of a mile east of Bell House and built on the site of the old workhouse and a harnessmaker's shop owned by a Mr Goodman.

The White Hart is an attractive 17th century building and stands opposite the old primary school, built in 1876 and presently used as a youth club and adult education centre.

Chapel Lane is named after the Congregational, now United Reformed, chapel. There was an earlier church standing opposite the present building. One of its early ministers was the Rev J. W. Phair. He was a most industrious man with progressive ideas regarding education. He started a school in the village and ran a loan club and lending library.

The Anchor is the second public house of that name built on the site. The first was destroyed by fire and was a wooden building. Nearby is Anchor Cottage, the oldest building in the High Street, being 15th century.

Turning left into Common Road you pass the village pond, used in earlier times for the washing down of carts. The road continues through the common to the creeks at Mill Head. The surrounding creeks are a haven for many types of wildfowl and a large proportion of the world's population of Brent geese winter here each year. Here, at Mill Head, was situated the 19th century brickfield, where over 20 Thames barges were used to transport bricks to London. Gradually these were phased out due to the growth of motor transport in the 1930s. Unfortunately the beautiful sight of the barges is but a memory and the old brickfield is now a refuse tip.

The parish church of St Nicholas is a very unusual structure, plain but of good proportions. The Everard family have been responsible for the winding of the church clock since it was installed in 1913. 'Crowie' Everard, a former sexton and local wit, had a stroke whilst digging a grave, and as he was carried out he was heard to remark, 'I've sin a good few carried in, but never one carried out before!'

Great Wigborough

Beautifully situated on the top of a hill at the highest point of the parish, the tree-circled tower of the church is a landmark for many miles around. The large manor of Abbots Hall belonged to the important nunnery of Barking from at least the Norman conquest (1066) until the dissolution of that monastery in 1540, and with that ownership went the patronage of the parish church, so we can assume that there was a church here from at least Norman times.

The present church of St Stephen is built of septaria and rubble with tiled roofs; owing to rebuilding and restoration it has no features earlier than the 14th century. The nave and chancel were built late in the 14th century, but the chancel has been completely rebuilt, introducing other stone. Late in the 15th century a west tower was added and also a south porch, but the tower has been rebuilt following the extensive damage done by the 1884 earthquake. The nave, with its fine beamed ceiling, remains the only part of the original building, but the windows are mostly modern work. The now blocked north doorway is of late 14th century date, the south doorway is of mid 15th century date. In the north-east corner behind the pulpit is the late 14th century staircase which led to the rood loft above the chancel screen in the pre-Reformation days.

Wigborough had two martyrs, John Simpson and John Ardeley who were tried in London in front of Bishop Bonner on 25th May 1555 and burned at the stake on 10th June 1555. These two peasant farmers from Wigborough had committed no crime, but were condemned for their belief in the Protestant Church.

The other manor house in the village is Moulshams, dating from 1450 and extended in the early 16th century. It is a beautiful house, timber-framed and plastered with a red tile roof and exposed timber frame on the west side.

Greenstead Green 🐝

Greenstead Green is a small village in north Essex, three miles from Halstead and 13 miles from Colchester. There are no housing estates as such, though houses and bungalows have been built over recent years, filling in the odd spaces. There used to be a windmill in the village, but unfortunately the sails came off. For a number of years it looked like a huge pepper pot, but eventually it was taken down.

Farming was at one time the mainstay of the village. Nearly all the families were connected with the land in some form. Women would take part in the pea-picking, stone-picking and picking up of potatoes. A number of cows were kept and milkmen would bring the milk to the door straight from the cow – often it was still warm when put into the housewives' jugs. Meat, fish, groceries, bread, pots and pans were all delivered to the door. Gipsies were regular visitors, some families returning to the same sites year after year. Around Easter-time the scissor grinder would make his appearance.

The church was built in 1845 and has played a great part in village life. The local gentry would fill the pews in the front and lesser mortals would sit nearer the back. The tall church spire is one of its outstanding features.

One vicar who made a great impression on everyone was the Rev Herbert Fasson. He came just before the outbreak of the Second World War and stayed for around 30 years. Mr Fasson was a bachelor and never owned a car. He was a familiar sight on his bicycle, his hat in one hand waving to all and sundry with a cheerful 'Hallo you!' Everything that took place in the village was of keen interest to Mr Fasson. He would run up and down the touchline during a football match crying 'Come on the Green'. He was loved and appreciated not only in his own village but in surrounding places also.

Sadly the vicarage and the village school are now private homes. The school was built in 1846 and closed in 1963. The children are taken to schools in Halstead. It is a long time now since Greenstead Green children greeted Halstead children with the cry of 'Halstead Tom Cats' and Halstead's reply was 'Greenstead Green Water Rats'!

At one stage one of the charities from the church was for loaves of bread to be given to certain people in the village. The people who were to benefit always knew when it was their turn for a loaf. Children would take the bread to the people who were unable to collect it themselves. The 'Forty Shillings' was another charity from the church which was given out twice a year. Great secrecy was observed when this was presented, but somehow the word always got around who had had the 'Forty Shillings'.

Greenstead Green is still a friendly village, though the farm workers are very few. People now commute to the various towns to their work.

Hadstock

Hadstock is a small village of about 300 souls, situated in the north-west corner of the county, within hailing distance of Cambridgeshire on two of its borders, and close to Suffolk.

St Botolph's is the main feature of interest and is an early Saxon building. In AD 654 Abbot Botolph started to build a monastery at

Icanho. In AD 680 he died and was buried there. From ancient documents in Ely Cathedral it would seem that Icanho was the early name for Hadstock. During extensive archaeological excavations inside the church in 1974, an empty early Saxon grave was found against the east wall of the south transept. It was very shallow, so that most of the coffin was above ground and that fact, and its position, denoted that it had been the burial place of a very important personage. The body had been exhumed at a later date, and it is known that the body of St Botolph was removed and his relics distributed to the monasteries of Ely, Thorney and to the King's reliquary.

From circumstantial evidence, therefore, it would seem that this was the site of St Botolph's monastery. The chapel where the coffin was found has always been known as St Botolph's chapel. From further finds during the excavations this feeling has been reinforced. For instance, 20 floor levels were found in the north transept and for that period it must have been an impressive church of minster proportions. Icanho was destroyed in AD 870–871 by the great army of the Danes and rebuilt on a lesser scale. A third rebuild took place, probably in the 11th century – seemingly an expensive major reconstruction caused by an important event. This leads to the possible conclusion that after his victory over Edmund Ironside, Cnut the Dane built his minster to commemorate the battle of Assendaum which is thought may have taken place on the ridge of higher ground between Hadstock and Ashdon. The battle was purported to have been lost because of the defection of Eric Storna, one of Edmund's knights, and a small field in the village has always been known as Traitor's Field.

There are many interesting features of Saxon origin in the church, but the main door is of special note. It is the oldest door in the UK to be in constant use and is mentioned in the Guinness Book of Records.

A 'holy' well is situated by the western wall of the churchyard and was said to possess healing properties. It was known as a cure for scrofula. It is fed by a spring that never dries up, and until 1939 was the source of the village's drinking water. On a certain day a young girl would drop a 'ring' into the well and she was supposed to dream of the lad she would marry. This seemed like a fairy tale until two rings were found in modern days. In the late Victorian era, the rector of the day built a new rectory on the slope above the church and installed a 'modern' drainage system. It is said that one member of the rectory staff was a typhoid carrier, and leaks from the drains trickled downhill and into the well. Rumour has it that 40 folk from the village died, although no account of the deaths can be found in registers of the period. Presumably any illusion of the water's healing powers must have vanished!

When an ancient document came to light in the Ely Cathedral archives, it was found to be the charter granted to the village by Henry II to enable Hadstock to hold a weekly market and an annual Horse Fair on St Botolph's day. The Horse Fair has long since gone. The rector of the day was shocked at the debauchery that went on, and in 1872 he invoked an Act of Parliament to have it annulled, preaching a Blood and Thunder sermon at the time! However, the village still holds a fete each year in June on the Saturday nearest to St Botolph's Day, when the entire population usually takes part and a great time is had by all. It is the chief money-raising event of the village. The house at the scene of the ancient Horse Fair is still called Fair Hill.

From the 1950s to the 1970s the only mounted Scout troop in the UK was based in Hadstock. The troop was used by the Chief Scout as a Guard of Honour at Jamborees and when the Royal Show was held in Cambridge they gave a display. All Scouts learnt to ride and the troop only ceased when the Scoutmaster had to retire.

The village has changed considerably in recent years. There used to be 13 farms in the parish, now there is only one as the land has been bought by larger concerns and incorporated into farms managed by people outside the village. The farmhouses are now private dwellings. Cottages have been bought by folk from outside in the main and all have been extended or two or more incorporated into one house. Once there were three pubs, a blacksmith, a butcher, a wheelwright and a post office and shop. Now only the latter remains. The almshouses are now one dwelling.

The oxlip and bee orchid have always been found around the village, but nowadays in restricted numbers, although they are protected. The Essex Naturalist Trust owns a small reserve in the parish and there is a very ancient wood which is part of what was the great forest that covered the area in bygone years. It is in private hands and being well cared for. Many footpaths encircle the parish and lead to neighbouring villages, a significant pointer to the days not so long ago when journeys were mainly made on foot, whilst the bridleways were the horse 'lanes' of the area.

Halstead 🦢

In the 16th century many of the Protestants of Flanders and the Low Countries fled to this country to escape the religious persecution they were suffering there. Numbers of them settled in Colchester where they very successfully plied their trade of weaving woollen cloths. So much so that more came to join them until Colchester had become uncomfortably overcrowded with 'the straingers' and in 1576 some of them petitioned to be allowed to move to Halstead, twelve miles along the road, which already had a thriving cloth trade. Permission was granted, they came, they settled in and immediately set up their own strict system of quality checks on the cloths they made, 'bays and says' or the 'new draiperies' which were much finer and more in demand and better priced than the existing local product.

For a while the Halstead people and 'the straingers' co-existed happily together but eventually small frictions grew to discontents and arguments and relationships between the two parties became increasingly soured. The main controversy was over the system of inspection and 'sealing' of the bales of cloth, ie a seal that was attached as evidence that it had been inspected and was of marketable quality. This was normally done independently of the cloth makers but the 'Dutchmen', because of their reputation for producing high grade cloth and their scrupulous business dealings, were granted the rare privilege of sealing their own cloths. A second ticket bearing the name and trademark of the manufacturer would also be affixed and on this evidence alone the Dutch cloths would be passed through the London and Continental markets 'on the nod', such was their reputation.

Meanwhile the native Halstead weavers were seeking to improve the standard of their own cloths to emulate their new neighbours but with limited success and their products, though Halstead labelled, were not accorded the same high regard. So they thought of a way round this. Why not get an agreement that all Halstead-made cloths should bear a common seal?

Needless to say the Dutchmen were emphatic in their refusal to accept this ploy, being fiercely jealous of their own reputation in the markets and, of course, the increased profitability it engendered. The native Halstead weavers persisted in their demand and for a couple of years there were unseemly squabbles and recriminations, with the Dutchmen remaining adamant in their refusal to agree to what was, in their view, a

Halstead Mill, today a series of shops

monstrous invasion of their rights. The final showdown came when it was discovered that some of the local English weavers were counterfeiting the Dutchmen's seals to obtain a readier acceptance and a better price for their products.

It was the last straw. The Dutchmen had had enough. Finally, in 1589, they packed their wives, children, household goods and looms into wagons and made the tedious journey, as it then was, back to Colchester to resume their trade there.

They expressed their sorrow at leaving for, as they said, they had found Halstead 'one of the most convenient towns in England for their trade'. The townspeople were at first overjoyed at the departure of their 'strainge' neighbours but disillusion quickly set in when it was discovered that the Halstead labels were no longer synonymous with high quality and the demand lessened. There ensued great distress in the town, not only among the weavers but also for all the ancillary trades that accompanied the production of wool cloth.

Greatly alarmed, the town council swallowed their pride and petitioned Queen Elizabeth to ask the Dutchmen to return to Halstead and resume their trade with a guarantee that there would be no more trouble with the seals. Fifty of the principal inhabitants of the town signed the petition although nine made only their mark. This paper still exists and

113

lies in the State paper archives. The Privy Council sent Sir Thomas Gent to Colchester to plead with the Dutchmen to return but they were having none of it. Finally the Council wrote to the Bailiffs of Colchester ordering that six of the Dutch weavers (named) should be ordered back to Halstead. They did not, nor did any of them and that was the end of that.

Towards the end of the 19th century life in the town had altered beyond the wildest dreams of those who lived at the time of the Flemish weavers. Communications had improved, industries had been founded and developed, Courtaulds and the tortoise stove among them; the Halstead and Colne Valley Railway had been built in the 1860s; the electric telegraph had been connected to the town (via the railway) and compulsory education for all children had been established.

But on the morning of Tuesday, 22nd April 1884, something happened which none of the inhabitants could have foreseen or expected, in their most bizarre dreams – or nightmares.

At 9.20 that morning Halstead suffered the effects of a severe earthquake, the epicentre of which was a mere 20 miles or so away to the east. Colchester and its surrounds were the most severely affected but places as far away as the South Coast, Bristol, the Midlands and even Ostend over the Channel reported evidence of tremors.

Courtauld's factory was just a few hours into its morning shift when the blow fell. The looms shook, the weaving sheds swayed and the weavers, mainly female, rushed from the premises in terror, many of them fainting on the way. Clerks at a solicitor's office fled the premises fearing the building was about to fall down, and in houses articles were dislodged from shelves and tables. In the larger houses servants' bells were set confusedly jangling and one lady in Head Street said she had been tipped from her chair.

The feeling of alarm was intensified as the tremors were accompanied by a loud subterranean rumbling described as being similar to a 'passing traction engine', but it seems the most frightening aspect of the affair was that no-one knew what actually had happened. Rumours abounded and the favourite conjecture was that there had been a magazine explosion at Colchester barracks some twelve miles away. It was an hour or two before the news came over the telegraph wires to confirm that an earthquake had occurred near Colchester much, we may imagine, to the astonishment of the townspeople.

Little physical damage was done to the town but its shattering effects on the peace of mind of the inhabitants can only be supposed. No further tremors were felt then or since but . . .?

114

Harwich 🦐

The town of Harwich lies at the tip of the peninsula of north-east Essex where the rivers Stour and Orwell come together and flow out into the North Sea. It is known as the port for the cross-channel routes to Holland, Germany and Denmark but, in fact, all the passenger ferries now leave from adjoining Parkeston Quay. There is, however, a large volume of commercial traffic using the port and this sails from the Navyard Wharf which replaced the old Naval yard or shipyard. There is also a little ferry making the journey across to Felixstowe in Suffolk. This sails from the Corporation Pier, better known as the Ha'penny Pier because of the original toll charge. The original ticket office, built in 1854, still stands.

The present town of Harwich is tiny, only 95 acres, and it differs little in plan from the original medieval one of the 13th century. The streets run in comparatively straight parallel lines from north to south with cross alleys, staggered to break the strong east winds.

Harwich became an important Naval base in the 1660s. At that time Samuel Pepys was First Secretary for the Admiralty and also one of the two Members of Parliament for Harwich. Not unnaturally it was also a centre for ship-building and many wooden ships were built in its Naval yard. A unique wooden tread-wheel crane used there was built in 1667. This was operated by men walking inside two large oak wheels, 16 ft in diameter, rather like giant hamster wheels. It was still in use in the First World War, but in 1928 it was moved to the green where it now stands.

One particularly interesting building in Harwich is the Redoubt. This is a large circular fort built about 1810 to resist a possible invasion by Napoleon. It is part of a chain of Martello towers which stretch from Aldeburgh to Seaford. It is built on the top of a slight hill and is 200 ft in diameter, yet, surprisingly, it is not visible from the road. It is approached over a drawbridge (now fixed) over a dry moat. There are staircases to rooms at lower level. These rooms were used variously for soldiers' accommodation and stores. The gun positions on the upper level command a wonderful view of the approaches to the harbour. The garrison was equipped for six officers and 250 men. Although during the First and Second World Wars the building was used for minor purposes, no shot has ever been fired in anger from it. Over the period of the last 20 years it has been carefully restored by the Harwich Society and now contains an interesting museum.

There is a Maritime Museum in the Low Lighthouse. This is one of a pair of leading lights which, in earlier times, guided shipping into the harbour. They were built in 1818 to replace earlier wooden ones. They were owned by General Rebow who became very rich by charging one penny per ton light dues on all cargoes coming into the port. However, they were acquired in 1836 by Trinity House and in 1863 they became redundant as the course of the channel had changed. The High Lighthouse continued to be used by mariners as a landmark.

Trinity House was founded by Henry VIII in 1517 and there is an establishment in Harwich. In times past the welfare and maintenance of lighthouses and lightships was an important part of the work, but times change and now there are automatically operated light buoys. On shore there is a large maintenance yard and there one can see buoys awaiting their turn for servicing and others gleaming in a new coat of paint ready to be returned to sea. The pilot boats which take the pilots out to the incoming vessels are also the responsibility of Trinity House.

Harwich's parish church is St Nicholas. This was built about 1820 on the site of a much earlier church. It is noteworthy for its graceful slim iron pillars which are a product of the Industrial Revolution. The church registers date back to 1559 and contain the records of the two marriages of Christopher Jones, Master of the *Mayflower*, and also the baptism of some of his children. He made his home in King's Head Street and it is believed locally that the *Mayflower* sailed originally from Harwich. Capt Jones' house still stands as do many medieval houses. Near the church is 'Foresters'. This was built in 1450 and at one time was used as a pub. It is believed to be the oldest house in Harwich.

Another building of interest is the Electric Palace. This is one of a very

Ferry leaving Harwich

few remaining purpose-built cinemas of its age. It was built in 1911 as a result of the Cinematography Act of 1909 which demanded structural fire precautions. As Harwich was a poor town this little cinema carried on without modern improvements until it closed in 1956 – mostly as a result of the damage done by the floods of 1953. In 1970 the local council decided that the site would make a good car park. This spurred enthusiasts into action and now Harwich boasts a beautifully restored little cinema which, with the help of volunteers, shows films every week-end. Just behind the cinema is another more modern item of interest. A long plain wall has been decorated with a fine mural. This was designed by the art master at the Harwich school. The paint was donated by a large paint manufacturer and the work was carried out by the pupils of the school in 1982. It depicts some of the buildings of Harwich and also time changes from the Elizabethan era to the present day.

The river Stour, on which Harwich stands, is the border between Essex and Suffolk and the estuary, which extends westward to Manningtree, is important as the winter home of many wildfowl such as Brent geese, shelduck and wigeon. There is an RSPB bird reserve in Stour Wood between Wrabness and Ramsey, with bird hides along the shore.

Hatfield Heath ༄

Despite the address, (Bishop's Stortford, Herts), Hatfield Heath is four miles over the border. Upon entering the Heath on one of the six main roads you will circulate round the large village green, our pride and joy, upon which lies the cricket field spreading its green acres and stretching back in time beyond living memory.

In front of the Post Office Stores, on a grassy mound, is the ancient village pump, which used to augment the many 40 ft wells in cottages and houses around the green. From this there is a good view over the green of the church of Holy Trinity and its wooded graveyard, a little over 100 years old, small, but large enough for these modern times.

Opposite Holy Trinity is the village junior school, its foundation stone bearing the inscription: 'The Very Reverend Montague Butler, Master of Trinity College Cambridge, Wednesday 25th October 1899'. He was grandfather of R. A. Butler, Minister of Education whose Education Act of 1940 brought secondary education for all pupils. The log books, dating back to 1830, chart the progress of education in the village from the early dame school. Notably, one log book bears the signature of the famous poet Matthew Arnold (1822–1880) whose father, so well remembered in *Tom Brown's Schooldays*, was the legendary Doctor Thomas Arnold, headmaster of Rugby School.

Behind this is the splendid village hall, which the village built in 1970. It is the centre of social life, being host to many of the 30 organisations centred in the village.

A large windmill once graced the village hard by Mill House and Mill Cottage on the south side of the green. It was demolished in 1908, being overtaken by progress in the shape of a new, engine-powered mill to the west end of the village on the Stortford Road. This mill in turn was superseded by the larger mill in Bishop's Stortford, about 1970. It remains smartly decorated but redeveloped into small businesses and offices.

Why so many main roads passing through here? A record number for an English village we're told! They grew in the 17th and 18th centuries when London was expanding. Flour and produce from the wheat-growing parts of Suffolk was hauled in by large horse-drawn vehicles en route to the London markets, often staying here overnight. Hence, also, four inns supplemented by the many unlicensed alehouses prevalent in those days.

Many local trade are evident by street and house names. 'Little Brewers' hard by the mill, is a reminder of the brewery founded there which once supplied the local hostelries. Forge Cottage is where the blacksmith's hammer could be heard striking the anvil in bygone times.

Corringales, situated on the outskirts of the village, is a link with Saxon times as it was once a Saxon hall. The founder, a certain 'Curra', built a hall known as 'Curras Ing Hall' in AD 836. It would have been a large hall with a hole in the roof for smoke emission. Ongars was mentioned in the Domesday Book. Friars Farm, once paid its rent to the friary which was situated at Hatfield Broad Oak. Lea Hall, on the Broad Oak Road, was a moated manor, having still the remains of a moat behind which the stock was driven for protection when raiders from the sea were in the area.

There is still a lord of the manor who owns the soil of the village green and four houses whose owners, known as 'Commoners', have vested in them some 'Rights of Common'. These individual's rights are (1) right of loppage, to gather wood for burning; (2) pannage, the right to pasture swine on the common land; and (3) the right of the warren, the right to hunt rabbits on the common. Not, however, the 'right of chase', ie the hunting of animals. This was the prerogative of the lord only. In medieval times Hatfield Heath was but a clearing in the Great Forest which covered most of England, hence its name, Heath meaning 'a clearing surrounded by trees'. Hatfield Forest, but three miles away, is a reminder of days gone by.

King Robert Bruce of Scotland's forebears held land in the district. Legend has it that this hero of Bannockburn was born in a ditch by the side of the track from Hatfield Heath to Hatfield Broad Oak. It is also said that it was by Caesarean operation, his father's hunting knife being the instrument.

Hatfield Peverel 🦉

Draw two diagonal lines across a map of Essex and there, almost plumb in the centre, you will find Hatfield Peverel.

Hatfield is from the Saxon 'Hadfelda' meaning 'a clearing in the wild uncultivated ground'. William I took as a mistress one Ingelrica, a lady fair, and daughter of Ingelric, a Saxon noble and court scribe; she bore the King an illegitimate son, also to be named William and later to become owner of Nottingham Castle. Eventually the King tired of her and Ingelrica was married off to one of his knights, Ranulph de Peverel. Amongst his estates in Essex was Hadfelda and when Ranulph's own name of Peverel was added to 'Hadfelda', we have the name by which it is known today: Hatfield Peverel.

It is Ranulph's wife Ingelrica, and their legitimate son, again called William, whom we have to thank for the Norman church, at some later date to be dedicated to St Andrew. This was built as part of the old priory, for after the death of the King in 1087, Ingelrica began to reflect on the misdoings of her earlier life. To make atonement, she founded in the village, on land given her by her husband, a college of secular canons dedicated to St Mary Magdalene; here she spent the remaining years of her life. After her death around 1100, William her son carried on her work, changing the order into a priory of Benedictine monks subordinate to the abbey of St Albans and dedicated to the Virgin Mary. All that remains now of the original priory is the church; the present impressive building bearing that name was built in the 18th century.

The 17th April 1231 was a day of high drama in the village, for a great fire had broken out within the monastery walls. The main part of the monastery buildings were destroyed as was the east end of the church and its tower; so fierce was the heat that the bells melted whilst the original beams in the roof above the choir bear the scars of charring. It was not until many years later that, with the help of the villagers, the church was repaired; in return for this help, they were given the nave as their own parish church.

To round off the story of Ingelrica, a legend exists which says that the Devil vowed he would have her soul whether she was buried inside or outside the church. This problem, so we are led to believe, was neatly overcome by burying her in the wall itself – neither inside nor out. Believe what you will, but we all love a legend. A 13th century effigy, reputed to be that of Ingelrica lies on the window sill of the north wall, next the organ.

Hatfield Peverel has the dubious honour of being the home of the first three women in Essex to be tried for witchcraft: Agnes Waterhouse, her daughter Joan, and Elizabeth Frauncis. These three women were put on trial at Chelmsford in July 1566, each suspected of being a witch, and on the 27th July 1566, Agnes, aged 63, was hanged on the gallows; her daughter and Elizabeth Frauncis were acquitted.

Of the several old houses in Hatfield Peverel, the oldest is Vinehurst in the Street; it is directly opposite the post office (itself 15th century) and has been authentically dated to around 1350. The previous owners told of two ghostly presences, one kindly and affectionately known as Silas, whilst the other, unnamed, manifested itself, even on a warm day, by a sense of chill and a feeling of unease, and at which the dog would howl all night. On such nights the lady of the house would pull the bedcovers tightly over her head!

A further strange tale is that of 'Shaen's dog'. This creature, big and with glaring eyes, was said to haunt the road between Crix Corner and the bottom of the hill on the approach to the village from the Chelmsford direction. A waggoner who lashed out at him was consumed with fire – together with his waggon.

Whilst in the vicinity of the post office, spare a glance at Hill House, next to Vinehurst, which was reputed to have been built by smugglers and with a system of cellars. When Excise men became suspicious and organised a raid, it is said that the villagers lay on their stomachs to drink, as the spirits ran down Hatfield Hill.

On the other side of the Street and clearly visible is the tall spire of the Methodist chapel, but you will look in vain for the weathercock – on 22nd April 1884 it was toppled, a casualty of the earthquake in the Colchester area. Nearby is the William Boosey public house, formerly the Crown and mentioned in deeds dated 1607. Not only has it served as a place for refreshment, but almost 200 years ago it was a station for fish-curing. Big wagons rumbled in from Lowestoft and Yarmouth and deposited their fish at a building behind the hostelry. The owners, the Ong family, used sawdust to fuel the fires, and the villagers brought their hams there to cure.

There are now six pubs in Hatfield Peverel, fewer than in earlier years, whilst on the green there was, until around 1919, a thriving brewery run by a family named Brown; Brewery House still dominates the green. In a small house opposite (since demolished) was formed, exactly 100 years ago, the Hatfield Peverel branch of the Salvation Army, still active in the village and whose splendid band, on many a Sunday, can be both seen and heard on the streets.

From an estimated population of around 500 souls in the 1500s, it took 300 years for the number to double to 1,008 by 1801. In 1951 there were 2,175 people living here but this time it took only 40 years for that figure to again double, until today the village is home to more than 4,000 people.

There are many facilities here and despite the increased population it is still a pleasantly rural and convenient place to live. The towns of Witham, Chelmsford and Maldon are all within easy reach, whilst a trip up to London is a mere 45 minute train ride away – given a fast train, and British Rail willing! The station, first built in 1844, was totally destroyed by a disastrous fire in February 1849 and was not rebuilt for many years. On 1st March 1878 it was reopened by the Great Eastern Railway and today serves not only the local inhabitants but those of several surrounding villages. Parking for commuters, alas, leaves much to be desired.

An admirable doctors' practice with a surgery equipped for performing minor medical treatment is centrally situated near Hadfelda Square car park. There is a well-stocked library, two garages, a variety of shops, and a police station. One discerning gentleman who moved in from the suburbs of London some years ago remarked: 'Here I am and here I intend to stay; to my way of thinking, Hatfield Peverel is the next best thing to heaven!'

Helions Bumpstead 🌿

Helions Bumpstead is a border parish in many senses since it is adjacent to both the Cambridgeshire and Suffolk borders and is situated immediately below the watershed between the boulder clay uplands of Essex and the chalklands of Cambridgeshire, a geological border which once formed the northern boundary of the great forest of Essex, the remnant of which is represented today by Epping Forest.

It is difficult to assess when the village proper came into existence but the building of the church near the crossroads by the local benefactor, probably in the 12th century, obviously established the position of the village. The attraction of tradesmen such as a blacksmith and wheelwright, and the provision of a beerhouse and a bakery of course followed, thus creating the nucleus of a conventional village and a centre for the inhabitants of the outlying hamlets.

The Domesday Book records that the parish contained four manors, namely Horsham, now represented by Horsham Hall Farm at the Suffolk end; Bumpstead, now Bumpstead Hall Farm on the road, midway between Helions and Steeple Bumpstead; Helions, now Helions Farm, close to the village centre; and Olmstead, now Olmstead Hall Farm at the far Cambridge end of the parish.

In 1466 Sir William Blount, Lord Mountjoy and his wife, the Duchess of Buckingham gave Queen's College in Cambridge some 1,300 acres of land within the parish. The farms involved were Copy Farm, Drapers Farm, Horsham Hall, Ladysgate Farm, Perry Appleton Farm, Lancelots Farm, Haven Farm and Olmstead Hall. They remained in the college's possession for 454 years when they were sold in 1920, principally to the sitting tenants. In 1727 Queen's College bought Moon Hall Farm, which lies next to the lands of Horsham Hall, to add to their properties in Helions Bumpstead.

Apart from farming there was a cottage industry in the 15th century engaged in spinning, and to a lesser extent weaving. The area embracing the towns of Dunmow, Coggeshall, Braintree and Bocking became a virtual industrial centre for these activities. The villagers of Helions Bumpstead formed a guild known as the Guild of St Peter of Spinners and Weavers – a craft union – who held their meetings in their 'Yeld Hall'. But the prosperity brought to the area faded away and whereas in Colchester 20,000 had been employed, that number had dwindled to 150 by 1790. In 1750 in Dunmow the best spinners could earn eightpence per day, by 1790 they could only get fourpence. In the villages the situation was worse.

In the 19th century another cottage industry evolved, straw plaiting. It had its advantages since the raw material was freely available and all the female members of the family could participate. The plaits were collected at intervals by a travelling dealer who paid for them on the spot and passed them on to the bonnet makers in the surrounding towns. One particular type much sought after and for which a premium was paid was known as a diamond plait, when the straw was twisted as it was plaited, forming a small tent-like point which sparkled in the sun – hence its name. Since the straw bonnet was de rigueur for all females from all walks of life at work or at play, the demand was never-ending – until of course the straw bonnet went out of fashion. In the 1851 census no less than 74 women, wives and daughters of farmers and farm labourers alike, are listed as straw plaiters.

Herongate 🐓

Herongate has a great history. Heron Hall was the place of exile of the Tyrell family after one of them unfortunately killed William II (nicknamed 'Rufus' because of his red hair) in the New Forest, claiming that he mistook him for a squirrel! The Hall was originally moated, and in the fields behind it are the banks which formed the old heronry. The sign for the Boar's Head public house shows the Tyrell crest, a boar's head holding a peacock's feather in its mouth. There is a local legend that Dick Turpin, closely followed by those trying to arrest him, jumped from an upstairs window of the pub and got away.

Robert Graves, in one of his books about the Emperor Claudius, has the description of an ambush planned in this area by the 'Heron King' (a man on stilts) in an attempt to stop the march of the Romans on Chelmsford.

There used to be a windmill at the top of Mill Hill and the common once stretched from the south of Button Common to Common Road, Ingrave. Lord Petre owns most of the local common land and has the right, confirmed by Act of Parliament in 1979, to hold a manor court here. According to the Act, it is 'to manage the land' he owns, and it is one of only some dozen such courts still in existence in England. The Petre family take a great interest in Herongate and Ingrave.

The old Tudor Hall, replaced by Thorndon Hall in Ingrave, used to

123

stand in the woods west of Herongate. Instead of reconstructing it, the Petre family had it pulled down. It would have been too difficult to bring it up to the then modern standards; for instance, as at Weald Hall, all the bedrooms led off each other. There is a story that once it was badly damaged by fire as its owners were celebrating a marriage. The bride died in the flames. The present Hall was also almost destroyed by fire. A local man claimed that his great-aunt, the housekeeper, shutting up for the night, carried a candle which set fire to a curtain, with disastrous results.

There is a letter in the London Record Office from the then rector of Ingrave asking the Government to station troops at the foot of Brook Street Hill, Brentwood, to prevent the anti-Catholic Gordon rioters, in 1780, from marching against the Catholic Petre family.

There is a Tyrell Society in the USA and from time to time various descendants of the family have come to visit Herongate, the home of their ancestors.

Heybridge & Langford 🐚

Heybridge and Langford have seen many changes over the years but one thing that is unchanged are the beautiful walks by the canal and riverside. The long awaited bypass from Maldon to Heybridge opened in 1990, taking up a lot of the countryside, but the developers kept most of the footpaths where possible and in some cases have improved upon them.

At Langford, one can see an imposing red brick building built in 1879 to replace an earlier wooden building which was burnt down, and which is now known as Langford Mill. Next to it is the Mill House and the unique St Giles' church where the Norman apse is at the west end. Formerly it had an apse at each end. The church was restored in Victorian times by the Honourable Mary Byron, whose husband Frederick was the rector from 1890–1913. The family lived in Langford Hall, a large Georgian house that can be seen behind the church. Several members of the family are buried in the church grounds.

The chief occupation of the inhabitants of Langford was farming until the 1920s when the waterworks pumping and treatment plants were built and employed about 50 men. Langford today has no shop, no post office and no public house, just a small village hall that was originally the local school. This is still owned by the Byron family and used regularly. Langford is a charming and unspoilt village.

From Langford it is a very pretty walk to make your way towards

Beeleigh, either along the road towards the golf course or by 'The Cut', a disused waterway leading to Beeleigh Weir where fresh water from the Blackwater flows into the tidal estuary. This is a very picturesque spot, more so when the tide is in and the water in the canal high enough so that it cascades over the falls.

Rural tranquillity is captured by the sight of cattle grazing in nearby meadows and drinking at the water's edge as you make your way towards Heybridge and Heybridge Basin. Passing over and under bridges, some built recently with the development of the Maldon bypass, one is reminded of the days when the rumble of a steam train could be heard passing overhead but alas, now it is all part of the motorway. As one approaches the landmark known as Wave Bridge there are some riverside cottages looking very attractive, with their only access from the towpath and no traffic passing their door.

The name of Edward Hammond Bentall, who lived between 1814 and 1898, can be remembered by the older population of Heybridge. It was because of this man's invention that many local men were employed at E H Bentall Engineers making agricultural machinery to be sold all over the world. In those days it was a familiar sight to see horse-drawn barges on the canal, loaded with the machinery that had been stored in an enormous building at the water's edge that E H Bentall had built in 1863. These were taken along the canal and through various locks to be loaded onto larger ships at Heybridge Basin and exported to many foreign countries. The barges were also used to transport coal, corn and timber in the opposite direction to Chelmsford.

Leaving the Wave Bridge the towpath takes you past Heybridge Cemetery where some Heybridge Basin people are buried, having travelled in a funeral cortege by canal lighter. It is only a few years ago that this procedure was witnessed, presumably at the request of a very old resident of Heybridge Basin. Today there are many boats moored by the bank and it is a haven for estuary-going yachts and cruisers. There's always someone messing about on the water.

The Basin was dug out of Heybridge Marsh in 1793 and soon after that date houses were built. There are still some attractive cottages by the locks. Unlike Langford you will find the 'Basiners' have two public houses and two churches; St George's which stands isolated and the United Reformed. A village store was opened by Samuel Purkiss in the 1900s and with his son Clifford he started a mobile shop which allowed customers to have goods on credit. Anything in the drapery line as well as boots and shoes etc could also be obtained from Sam; one could more or less tell the time by his weekly visits. Sadly this all came to an end many years ago and only a yachtsman's shop now remains by the shore.

It is fascinating to watch the lock gates being operated during high tide and both old and young people are attracted to the variety of craft which go through either way. A short walk on the sea wall and you come to the Blackwater Sailing Club that brings visitors to the water front. The founder Commodore of the club was none other than E H Bentall.

Crossing over the footbridge on the locks, take the footpath along the sea wall heading back towards Heybridge. Looking across the river Osea, Northey Island can be seen and often flocks of birds in flight. In a short time Maldon Promenade comes into view on the opposite side with St Mary's church standing out against the skyline. The locals used to call this point of the sea wall Paddle Dock as it was a quiet and peaceful spot for taking a swim. In olden days barges en route to John Sadds timber wharf could be seen taking sawn timber to be unloaded by hand into the quayside warehouses. Timber was also tranported from Heybridge Basin by horse-drawn barges along the canal to Chelmsford; sadly Heybridge has lost that part of its heritage. Today we see timber-built holiday chalets where cattle used to graze and rabbit warrens flourished.

Eventually you leave the waterside and come into Heybridge Street, where the local shops cater for most requirements and the shopkeepers greet you on Christian name terms, which all makes for a warm and friendly community. In common with most places many changes have taken place in the village; buildings knocked down to make way for industrial sites and building sites cover many a green field. Most of the public houses and some of the shops have retained their external appearance but what was the Square is now a roundabout.

A prominent landmark is St Andrew's church, with the church hall on the opposite side of a busy narrow road. Locally known as the Waring Room, it is so called after a former vicar, Francis Waring, who died in 1833 at the age of 62. He had a son named Walter who had the original St Andrew's school built in 1869 in memory of his father. The school closed in 1900 but the Waring Room remains today as a centre for so many social events and meetings, having been brought up to date and modernised.

High Roding 🌿

The Rodings (or Roothings) are a group of eight villages said to take their name from a Saxon chieftain named 'Hroth', and from the Saxon 'ings' or 'meadows' by the river Roding, a small stream which eventually flows into the Thames at Barking Reach.

High Roding is so called because it lies further upstream than the other Rodings, and is on slightly higher ground. It was at one time considered to be the most important of the Rodings and on that account is sometimes referred to in ancient records as Great Roding. This may account for the fact that High Roding church is larger than the others in the Roding group. The village consists of several old thatched cottages.

At the beginning of the 20th century Gowers Farm, as it is known today, was connected with Tryphena Mission, a holiday home for East London's poor children, and was supported by voluntary contributions. So was the clock on the school tower, which was purchased and erected in commemoration of Queen Victoria's Diamond Jubilee. The building is no longer used as the village school and is now a private house. The Youth Hostel in the village has also been made into a private dwelling.

In the early 1900s High Roding had several public houses, a post office and two general stores, a bakery and butcher's shop. Today there are just two public houses and, like so many other villages, the shops and post office have gone.

Hockley 🌿

Hockley used to be a village and, despite its increasing size, does not really qualify to be a town. Since the Second World War growth has been rapid, especially since 1957 when the railway was electrified giving a ten minute interval service to Liverpool Street during the rush hour, instead of one train an hour.

Where there were grass paths there are now made-up roads with pavements, street lights and houses each side. The field opposite the public hall was known as Horslin's Green and there every May there was dancing around the maypole after the crowning of the May Queen. In May 1935 a pageant was arranged to honour the Silver Jubilee of King George and Queen Mary. This was staged by Mrs Wragg in the public hall. A girl with fair ringlets was enthroned as Britannia, but there was some difficulty in finding a John Bull as no boy was really tubby enough! The celebrations came to an end with an enormous bonfire on Spa Meadow – everybody seemed to be there.

Spa Meadow, the triangle of land behind the Spa and bounded by Spa Road, Southend Road and Great Eastern Road, was the scene of many village fetes and also the home of the highly successful Hockley Football Club. It, too, has disappeared beneath bricks and mortar, and the building of a row of lock-up shops on its north-west side was the start of the movement of the village centre from the Rayleigh side of the Spa to Spa Road. Many new shops have been built and many seem to change hands regularly. The old shops have gone: Mr Quy's sweet shop, Mr Redbond's fish shop (frying on Friday evenings after Guides) – his shop had once been the toll house, Mrs Smith's general store (especially bread pudding) in the Forge Cottage opposite the Bull Inn, all these are but memories. The butcher's from which Mr Emery could be heard declaring to customers that lambs only had two legs apiece and so not everyone could possibly have a leg of lamb for their rations – that is still a butcher's shop. The large hardware store 'Inifer Potter and Son' has a long history. Inifer Potter opened a grocer's shop opposite his greengrocer's (later to be Mr Redbond's fish shop) and used to run across the road serving customers in each shop – something he certainly couldn't do now as traffic congestion is a serious problem.

In 1989 the parish hall, which is next to the Spa Hotel, where the main road divides for Ashingdon and Hawkwell, was completely refurbished and resumed officially its descriptive name, The Old Fire Station, and an appropriate sign was erected. Many old photographs of fire engines and the crews that manned them were hung. Then in October 1989 Hockley received its first Royal visitor. The sniffer dogs went down the drains, and even the milestones were repainted, and HRH the Duchess of Kent landed from a helicopter on Greensward School's playing field and was driven a short distance. She declared open the Old People's Day Centre, charming everyone, both old and young. The centre was built after a great fund-raising effort lasting several years, and is much appreciated by the older citizens of Hockley and Hawkwell. But it is tucked away behind the doctors' surgery and has been subject to vandalism – ironically it is nearly opposite to where the police station used to be.

Most of the development has been to the north as Green Belt regulations have restricted building to the south, and this, thankfully, has preserved Hockley's greatest glory, the woods, changing constantly and yet unchanged since the end of the last Ice Age. They have been designated an area of Special Scientific Interest and are the most extensive area of ancient woodland in the county. They contain many species which are only found where the soil has been undisturbed for hundreds, if not thousands, of years. Although the soil has been undisturbed, from Saxon times the woods have been managed as a valuable resource, not just for Henry VIII's hunting, but also by coppicing, especially of hornbeam. These stately trees which are growing almost at their northern and western limit, provide a very hard wood which has been used for policemen's truncheons and cogs in machinery.

Once, different parts of the woods were in separate ownership and the low banks, which marked the boundaries, are still an obvious feature. On the southern edge of the woods there are the remains of two parallel banks, which are all that remain of the old road from Rochford to Rayleigh which fell into disuse with the construction of the turnpike road (now the B1013) to Shenfield. Access to the woods is unrestricted, except for that area belonging to the Prison Commissioners, and both foot and bridle paths are well marked – there is no need to take a compass, as one guide book advises, if you remember that if you go uphill, you will come to the edge of the wood.

Despite the changes, from Plumberow Mount with magnificent views over the Crouch valley, it can still be appreciated that Hockley is built in woodland as the house-tops barely emerge from the surrounding trees, and across the great field (no hedges now) on another hill the top of the octagonal tower of the 13th century church is just visible above the trees, as it has been for nearly 800 years.

Holland-on-Sea ✒

Holland-on-Sea is situated on the East Coast between Clacton-on-Sea and Frinton-on-Sea, a friendly, neighbourly relaxed area. Hoilanda, once owned by Count Eustace of Boulogne, is recorded in the Domesday survey of 1086.

Spacious greenswards flank the clifftop Kings Parade, with terraced cliffs and beautiful soft sandy beaches. Along the Promenade are two kiosks open during the holiday season selling refreshments, buckets and spades, deck chairs for hire and everything that goes to make a seaside holiday. The residential area is mostly tree-lined avenues with generous open spaces for picnics and recreation.

A centre for sailing, power boat racing and wind-surfing is adjacent to a car park and unspoilt cliffs. Even in the height of the summer, it is always possible to find a quiet corner. There is an excellent bowling green, a very well run caravan park, tennis courts and a number of guest houses.

There is a coastal walk through to Frinton-on-Sea which is invigorating and free from traffic, passing fields with cattle contentedly grazing. Holland Brook is very popular with anglers, and there is also a golf course.

Holland-on-Sea has four churches, Methodist, Church of England, Baptist and Roman Catholic. Two sub-post offices, a public library and many restaurants and shops cater admirably for the community. The public hall is used by 20 organisations.

Although mainly a retirement area, there are many children and young folk around and they are much in evidence at the yearly carnival, which is successfully run for charity. The adjoining areas support the procession by entering their Beauty Queens and attendants, all making a colourful display complete with local marching bands.

The beaches and sea have been declared pollution free and swimming is safe for young and old and many take part in such enjoyment. Being within walking distance of holiday entertainment, theatres, night clubs and amusement arcades, it is ideal to be separate and have the choice of a quiet holiday or the excitement as one wishes.

Hornchurch

The London Borough of Havering, created in 1965, originally comprised 14 manors all owned by William I. In 1086 Hornchurch was part of the Becontree Hundred; before 1066 it was held by King Harold at a value of £36.

St Andrew's church existed by 1163. The church was originally given to the Hospice of St Bernard in the Alps for helping envoys of Henry II, as an endowment. The Hospice administered their lands in Hornchurch for about 230 years, then church and property were passed to New College, Oxford about 1392.

There is evidence of early occupation near St Andrew's church and Roman occupation was discovered at Mardyke Farm, possibly one centre of pre-Christian worship. In the Middle Ages the leather trade was important. In the Royal Charter of Henry II, the church was still called 'Ecclesia de Havering' as it was the main church of the royal manor. The High Street was called Pell Street or Pelt Street and there were tanyards behind the King's Head. Goods were exported but many were sold in Romford Market. Thomas Witherings was the earliest Postmaster General, buried in St Andrew's.

At the back of St Andrew's church and adjacent to the cemetery situated in an area known as 'The Dell', is Mill Cottage. The mill no longer exists, but two millstones from it were used as ornaments in the garden of Mill Cottage. It originates from the 16th century and contains many original and interesting features.

The Harrow Inn in Hornchurch Road dates only from the 1890s, but a previous building of that name occupied the same site. The old Harrow was extremely picturesque, partly weatherboarded and with three dormer windows set in a low thatched roof. The building was erected probably in the 17th century and may well have been originally a private dwelling house as the brewery records go back only to the 1850s.

Harrow Lodge was originally a small country seat cum farm, built in 1787. In 1886, 86 acres of Harrow Lodge estate were purchased by the Board of Guardians of Shoreditch for the erection of cottage homes for the orphans and other needy children of the parish of St Leonard, Shoreditch. This virtually self-contained 'village' remained intact until recently when it was redeveloped for residential use. Some of the original buildings still remain and have been converted for private use, and the new buildings have been built in character with the original dwellings.

131

With the development of Hornchurch between the wars the 120 acres forming Harrow Lodge Estate were saved from development and now form a fine public park. The house, approached by an impressive avenue of horse chestnut trees (some were lost in the 1987 gales) served for many years as the public library for Hornchurch. It is now used by the Borough Council as offices.

In 1621, Anthony Rame bequeathed two cottages on Church Hill to form Rame's Charity Estate. Up to quite modern times these two cottages (now forming the single dwelling known as Wykeham Cottage) were let, with the proceeds from the rent going towards the funds of the Consolidated Charities. Anthony Rame was the son of Francis Rame, steward to Sir Anthony Cooke of Gidea Hall who was tutor to Edward VI. Francis Rame was buried in Hornchurch church in 1617 and his interesting monument is well worth inspecting.

Langtons, a fine house set in six acres of ornamental gardens, was the largest private residence in the village. The centre part of the building was erected in the 18th century as was the small bath house by the lake, and the orangery. The name, however, goes back a great deal further, being recorded as 'Langedun' in the middle of the 13th century. In 1899 it was sold to Mr Varco Williams. He was Master of the Waterman's Company and the family lighterage firm of Samuel Williams and Sons of Dagenham Dock was almost a household name. Present day residents of Hornchurch owe a good deal to this family for, in 1929, Mrs Fraser Parkes (nee Williams) presented Langtons, complete with its beautiful park, to the town. Langtons is now the district Registry Office, probably the finest in the country. The extremely attractive park, with its ornamental lake and wildfowl reserve is open to the public – a delightful oasis where one may still recapture some of the atmosphere of more peaceful bygone days.

There had been an aerodrome at Hornchurch since 1915 when the War Office leased some meadows at Suttons Farm. In the mid 1920s its unique position resulted in a compulsory purchase order and in 1928 the enlarged aerodrome became known as RAF Hornchurch.

Ideally situated to cover the Dunkirk evacuation, the Hornchurch squadrons were heavily engaged across the Channel all through the last week in May and early June 1940, and from the opening stages in July were in the thick of the fighting throughout the Battle of Britain. All through September and on into October the battle raged and when it finally ended with a narrow but decisive victory for the RAF, the Hornchurch squadrons had claimed 411 enemy aircraft destroyed since the early actions over Dunkirk.

Apart from a length of perimeter track, the remains of a dispersal bay and a stretch of overgrown grass, RAF Hornchurch now lies under housing estates. In neat, well-tended gardens children play happily where the Spitfires, deadly yet as beautiful as butterflies, once 'scrambled' from the grass flightways. Some of the men who flew them are remembered by the names of the streets – Malan, Tuck, Deere, Gray, Franklin, Lock and Mungo Park. Others are remembered now only by relatives, by old friends who grow fewer with the passing years.

If the sky is blue today look upward and spare a few moments thought for the young men who flew day after day against overwhelming odds, and remember especially all those who took off from that Essex airfield and did not return.

Hutton

There is evidence of Roman occupation in Hutton, as coins have been found near the church. The Domesday reference mentions Hutton as a place where many pigs were kept. Epping Forest then covered many square miles, and Brentwood (a charcoal area – Burntwood) and nearby Hutton were all in the forest clearings.

The church of All Saints stands on the site of a crossed spring, which suggests pagan rites even before the coming of Christianity to Essex. The list of rectors begins in 1325, when Hutton was part of the Benedictine foundation of Battle Abbey. Unlike most village churches this one stands alone, away from the old properties and in recent years a new church (St Peter's) has been built nearer the 'new' population. Because the church is away from the mainstream of human activity it is a refuge of peace and has remained undisturbed by this century's upheavals.

A moated house, Hutton Hall, has existed from medieval times with its cottages nearby and, until the 20th century, many farm lands and tenant farmhouses. Some of the lords of the manor were very good to their people, others achieved notoriety. After the Dissolution of the Monasteries by Henry VIII, the manor left the ownership of the Benedictines and became the property of Sir Thomas D'Arcy. Another occupant was named Surman, secretary to the South Sea Bubble Company, and his lands were sequestered by Walpole. Another man named White helped to found the first school. The Hall was rebuilt in 1720, using local brick. Hutton had good clay deposits for brickmaking and some are still to be seen in the present house. The moat can still be seen around the pleasant grounds and house, now a private home but a walk round the lane in daffodil time is quite an experience.

There is evidence of education in the village from the 1600s and by 1807 there was a day school with nine or ten pupils, supported by the lord of the manor and the church. Six poor houses were sold to raise money for a school and the old school (1844) is now a modern nursing home but retains the facade and one original building. In 1900 records show that, where possible, parents contributed one penny per week to their child's education. In 1840 William Offin who lived at Hutton Park gave £500 for the school building and the Cross family at the Chequers public house built the school. The thriving village, still so small, enjoyed much care from the community. Interesting church records reveal how much was given to parishioners in difficulties.

At the beginning of the 20th century, changes loomed on the Hutton and Shenfield horizon. Hutton was a very small community, in green fields far away from city influences. Its row of cottages, its farms, the few larger houses, the Hall and church moved into the 20th century but even now remain slightly aloof from the busy commuter world.

In 1907 Hutton Poplars was built as a large institution for orphans from a London Borough. The population of Hutton literally doubled when George Lansbury decided on this site, with 500 children to be housed and educated. It stayed for over 50 years but when legislation decreed that children should be cared for in smaller units the homes were demolished. The school remains for adult education, the land developed with houses suitable only for the wealthier 'commuter' pockets.

The word commuter is the clue to the tremendous post-war growth in population, together with another jargon term 'Metropolitan overspill'. The railway at Shenfield meant wholesale disposal of lands; Hutton Mount, once all farmland, became the mecca dwellings of the railway bosses. Hutton and Shenfield became part of a great movement east of the capital. Since the Second World War many estates have been built near the main road, near to the station, and the population has risen dramatically. A good example of this is the change in education. In Hutton alone one small village school was outgrown by 1961, when five schools were opened and another was being built.

In 1986, Hutton village was designated a conservation area, ie the ancient grassland and fringe of older houses. Opposite the church is an open space, the centre of village life once. Queen Victoria's Jubilee tea was held there, a path from it is an ancient bier path. There are ponds and lakes near the church and clay from the area made bricks.

As you go from the church to the left into Church Lane you pass one entrance to the Hall and will have noticed the moat remnants. To the right you would have walked past The Willows, originally a Tudor farmhouse, and Humes. The Hume family were tenant farmers for 150 years. Sadly most of the farmhouse was demolished after bomb damage but it retains a wonderful piece of history. Look to one side for traditional Essex boarding and you will see a cottage built before the 1500s, attached to the main farmhouse.

Where Church Road meets Rayleigh Road there is a row of cottages, one of which was the last village shop, and Tomlyns, a lovely old house once lived in by Lilias Rider Haggard.

Kirby le Soken ॐ

The small village of Kirby le Soken has a long and chequered history, dating back to the Romans and believed to have been used for shipping as far back as 1326. Certainly by the mid 1800s Kirby was a thriving area with Kirby quay handling everything from sand, gravel, chalk, lime and fertilisers to wheat, copperas and of course fish. In fact, everything needed for a population of around 900 people, at that time more than Walton on Naze itself whose population had only reached 500.

Apart from the legal trade, Kirby was a great place for smugglers, very well organised and quite extensive, not just the odd bottle or 'baccy'. If today you walk along the high path of the sea wall on the backwaters, it is not difficult to imagine it would have been a perfect place to carry out 'private' business. It can be a wild and lonely place on a winter day.

The fine Norman church of St Michael set spaciously in well kept grounds has many beautiful windows. Its polished pews and tapestry kneelers give a warm feeling of a church well used. The full peal of bells rings out for Sunday services and on Tuesday for practice. Quite often visiting bell ringers ply their hands and once again the lovely sound rolls across houses and fields.

Like most villages there is a mix of lovely old houses, small cottages and two reasonably new estates. Luckily there is a sub post office, which is also a mini supermarket, and two pubs, without which no decent village could boast existence. Both the Red Lion and the Ship, like the village itself, have long histories, and were certainly suspect in the smugglers' days. Now of course both offer good food, good beer and pleasant atmosphere.

The stretch of backwater upon which the village grew is no longer used commercially, but is much used and loved by naturalists and watersport users. Yachts, rowing boats, windsurfing boards and light craft take the place of the barges. It is a tidal river running to the east of the village and at its source has Walton one side and Harwich the other, where of course it remains very commercial. The walk along its bank to Walton is ever changing.

The backwater area is unique as it is totally salt, having no river sources or entries of fresh water. It is regarded as a 'Jewel in the Crown' of Essex, is a national nature reserve and a registered wetland of Europe. Apart from the wildfowl which include Brent geese, pintail and shelduck, the flora and fauna is prolific. To add to the interest, it boasts oyster farming and on an island called Horsey, thoroughbred horses are bred, reared in an ideal situation and exported around the world.

Langham ✣

Langham is a long narrow village, about four miles from north to south and not much over a mile wide. Some say that the original name was Longham, now corrupted to Langham, but in the Domesday survey it is referred to as Laingaham, meaning the home of Lawa's people. Its northern boundary is the river Stour, and on the opposite river bank is Suffolk. On the south is Salary brook and the Colchester borough boundary, while the A12 forms the eastern boundary. At the northern end of the village is the church of St Mary, standing in the private grounds of Langham Hall. The earliest parts of the church date back to the 12th century, and in a recess in the southern wall is an oaken dug-out chest, said to be the oldest church chest in Essex, and one of the oldest in the country. The solid baulk of timber measures 4'7" × 1'6" × 1'3" but the cavity inside is only 13" × 7" × 6". Its lock, plate and hasp have at some time been broken from the heavy iron-bound lid.

Langham at one time had three working mills, including two wind-mills. One in what is now Mill Road near the Boxted boundary, is recorded as belonging to a Charles Whiley in 1594, and is thought to have been demolished in 1907. About the other a rather wonderful tale was recorded in the *Ipswich Journal* of November 1820. This stated that a post windmill, owned by a Robert Baines, of a large dimension, was moved nearly three quarters of a mile over five ditches and a road, the operation taking six days, and the mill was kept working the whole time.

This must have been some feat in those days! The mill was situated somewhere near the top of Nightingale Hill, and was moved to be nearer the Ipswich Road for the convenience of the farmers and merchants.

The other mill was a water mill on the river Stour. This was working up to the First World War, and sold to the South Essex Water Works when they came to Langham. This project, to supply water to the Southend area of Essex, was started in 1928. A large reservoir was built in the valley with houses for the workforce, and a large pumping station a little further down the river at Stratford St Mary. Water is pumped from here via reservoirs at Ardleigh, Abberton and West Hanningfield, on its way to Southend. The whole concern, since water privatisation, has now been sold to a French company.

The impressive building in School Road was built in approximately 1888. It was a large private residence, standing in its own grounds. Rumour has it that the Prince of Wales (later Edward VII) had it built for one of his lady friends. During the building's lively history it became home for the pacifist group the 'Adelphis', this was in 1936. The Peace Pledge Union was founded, and under the leadership of Max Ploughman a group of the members lived at 'Langham Oaks' until 1941. Vera Brittain, authoress, recorded in one of her books 'Staying at Langham Oaks' during the early war years. From 1937 until 1939 a group of some 60 Spanish refugee children from the Spanish Civil War stayed here. Some of these 'children' returned in 1987 to commemorate the 50th anniversary of their first arrival. From 1943 to 1956 Langham Oaks was an approved school for boys run by the Society of Friends. It has since been taken over by the Essex County Council as a special school for boys, and is now renamed Homestead School.

The Langham scene was changed drastically when Boxted Airfield was built in the Second World War. Householders and landowners received a nasty shock in January 1942 when letters were received from the Air Ministry giving notice of their intention. It was called Boxted as there was already a Langham Airfield in existence in Norfolk. Compulsory purchase notices were served, and a large workforce, of mostly Irish labour, moved in. Trees were felled, hedges disappeared, and in some cases houses too. Concrete runways were laid, and buildings of all shapes and sizes appeared. The first planes, American Marauders, arrived in May 1943. Park Lane was closed as one runway extended right across it, and it was not reopened until 1954. The present owners of Langham Lodge, the farm of over 300 acres which was completely swallowed up by the airfield, still get frequent visits from American airmen who flew from there.

Other changes that have taken place in the village are the disappearance of the local pubs and shops. There is still the Shepherd and Dog standing on Blacksmiths Corner, but the Greyhound and the Fox have gone, as have three of the shops. There used to be Lilley's on the corner of Perry Lane, Pickering's opposite the Shepherd and Dog, and Biggs' in Moor Road – which did not close until the early 1980s when the sisters Flossie and Phyllis Biggs retired. It had been in their family from the time it was built. The post office and village stores, run by the Forder family, is still flourishing, as is Thorpe's the butchers. There is also a new community centre, opened in June 1988, which is a great asset.

A great loss was the ancient oak which stood on Langham Oak Corner, the turning into the village off the main Colchester to Ipswich road. This had to go when the A12 was widened to dual carriageway. A new oak has been planted, but it will be many years before it can in any way replace the old warrior.

Layer de la Haye

Before the Second World War, the milkman delivered on a sturdy old bicycle with churns and measures, except to those who worked on the farms and thus got the dairy produce direct from their employer. Most people were farmworkers; the modern tractor had taken over from the horse-drawn ploughs etc, but it still entailed a lot of manual workers. Wives were glad to earn extra monies when the season demanded more labour; after the first agonies of backache, armache, legache and every other ache, young Mums picked potatoes, hoed the root veg, picked the beans and peas – and anything else that was going, while the babies watched from prams, or toddlers learnt where to keep out of harm's way, and seemed to revel in the grubbiness.

Rules were that children *must* go to school, of course, but in pea-picking times the school was closed because parents would pack the family's dinner and off they would all go. The coloured cottons of dresses and overalls made bright splashes along the 'stetches' in the fields.

It was a tiny school in those days, when families were larger and many were inter-related. Sanitary arrangements were primitive but by the 1930s the cesspit was an improvement. It was a real red-letter occasion when the main sewer-system was installed! Electricity replaced the oil lamps, which meant the modern cooker could replace the old pressure-stoves and kitcheners; but one heavy storm and the power would cut off, and hard luck for the dinner or cup of tea!

Progress brought in the buses, which were run by a family firm who started it all with horse-drawn vehicles many years previously. No one was left behind. Double-deckers were crammed full at holiday weekends, standing on top, squashed down below, holding tight on the platform. Yes, they were reprimanded, warned and called to recant, but every fare was taken aboard at a few pence return-ticket. It was only Christmas Day when they did not run. Everybody knew each other in the squash, and the noise was terrific as the Suffolk and Essex dialects intermingled.

Layer Marney 🪶

Layer Marney lies south west of Colchester, between Birch and Tiptree. It is one of three villages which bear the name 'Layer'. The other two are Layer Breton and Layer de-la-Haye. It is a village of about 70 dwellings, with no real centre, comprising dispersed farms and small clusters of houses.

Very little development has taken place over the years, because of planning restrictions, and, apart from restoration work to a number of dwellings, the village looks much as it did in the 1940s. Comparatively few of the once numerous Tudor cottages survive today. The most permanent entities in the area are the farms, despite the changes in farming methods which have resulted in the removal of hedges and the consolidation of some farms in to larger units.

The village once boasted a school, rectory, bakery, workhouse, off-licence, grocery and butcher's shop, slaughterhouse and fruit farms; a vet, blacksmith, wheelwright, bricklayer, and a dressmaker, although not all at one time. Alas, the majority of these have long gone, leaving only Parish Records as a testament to their existence. The school closed during the two World Wars 'in consequence of the decrease in child population of the parish', and now Layer Marney's only amenities are a garage, a public house and the church.

The few sources of work in the village itself, apart from agricultural occupations, come from an horticultural nursery, a window manufacturer and a fencing company.

Layer Marney is situated in a very pleasant, rural part of North Essex. Its country lanes and flat open fields are complemented by the Tower – the enormous gatehouse built by Henry, first Lord Marney in the early

16th century. The Tower itself is 80 feet high and was to be the entrance to a central courtyard of a house to be built to the north. Unfortunately, Henry died in 1523, bringing the building operation to an end and leaving the Hall much as it is today, with East and West wings to the gatehouse and an isolated South range, but no completed courtyard. During September 1579, Queen Elizabeth I stayed two days at Layer Marney Tower during a progress through Essex. Both Tower and Church are open to the public, and can also be enjoyed when the grounds and buildings are used to host Country Days and Antiques Fairs.

The Church of St. Mary the Virgin, build at the same time as the Tower, and within the extensive grounds, replaced an earlier Norman church on the site. The Marneys were a Norman family, who followed William the Conqueror, and the Marney chapel contains the tombs of Sir William, Lord Henry and Lord John Marney, as well as an original Tudor fireplace. In the nave there is a wall painting of St. Christopher, and a Jacobean pulpit. The earliest tombstone in the churchyard, and the only one to mention a craft – that of blacksmith – is dated 1784.

For the walker, numerous footpaths criss-cross the village, three of which converge on the Tower. By following the footpaths, it is possible to walk through Layer Wood, Pods Wood and Long Wood, radiating out to the adjoining villages of Messing, Tiptree and Tolleshunt Knights, respectively. From various vantage points, the lie of the countryside affords the walker a panoramic view of the River Blackwater, with tiny boats visible in the distance, and the Nuclear Power Station at Bradwell dominating the horizon.

Leigh on Sea ✄

The earliest written record of Leigh is in the Domesday Book of 1086 although from archaeological evidence we know it was in existence from a much earlier date. Two hoards of Bronze Age objects have been found – weapons of the West Alpine type dating from between 1000 BC and 750 BC. There is much evidence of Roman occupation and Saxon coins of the time of King Alfred were found in 1892.

There is reason to believe that the Pilgrim Fathers' ship *The Mayflower* was either built or owned in Leigh. There was much boat building in Leigh during the 16th century although it was during the next two centuries that so many Leigh sailors achieved distinction.

For some centuries Leigh has been concerned with fishing in general then later shellfish such as oysters, mussels and winkles were the most marked features. Nowadays Leigh is best known for shrimping, cockling and whitebaiting, these dating from the 19th century only.

Fishing being a precarious means of livelihood, Leigh men took advantage of any opportunity to make more money. When the Peter Boat, in Leigh High Street, dating from before 1695, was burned down in 1892, a large underground room was found. This has a waterside entrance and relics showing that it had once been used for contraband. It is believed there was a thriving illicit traffic in brandy and tobacco by the Leigh fishermen.

There is much evidence of the past in old Leigh. Many of the old buildings still stand whilst many others were rebuilt on sites retaining the original name – not least the parish church dedicated to St Clement. For 500 years its 80 ft high tower has been a landmark to generations of mariners. Records show that a church must have existed before the present building which is of late 15th and early 16th centuries.

Little Burstead 🐑

Little Burstead is a rather straggly and widespread village south of Billericay, the boundaries of which have changed over the years. It is only a mile from the A127 and six miles from the M25, and is approximately 24 miles from London. It has been designated a Green Belt area, and within the last ten years the main part of the village has been created a conservation area, so there has been very little new building and the appearance of the village has not altered since the early 1920s.

The name Burstead comes from the Saxon word 'Burghstede' which signifies a fortified place. During the Saxon period Little Burstead was part of the great estates of Earl Godwin, the father of King Harold.

There are several fine large old Elizabethan houses in the village (including the Old Rectory) which are privately owned. The most prominent one is Stockwell Hall, dower house of the Mexborough family. Lady Mary Savile, a lady in her own right, lived there until after the war, when it was sold. This house is also known as Clock House, so called because of the large clock on the end of the house, and it is said that the hands and figures were made from human bones, but were later changed to sheep bones. The house belonged to the Earl of Mexborough, as did a lot of properties in the village, farms and cottages. It was said that when Lady Mary Savile lived in Stockwell Hall, they used to go with an old cart and a mule to Billericay railway station (about three miles) to collect the coal to heat the Hall. The coal was sent to Billericay from her own coal mine in Yorkshire. They were called the Mexborough Mines.

Up until the first half of the 20th century these houses provided employment for many of the villagers, as did the farms and other local enterprises. Among these were a wheelwright, blacksmith, bakers and a general store. Also in the village were several poultry farms, a piggery, market gardens and an orchard, so people lived and worked in the village.

Unfortunately only the blacksmith remains (now called an agricultural engineer). In several instances, two or three small farmworkers' cottages have been made into one large house. Originally the village had two public houses, the Wheatsheaf and the Duke's Head. The latter is still open to the public, but the Wheatsheaf is now a private residence.

The village school closed around 1947 and is now used for activities connected with the church. Just past the school is the village pond. Much work has been carried out recently, eg excavation and clearing of duck weed, to make a pleasant spot to sit and relax. This was a project undertaken by the Little Burstead Conservation Society. Children once played hop-scotch, skipping, ball, whip and top and hop in the main street, mostly by the village pond which was the favourite meeting place. Another favourite pastime in the spring was catching newts and tadpoles in the then clean pond, and in mid-winter sliding on the ice was great fun enjoyed by all the youth of the village.

Almost next to the pond stands the property which used to be the village shop and post office. This business ceased in 1973, although many villagers found it invaluable. Opposite the old shop stands the village hall. This was built by Mr Weedon in 1926, on land donated by the Johnson family from Hope House. Many happy hours are spent in the hall by the villagers participating in the whist and beetle drives, parties and coffee mornings; and of course the Christmas party.

The main part of the village had a few street lights, but many people once cooked by oil stoves or kitchen ranges. Not everyone had main water and so had to rely on wells. During the summer months, a water cart would come down the road to provide people with water if their own wells had run dry. There was no electricity until the early 1950s and mains drainage did not arrive until 1981. Some areas still have no mains drainage today.

The church of St Mary the Virgin is quite an interesting small church, the structure being a survival from late Norman times, although most of the church dates from the 14th century and is well worth a visit. One rector of the parish became Bishop of Norwich in 1499, and another rector became Bishop of Gloucester in 1789 and of Bath and Wells in 1802.

As the road rises towards the church of St Mary the Virgin, it takes a sharp bend. This is Broomhill and there are still some properties called 'Broomhill' or 'Broomhill Cottage'. The records show that there has been a church on this hill since about 1142. The rectory is further along Rectory Road towards the village of Little Burstead. It is interesting to remember that in the late 1950s one could stand in the churchyard and look towards London, Grays and Southend without seeing a single light. Now the whole area is one mass of lights.

Another pretty place is opposite the Duke's Head, part of Laindon Common, an area of woodland which is much explored by people from the surrounding district.

Despite the loss 20 years ago of numerous beautiful elms due to Dutch elm disease, and hurricanes in October 1987 and January 1990 destroying masses of trees of all species, Little Burstead is still a 'green and pleasant place to live'. A friendly, neighbourly atmosphere prevails, and it is a truly rural village.

Little Wigborough 🐚

Little Wigborough is a small village overlooking the salt marshes and the estuary of the river Blackwater, eight miles south of Colchester between Great Wigborough and Merea.

Little Wigborough is mentioned in the Domesday Book under the name of Wigheberga, with the land belonging to Hamo Dapifer. The manor of Copt Hall, now owned by the National Trust, was held by the Earls of Gloucester. In the early 17th century, Sir John Cotton sold the manor to the Governors of the Charterhouse and it was held by them until recent times.

Being so close to the sea, it is appropriate that the church is dedicated to St Nicholas, the patron saint of sailors. There has probably been a church here from Norman times; the list of rectors goes back to 1272. The parish is now united with Great Wigborough (since 1878) and this parish was joined to Peldon in 1975. The church is small but attractive consisting of chancel, nave and west tower. It had probably been rebuilt in the late 15th century. Much restoration work had to be done between

1885 and 1888 following the severe damage caused by the local earthquake in 1884, especially to the tower. The church has a piscina and
chancel screen.

Little Wigborough's other claim to fame relates to the German Zeppelin L33 which crashed across the lane at one am on Sunday 24th
September 1916. This was one of the first airships to fall on English soil
in the First World War. The countryside was suddenly lit up by flames
from the huge gas bag as the commander fired his ship. Nearby cottages
at New Hall Farm narrowly escaped being hit or burnt. A framed
account of the destruction of the Zeppelin hangs in the church together
with a section of the airship.

Loughton ✧

The town of Loughton lies to the east of Epping Forest and west of the
river Roding, adjoining Chigwell and Buckhurst Hill. It is 12 miles from
the centre of London, easily accessible by both train and car, yet it is
surrounded by countryside and of course Epping Forest.

Rudyard Kipling as a boy spent much of his childhood here, making
his home with a farmer in Goldings Hill. Sir Jacob Epstein had a cottage
here for over 20 years and in his garden shed overlooked by the Forest,
carved 'Rima' in 1924/5, followed next year by 'The Visitation'.

Back in 1770 Loughton consisted mainly of dwellings along the High
Road, Church Hill, and Goldings Hill. Roads were eventually cut
through the Forest to Epping and much later the Epping New Road was
built by-passing Loughton, being a route from Woodford to Epping. At
that time herds of deer were still roaming free in the Forest, but sadly
they became a danger to the users of the New Road and were rounded up
and taken to a large penned-in area of the Forest at Theydon Bois, where
they still are.

The population in 1801 was 681, in 1831 was 1,269. In 1850 the
railway line was built London to Loughton and by 1871 the population
doubled. In 1911 it was 5,433. By 1916 Loughton changed from a village
to a residential town. 1931 it was 7,390, 1951 29,974. Today one tells a
local, because they still refer to 'the village', although population stands
at over 86,000.

The Forest also has evidence of early settlements. One such is
Loughton Camp; it is only about 1½–2 miles from the station going
north. It is a rough oval of some 6½ acres on a hill, enclosed by a single

rampart and ditch. It is thought to be pre-Roman. Also in the 18th century the notorious Dick Turpin was one of many highwaymen to haunt the Forest. It is said he roasted an old woman over a fire at Traps Hill Farm to make her reveal where her money was hidden. As a result many homes contained 'Turpin Traps', old wooden flaps let down over the head of the staircase and kept there by a pole placed against the ceiling, so they could not be raised from below. These were said to have been seen as late as 1891.

In the 19th century, some wanted the Forest or 1,000 acres of it enclosed. These supporters believed the poorer people of Loughton were idle and had a tendency to crime by custom of 'Lopping' for firewood during the winter. Actually the inhabitants of Loughton had an ancient right to lop wood from the Forest from 12th November–23rd April each year. Enclosures took place, roads and houses were built. Around 1860 the Willingale family were leaders in the pro-lopping rights and several actions were taken against them, and yet it is said their claims to fame were as preservers of Epping Forest. 1875 saw the Epping Forest Commissioners making their preliminary report and they found enclosures made between 1851–1871 were illegal as they contravened the rights of commoners.

In 1878 came Epping Forest Act appointing the Corporation of the City of London as Conservators of the Forest, keeping it open for public recreation, they bought up the lopping rights of Loughton. The Forest was saved, but the City of London paid £7,000 for the extinction of the lopping rights and from this Lopping Hall was built in 1884.

Until the 19th century most inhabitants of Loughton were engaged in agriculture. Debden estate was built in 1945, pasture land disappeared, although two farms still remain – Hill and North Farms. Today the estate is extensive with its own shopping centre and a large industrial complex.

Loughton has grown and now with the Forest/Green Belt surrounding it there is little or no land available upon which to build. The only option left is to demolish modern houses and even schools, to provide the area for several new buildings on the same site. The Century Cinema is such a building, built in 1928 and opened by Miss Evelyn Laye; it gave much pleasure to many and indeed was the only place of entertainment, but in 1963 it was demolished for shops.

The new Motorways, the M11 and M25 have made Loughton very accessible and of course have made other places more accessible from Loughton. Loughton is steeped in history but little evidence can be seen today. It is now a large town from which many people commute to London daily and yet it is a breath of fresh air nestled in the Green Belt.

145

Maldon Church

Maldon 🦋

Maldon is the lowest bridging point of the Chelmer/Blackwater estuary, and where they meet is the port area known as the Hythe. The settlement probably began here. Maldon is mentioned as far back as AD 913 when Edward the Elder stationed his fleet there. It is thought that the medieval quays lie behind the modern ones. St Mary's church on the hill leading from the quay is Norman built on a Roman site.

Maldon is not much used as a port now. The barges at anchor at the Hythe quay are a reminder of the days when these gentle giants raced to London and other ports and back, loaded with grain, hay or coal. They raced each other because to be there first got the loads. No load, no pay. The remaining few race today, once a year, not for cargoes but for the honour. Barges and fishing boats were built at the Hythe, and there are still boat builders there and sail lofts, mostly maintaining the barges.

Westward along the river from the quay, standing at the river's edge, is the salt works, Maldon Crystal Salt Company. According to legend salt was made here almost 2,000 years ago, when the Romans ruled Britain. Documentary evidence lists Maldon's salt pan in the Domesday Book. On the same site grew the Maldon Crystal Salt Company which has been in operation for 200 years, and has been run by the Osborne family since

1919. The modernised works sends salt all over the world. The original methods are still used to make salt today, although the salt pans are heated by modern means – British Gas.

A mile or so westwards along the river from the salt works lies Beeleigh, where stands the 13th century abbey. This famous old abbey houses original illuminated manuscripts. The abbey and its beautiful gardens now belong to Christina Foyle, of bookshop fame.

The market area of Maldon was east of the river at the top of the two hills, now known as Market Hill and Cromwell Hill. It is thought that the 13th century church was built when this area was flourishing and space at a premium. This church has a three cornered tower, owing to the space problem, and is one of only two such towers in the country today.

The Carmelite friars had a priory in the 13th century adjacent to what is now the adult education centre known as the Friary. Only a small ruin facing Longfield remains.

The D'Arcy family managed to acquire space during the 15th century in the High Street, between All Saint's church and St Peter's church, in which to build a grand town house. All that is left of this scheme is a corner tower now known as the Moot Hall. St Peter's church tower houses the famous Plume Library of rare books. Almost in St Peter's churchyard is the house where lived Edward Bright, the famous fat man, who was so large that seven tailors could be fastened together in his waistcoat.

On the edge of the town are the ruins of St Giles, all that is left of the 12th century leper hospital.

Margaret Roding 🦚

Margaret Roding straddles the busy road from Chelmsford to Dunmow. In ancient times there were two places here, Roding Masy and Margaret Roding. Roding Masy or Marcie Fee (Monks Hall) paid its tithes to Stondon Massey and hence the Masy. It also had a private chapel. Margaret Roding consisted of Garnish Hall or Olives and Garnetts as it was then known. Nestling hard by the grounds of Garnish Hall is the beautiful little church of St Margaret with its magnificent Norman Doorway. This little church has inspired a tale as the following letter will tell.

40 Hygeia Parade
Ringwood 3134
Rev G. F. Bartlam B.A.   Victoria
Aus

Dear Sir,   1986

This bible was preached from by Rev William Shepherd at Margaret Roding for many years preceding 1851. In that year, it was presented to his son 'James' who, as a midshipman was wounded at the Capture of Rangoon; was invalided home and in the same year, set forth with his nephew and two brothers to seek his fortune on the Australian goldfields.

Upon arrival at Melbourne the party equipped themselves and set out on the muddy road to the famous and wild diggings of the Buckland Valley, some 120 miles distant. Here it was, eventually, that James was called upon to press the bible in to service.

Here, where gold was plentiful but fever ran riot and the diggers were later to riot against the Chinese fossickers. Wild as they were, those diggers were extremely pious and, they gathered around the Shepherd campfire for the 'reading' as the boobook owl hooted on the ridge, night after night. This was later to become standard practice during the fifteen years of James' domicile on the incredibly rich fields of Ballarat and Bendigo; his ramblings to the Foster and Turton's Creek nearer Melbourne and on the fabulous field at Walhalla in distant Gippsland. In various parts of this area, James was to live out the latter half of his life and raise a family of eight children, all of whom were read to nightly from this bible and, when he passed away in 1911, it passed to my father, James Bentley Shepherd. Thus, eventually, it was placed in my care.

The conditions in which bush people lived in those years and continuous usage and handling, are reflected in the condition of the bible itself as I return it to its Margaret Roding home, 135 years after the commencement of its colonial sojourn.

James Keith Shepherd

Mayland 🦋

Today Mayland is a fast growing village and is known as 'The Maylands', the area down by the river Blackwater being referred to as Maylandsea. Now there are two sailing clubs, two public houses, several shops, including a post office, a small supermarket and a fish and chip shop.

Years ago it was very different, a small village with a farming and agricultural community. There was just one shop which sold everything from bread to paraffin and was also the post office. At one time the proprietor kept a parrot which would call out 'Stop thief!' The shop is still there, but is no longer a post office. It is on the Steeple Road next to the Henry Samuel Hall. The hall was given to the village by Mr Henry Samuel, and is used for WI meetings, playgroup, and many other community functions.

Nipsells Chase had six market gardens down the eastern side, and cornfields on the opposite side of the road. Acres were planted with fruit trees, some of them underplanted with bulbs, daffodils and narcissus, which looked lovely in the springtime when they were all in bloom. There were red may trees along Nipsells Chase, and walnut trees at the top end. What a pity the developers didn't think to leave some of those may trees, and so give the name 'Mayland' a meaning.

'I started school in 1915. My sister, two brothers and I had to walk the two miles to the old Mayland school, which was then up on the hill, past St Barnabas' church. The school was run by Mr and Mrs Jeffries, both teachers, and Miss Raisen who taught the infants. On our way along Grange Avenue there was a thicket of trees, with a hut in which lived a man said to be a hermit. We girls were very nervous about going past, until one day we saw him. He had long hair and a beard, but when we said 'Good morning' to him, he answered in a polite and cultured voice. He was said to be 'crossed in love', which we didn't quite understand, and was also said to be a member of the wealthy Fels' Naphtha Soap family, and thus a relation of the Mr Joseph Fels who had started the market garden scheme and also the 'French farming method' which at one time was practised at Mill Farm.'

The roads were just country roads with no pavements, but as there were no cars or buses it didn't matter. Sometimes there would be a horse and trap, but most of the time people walked – to church, to Althorne railway station if they wanted to go to London or Southend, or to the Huntsman and Hounds, which was the nearest pub, as the Mayland Mill was not a licensed house then but just two cottages. The tradesmen came round by horse and cart – the butcher and fishmonger from Maldon, the baker and general stores from Southminster. The nearest doctor was Dr Light, senior, who had a horse and trap.

Life is much easier these days, with electricity and gas laid on, made up roads with bus services and many car owners. Lots of people commute to

London and to other towns. There is a new church, St Luke's, down in Maylandsea, with a family centre, and a new primary school in The Drive.

Middleton 🌿

In the Domesday Book, Middleton was known as Midletuna, 'middle farm' being the literal translation. It was midway between Liston and 'Alphamstone', so was named for its situation.

The village church dates from at least the 12th century, as the list of priests hanging just inside the door demonstrates. Inside the little church there are many windows and plaques commemorating the Raymond family. This is a well known name locally, and indeed Oliver lived to be 95 years old and was priest here for 70 years. The Royal Arms of Elizabeth I are displayed on the chancel wall. It is said that there was a tunnel from the church to the big house, but no actual proof has ever been found.

The squire, of course, once lived at the big house and there was a time when every villager would have to mind his manners and touch his cap when the squire went by. However, there are many more tangible reminders of the past – the Ice House Meadow where food was once kept fresh and ice made; the sign in front of the lake 'Cave Stagnum' which was a warning to carriages coming up the drive and was erected after one driver made a mistake and went straight in; the old archway in the field commemorating the birth of a past Prince of Wales; the old school bell which still hangs outside the school door.

Villages everywhere have changed, and the saddest part of this change is the departure from the village of the old families. A farmworker leaves the village where his great-grandfather worked and his father and grand-father, covering well over 100 years between them, and the pleasant Essex accent is being overlaid by importations. The Tuffins have gone, and the Galleys have died out – Fred the horseman, friend of all the children, and his father Nathan, who was sexton for 40 years. When he retired he was presented with a cheque and the rector praised his long service. 'I can't rightly hear what you say,' said Nathan, 'but I thank you all the same.' However, when something stirs public opinion, there is still a corporate voice to Middleton.

Mistley 🦢

The name Mistley is said to be derived from two Saxon words, 'Mistel' the herb basil, and 'ley' a pasture, so perhaps there were great pastures of basil hereabouts.

Mistley is a unique village – the old part mainly Georgian with a street, a green, cottages and fields to the church. That is Mistley Thorn. Then comes New Mistley, Victorian cottages and houses, and then the modern developments. In between are the Maltings, and behind is the river Stour. It is tidal here and there are quays, with boats loading and unloading, and at low tide many wading birds and always the swans, and the ever-changing reflections on the water, with the Suffolk shore on the other side.

The walk to Manningtree, the shopping centre, is along the beautiful 'walls' – a stretch of wide grass along the river, and past the famous Mistley Towers. These were built in 1776 by the well known Adam brothers to enhance and beautify the new church built in 1735. The towers are now the only remaining part of this church, but are landmarks, and well worth seeing.

Mistley has had, like most other villages, a somewhat chequered history, but its worst period was in the middle of the 17th century when Matthew Hopkins the notorious Witchfinder General, waged his ruthless hunt for simple women he could condemn as witches. It is understood that some 3,000 were put to death in England between 1640 and 1660 and Matthew Hopkins caused 60 to be hanged in Essex in one year alone.

This is the story, which to us now seems ludicrous, of how Anne West who lived in a local cottage, was accused of witchcraft. The person who testified against her was Goff, a glover, from Manningtree. He was passing Anne West's cottage, so he said, at about four o'clock in the morning. The moon was full. He looked into the cottage and saw Anne sitting spinning. Suddenly four 'little things' in the shape of black rabbits, came leaping and skipping around him. These must obviously have been Anne West's familiars – evil spirits sent by Satan. Goff struck at the rabbits with his stick, but missed them. He seized one and tried to beat it to death, but it immediately turned into a ball of black wool! Next he tried to drown it in a stream close by, but he fell down (obviously this was also caused by evil spirits) so he crawled to the stream, still keeping a tight hold of the thing. He held it under the water a long time until it must surely be drowned, but no sooner did he release his hold than the rabbit sprung out of the water and vanished away. On this so-called evidence Anne West was taken before Justices of the Peace Sir Harbottle Grimston and Sir Thomas Bowes, convicted, and executed at Manningtree.

The probable explanation is that Anne West had got up early to finish some spinning. Goff the glover was returning home after a night of drinking. He stumbled along, past her cottage and looked in. To his drunken bleary eyes the balls of black wool on the floor seemed like moving rabbits. He stumbled and fell into the ditch. As he sobered up he slowly realised that he was in some difficulty. He was sure Anne West had seen him – if it became known that he was drunk and out at such an unseemly hour – what would happen to his reputation? He was known as a pious and industrious man! So he spread the tale that was to cost Anne West her life. Who knows if she had seen him, or if she would have gossiped about him if she had? In those days the lives of many other women hung on such a slender thread.

But that was a long time ago, and ladies who collect herbs and dried flowers are no longer suspected of being witches!

Gone also are the days of lavish entertainments at Mistley Hall. Of visits by Frederick Prince of Wales and the Duke of York, and of Horace Walpole who said of Mistley Hall 'It is the charmingest place by nature, and the most trumpery by art that ever I saw'.

It is rumoured that at one time Mistley Hall had two lots of servants – a day time staff, and a night staff to cope with the late, late parties and 'goings-on'. And there is also talk (but keep it to yourselves) that a certain clergyman fell in love with an actress there. When she treated his advances with disdain he followed her to London (that city of ill repute), entered the theatre where she was appearing – and shot her!

But to better things . . . In 1785 John Wesley visited Mistley on one of his tours and stayed in one of the houses in the High Street. He preached here, probably by the river, and now there is a little Methodist church in Chapel Cut, and in Manningtree one of the oldest Methodist churches in Essex.

When Horatio Nelson went into battle, one of his fighting ships had been built at the boatyard here. And did John Constable himself come to Mistley on one of his father's barges and help unload, or sit on the quayside with his sketchbook? Flatford Mill is only a few hours walk away.

In the late 1840s Mistley Hall was demolished and the estate sold to pay debts, but the woods are still there, and the huge oak trees to stand beneath and wonder.

In 1869 a new St Mary's church was built and consecrated in January 1870 with great ceremony and a public luncheon where 350 people sat down to a repast. No-one goes to church now in a chaise or governess cart, and there is no coal club or night school for men and boys. The dame school and the genteel lending library have long since closed, as have several of the shops, although there is still an antiques shop, grocer's and general store, and a post office.

The quietness has gone too, with the advent of the car and buses to Colchester and Harwich, and the lorries loading at the quayside, but the neighbourliness is still there, the chatting, the visiting and the cups of tea.

Mount Bures 🐾

Mount Bures is an Essex village whose very existence is doubted by many Essex people. Those who know the valley of the river Stour and 'Constable Country' know that the neighbouring village of Bures St Mary is in Suffolk . . . and who has ever heard of mountains in Essex?

The village does lie in north-east Essex, enclosed on the north by the river Stour and on the west by its tributary the Cambridge brook, raised above both on the 46 metre contour.

It is known that early Stone Age man came to this area before the last Ice Age because a flint hand-axe of that era has been found. Bronze Age tribes too lived here. The crop marks from their burial mounds and other sites can be seen in aerial photographs. The burial place of an Iron Age noble was also found when the railway line from Marks Tey to Sudbury was being constructed in 1849 through the middle of the parish. Although it is dated about 10 BC, too early for Queen Boadicea's revolt, this may have led to the legend about the mount.

The mount is a tree-grown mound, nearly as high as the church tower, believed by the local children to be the burial place of Queen Boadicea's warriors. It is in fact the remains of a great moated Norman motte, built by Roger of Poitou, one of the sons of Roger of Belleme, a companion of William the Conqueror in many battles. A wooden tower would have been placed on the summit of the impressive mound to form a rapid defensive point, essential during the early years of the conquest.

The church itself, near to the mount, also has an early Norman origin. It is dedicated to St John the Baptist, so perhaps it was erected by Roger of Poitou in memory of his mother, Mabel, who was foully murdered in 1077. She was decapitated by a vengeful neighbour whom she had wronged.

Unlike many churches in the area the church was not extensively rebuilt in late medieval times. It is not a typical 'wool church', but still shows its early origins. Its walls are of coursed flint-rubble, with Roman brick quoins, and the roof is tiled. It has windows dating from the 12th, 14th and 15th centuries and a 15th century south porch. The church retains an extremely attractive simplicity and when the flower festival is held for the feast of St John in June it looks outstandingly lovely.

The word Bures or Buers seems to be derived from the Old English place name Bura – a dwelling. The Domesday Book records the overlord Ulmer holding the Saxon manor of Bura before the Conquest. From about 1119, when the family of Roger of Belleme were stripped of their lands, until 1578 the manor of Mount Bures was held by the Sackville family. It is their arms which are depicted in stone on the church porch. In some documents the manor is referred to as Sackvile Mont Buers rather than Buers ad Montem or Buers Sancti Johannis (after the church). The lord of the manor meted out summary justice to the villagers, sometimes without obtaining the proper authority first. The villagers complained about Jordan de Sackville in 1274. They must have been anxious as he not only charged fines but possessed a gallows.

Glimpses of the lives of the people who lived in the village can be found in old records. Perhaps the one with the greatest claim to fame is Hugh Constable, great grandfather of the famous painter John Constable, buried in the churchyard in 1715 (though no-one knows exactly where).

Nowadays the village occupies 1,400 acres and has about 400 inhabitants. It has always been based on agriculture, and farms and houses are scattered throughout these acres, many of a great age. Records exist for over 400 years and are confirmed by the ancient timber-framed construction of the buildings.

The village hall was built as the school, which opened in 1873 but closed in 1938. It forms a meeting place for the lively parish council meetings and for such activities as aerobics and the meetings of the Morris men and the Bures and District Agricultural Club. Each year the Harvest Supper is held there. It forms the centre of the village in more ways than one.

The largest cluster of houses is around the village hall, stretching to the level crossing where the Sudbury line crosses the main road. These houses have mostly been built in the last 60 years but one very old house shows signs of having held an important position in the village, perhaps a court room, and the wheelwright's shop used to be nearby. At one time there was a shop near this and in living memory there was another at the south-east end of the parish, conveniently opposite one of the windmills, in a road which terminates near the war-time Wormingford airfield.

Now there is no shop but beyond the mount and the church is the Thatcher's Arms where good food can be obtained as well as drink and which has often been the venue for enjoyable charity fund-raising activities. Beyond that again, the water tower stands out as a landmark on the road to Chappel, though the two windmills which used to serve the parish have both gone.

The patterns of agriculture and country life are changing. Many people in the parish still make their living from the land in a variety of ways, including a deer farm. Others earn their living outside the village, commuting, often within Essex to Colchester, Maldon or Chelmsford or to towns like Sudbury in Suffolk. London too is accessible via the branch line to Marks Tey. The train's two carriages are full on the seven am run and the atmosphere is that of a friendly but select club. There are still families who have lived in the village for generations, while others are more recent arrivals, settling, as people have through the ages, in the parish, which though scattered has a strong sense of identity.

Mucking 🦢

Mucking is a small village near the river Thames, one and a half miles from Stanford-le-Hope and about the same distance from Linford.

In 1959 an important discovery was made from an aerial survey, which demonstrated the continuity of occupation in this area. In some fields at Mucking, now destroyed by quarrying, identified by the colouration of ripening barley, was an integrated pattern of rectangular and circular markings. Excavation showed that the area contained hut circles, iron-working hearths, and graves, in a chronological sequence from Neolithic to Roman times.

A railway line bypasses the village but there is no station, nor are there any buses. The milkstop used to allow passengers on or off the train but this has long since ceased.

There is a bird sanctuary between Mucking and the nearest small town of Stanford-le-Hope, with fishing and sailing on what are disused gravel pits. This makes a pleasant stroll and is the quickest way to walk if one has no transport.

Years ago Mucking was a busy village with a 12th century church, school, pub and many more houses than it has today. The last children were christened in the village at the end of 1981, when people came from several surrounding villages to sing in the choir. Now the church has been sold and is a house. Some of the Bibles and kneelers are at Great Braxted church.

The school used to be next to the church but as the population declined it was no longer needed and was used instead as a village hall. Sadly it is now disused. The Crown pub is now offices for Cory's Sand and Ballast and the beautiful orchard is their car park. Illegal bareknuckle fights once took place in or near the Crown, with people escaping over the marshes when police arrived. It is also said that a secret passage ran from the Hall to the pub, used long ago by smugglers who came up the creek to hide their contraband. The Hall is nearly 300 years old and now also belongs to Cory's and is used to house employees.

One of the vicars, Rev A. M. Morgan, wrote the words of several hymns. One of these, *The Name Of Our Village*, was based on the mistaken belief that Mucking meant 'the place of much grass'. This hymn achieved some fame and was published in New York.

Today Mucking is bypassed by the road and only used by the sand and ballast lorries and for waste tipping. One cannot stroll down its road in safety and sadly the sense of community no longer exists, but it is still beautiful in the spring and the old buildings still remain.

Mundon 🍂

About three miles after leaving Maldon on the Burnham road is Mundon, a village of some 200 souls (many less than there were in the middle of the 19th century) which spreads on both sides of the main road. Well into the village is the Victory Hall on the right where the visitor can leave the car and explore the boundaries on foot. Next to the hall is a small wood which was dedicated to the Parish Council in the autumn of 1990, a peaceful place where conservation and preservation are the order of the day. This wood is the largest remaining area of the Royal Forests which originally spread right through the Dengie Hundred.

Mundon no longer has its own church but is affiliated to the church of St Mary in Maldon. The original parish church, which dates back to the 13th century, can be found down a long lane almost opposite the wood. About half a mile on, the lane bends to the right by Mundon Hall and the church is almost hidden by the trees. Near to Mundon Hall was a plantation of oak trees planted to supply wood for battleships. The last one to be built from Mundon oaks was the battleship *Jersey* when Samuel Pepys was First Lord of the Admiralty.

A benefactor of the village was Thomas Plume (1630–1704) who owned Iltney Farm and is also remembered in Maldon for his library. He left money in trust, the interest from which was to support two boys to be educated at Maldon grammar school, with preference to be given to any applicant residing in Mundon. There is still a Plume Educational Trust used now to encourage pupils with GCSE levels to stay on in the sixth form. A member of Mundon Parish Council represents the village on the committee of this trust. Documents in the Essex Records Office show that the land around Iltney Farm was once a vine growing area.

It is generally thought that the village was once centred around the church but that during the time of the Black Death the villagers moved to higher ground. Legend has it that Tolstoy wrote part of *War and Peace* at Stud Farm in Mundon, where he stayed whilst visiting the Russian community at Purleigh, close by.

North Ockendon 🐿

North Ockendon is a ribbon development village situated on the outskirts of the London Borough of Havering, at its south-eastern edge. One claim to fame is a ghost that appears along St Mary's Lane in the form of a hooded monk. There is also Stubbers Outdoor Pursuits Centre.

The history of Stubbers goes back to 1334, the date on title deeds of the land. It was named after William Stubbers, a yeoman farmer who lived there around 1440/63. One of its owners, William Coys established a botanic collection preceding Kew by 100 years and it is from there that many plants were first introduced into this country, for example the yucca, rhubarb, yellow figwort, tomato and Jerusalem artichoke. At a later date it passed to the Russell family (one of whom introduced the variety of lupin) and this family made various alterations both to house and gardens. Unfortunately, the house, which had survived right up to 1955, was then demolished and all that remains now is the walled garden and a crinkle-crankle wall – a rare construction in Essex. The walled garden is currently being renovated to its former Elizabethan glory by a team of volunteers. A May Day fayre is held to raise funds each year and there are also various open days during the summer. The land is owned by Havering Council who are running an Outdoor Pursuits Centre for the young people in the borough and they also allow a canoe club and a sailing club for youngsters to use it at weekends.

There are many monuments and memorials in the church which relate to residents and landowners throughout the years, among them the family of Poyntz who have life-sized effigies in the lying position, carved in great detail in the costume of the period, circa 1600. There are also some fine memorials to various members of the Russell family. It is thought that the original church dates back to St Cedd who was Bishop of the East Saxons around AD 630, who used the well on the churchyard boundary as a place of baptism.

The village hall is known as the 'reading room' and was originally provided by the lord of the manor for his workers to read the papers. It is over 100 years old and was purchased by the villagers for the princely sum of sixpence per household to cover the cost of £20 (negotiated down from £2,000) plus expenses. This was in 1964 and was from the estate of Mr H Benyon whose family had been landowners in the area since 1758.

There only remains the Old White Horse, which is relatively young compared to the general history of the village. Nevertheless, there are villagers who remember horses being tethered outside while the workers went in to quench their thirst by quaffing a cup.

North Weald 🐗

Few people would claim that North Weald Bassett is a pretty village. In fact it is no longer truly a village, so much building has taken place over the past few years. About 4,500 people now call it home. There are a few buildings of note in the parish, the most attractive the King's Head public house which is a fine Tudor building.

Only a few minutes walk and you can be in open countryside. This is probably why many residents were ready to fight British Telecom's attempt in 1988 to build 900 houses on land where the radio station was from 1921 until 1985. From here there is a marvellous view of the village and surrounding countryside.

People who live in the centre of the village can now feel safer when there is a sudden downpour of really heavy rain. For years North Weald (few people give the village its full title; Bassett came from the principal landowner in the 13th century named Philip De Basset) has suffered from flooding. A huge flood alleviation scheme has taken place. There is also now a reservoir which should be a real nature reserve in a few years time.

A new hall has been opened on the Memorial Playing Fields which will be a great asset to the village. It has replaced the Queen's Rooms, two smaller halls that stood in the centre of the village and were built to commemorate Queen Victoria's Jubilee.

The village is fortunate to still have a school and a sub post office, a chemist and a few small shops. There are three different homes for the elderly. The Leonard Davis Home (named after a prominent one-time member of the village) has recently been updated after over 20 years of service. Wheelers Farm Gardens is also home to many elderly people and the latest home is Cunningham House, which was opened in 1987 by the Princess Royal.

St Andrew's church is worth a visit. The inside will surprise visitors. The building dates from around 1330 and the tower was added in the 16th century. There was a fire in 1965 and the inside of the church was rebuilt in a much lighter modern style.

The railway station is part of the Central Line, and at present there is a full service. Once a year, usually a weekend in May, it is very well used, when special trains and buses are run to bring thousands of people to the airfield for the annual air show. Those old enough to remember the Second World War may have memories of North Weald as a famous fighter station. The young ones just enjoy watching the planes or taking a ride in a helicopter. For the rest of the year the airfield is quiet, and it's very pleasant to see the gliders and those taking part in parascending.

Each Saturday there is a market on the old runway. It is said to be one of the biggest in Europe and free buses are run for people from various towns in the area.

There is still a Horticultural Society and an Allotment Association, so there are still some rural aspects to the village. The Horticultural Society has been in existence since 1902, and they once held a really big annual show that attracted people from miles around, rather like a miniature Essex Show. There is still a fine Annual Show usually in August, where people show their talents not just for growing vegetables, fruit and flowers, but for many other crafts.

Thornwood Common and Hastingwood are the other two villages in the parish. The most direct way to Thornwood Common is past the Tollhouse, now a stone's thrown from the M11 motorway, and along Woodside which is an attractive route, especially in the spring when many gardens are colourful with bulbs. The two public houses were named after the trades of many people of the time, the Blacksmith's Arms and the Carpenter's Arms. There used to be a Methodist chapel until just before the Second World War and the only church was pulled down in 1979.

Hastingwood still has its church building but it has been converted into a really attractive home. Hastingwood is a pretty village, but it is so near Harlow that it is doubtful whether it will remain so for many more years.

Orsett ﷼

In modern parlance Orsett would be described as 'The Gateway to the Fens', and here that old chestnut can genuinely be told that the proprietor of the Foxhound sells his beer by the pound, that is if you have noticed the tiny stockade on the green that once sheltered stray animals. Adjacent to this product of a bygone age stands a rural lock-up, which must have seen its last drunken customer sometime at the beginning of the century, and together, they make an unusual spectacle in Essex. Lost to present day view is the quoits pitch which was situated immediately behind the Foxhound, formerly the Swan, and until the advent of licensing hours, quoits was a very popular sport in rural areas. The cause of the decline of that popularity has been attributed to there not being enough 'open' hours in the day in which to complete a good game of 41 up.

In 1880 Mr Robert Ridgewell uncovered a red earthenware pottery jar of Roman origin in the churchyard, and further evidence of such activities are on display inside the church, a pair of funerary urns of possible pagan origin restfully residing in a Christian building. Of other church matters, it is believed that the remains of Bishop Bonner's house, that stalwart upholder of the Roman Catholic faith who possessed precious few other attributes according to common talk, is somewhere in the north of the old Orsett estate, and some odd stonework uncovered from ancient buildings in the High Street could possibly have been stolen from the gateway of this palace when the owner was languishing in Marshalsea prison.

As all rural villages worth their salt should boast of a ghost or two, Orsett offers the old rectory which stood in Herga Hill, now demolished, as a good example of what a haunted house should be. Considered to be a 'queer' place, the serving hatch in the rear hall was often unaccountably opened at night and a bedroom doorhandle was observed to turn and the door open and close of its own volition. Lastly, one downstairs room appeared to closet a 'presence' which caused some people to feel uncomfortable.

The figure of a woman dressed in a grey cloak appeared in Blacksmiths Lane on a regular basis, always between two milestones that once graced the road. Tradition has it that she and her male companion were held up and murdered at that stop by a highwayman of evil repute. Although she was frequently seen by many passers-by, her companion, if he were still with her in spirit, remained invisible to we mortals.

Basketry, a smithy and a fruit farm which produced amongst other things Orsett cider, seem to account for all of Orsett's industrial efforts, but these enterprises have long since gone. Orsett was one of those villages that possessed every advantage, being the administrative centre for the area, but as the years passed so did its importance, and Orsett, although the first village in the district to have street lighting, became a back-water. Lying off the main road the railway companies after failing to master the technology needed to cross the fens, totally ignored it, whereas all the villages hugging the north bank of the river Thames were connected by rail to both London and Southend. In many respects this isolation has helped to preserve the general aura of peace and quiet.

The main roads in Orsett boast of only three shops, a general store, a butcher and a post office. Any other requirements of the household can be obtained from a number of shopping centres surrounding Orsett, including Lakeside.

Orsett Hall was once an imposing and, for Essex, an important edifice. Time and circumstance has changed all that since the death of Sir Francis Whitmore, Lord Lieutenant of Essex, Francis Whitmore was lord of the manor from the early days of the century and he died in 1962. His son succeeded and worked hard for the estate. He was known as a racing driver and aviator, using the grounds of the Hall to take off and land, to the consternation of the owners of chimney pots in Maltings Lane. After six years he decided to sell up and the old house is now a restaurant, where one has the privilege to eat where once only the privileged ate. The gates are passed with a feeling of regret for the loss of its former glories. The famed Orsett Show, held on the first Saturday each September, was long held in the grounds of the Hall, but a fresh venue has been provided for the event, stark and open, with no trace of the elegance of yesteryear.

In honour of the family, the local innkeeper changed the name of his hostelry from 'The George' to the Whitmore Arms, and the inn sign proudly sports the red, blue and gold colours.

Following the road on from the village hall, first farmhouses then

161

ribbon-built bungalows and houses are passed until Baker Street is reached. Named after a former lord of the manor, Baker Street must at some time in the past have been a main thoroughfare, because alongside is a restored sail-less mill, with a machine house adjacent. The present buildings replaced a much older edifice in the early 1800s, which went into dereliction until quite recently. Here, at the crossroads, stands the King's Arms, where meals can be purchased. Opposite is the lane to the fen, a narrow, lonely way, passing through reclaimed wet-lands until it finishes at the edge of the fen.

Paglesham 🐚

Paglesham's fame came from smuggling, the large oyster industry and boatbuilding. In the early 1800s, there was a famous smuggler called 'Hard Apple, William Blyth, who kept the village shop at Church End and was also churchwarden. The river and creeks round the parish provided ideal conditions for smuggling. Three old pollard elms, which survived until ten years ago, stood by the main road where it is joined by East Hall Lane and £200 worth of silk is reputed to have been hidden within their hollow cavities. Several houses were also said to have been used for storing smuggled goods; Cupola House, a three-storeyed Georgian house near the Plough and Sail, was said to have been built with money from smuggling.

In early days, some of the smugglers were oyster merchants and dredgermen and their boats would have been used. Oyster cultivation was big business, both here and on the Crouch. In 1870, 80 to 100 boats and 160 to 200 people were engaged in the fishery. Paglesham oysters were very well known and liked.

The industry began to decline at the beginning of this century. Then, in 1921, there was a 'death' in the oysters and it was not known why. From the 1953 floods and the hard winter of 1962/63, the industry never recovered and finished in the 1970s. An attempt to revive it again in the 1980s was not successful. Today, the remains of the oyster pits are clearly visible along the saltings below the sea wall. The old railway carriage and shed, used until the 1970s, are fast disintegrating, while the meshed enclosure also stands forlorn.

For many years people came for miles – even from London – to eat oysters in the Plough and Sail. Between the wars they cost three shillings and sixpence per dozen. For a long time the tradition at the Village Produce Association supper was steak, kidney and oyster pudding.

Boatbuilding has been carried on at the river from 1848 when White's Directory gives Kemp as the boatbuilder. William Hall was there in 1883. Then James Shuttlewood took over. He built the *Ethel Ada*, a 48 ton barge, still to be seen, but converted to residential use. Many fishing smacks and some private yachts were built there by James and later by his son, Frank. Today it is no longer owned by the Shuttlewoods, but the name is still above the boatshed.

Farming has also seen many changes. From the sea wall, at one time one could look out over many acres of grassy marshes grazed by cattle and sheep. These have now been drained and ploughed and grow hectares of wheat, rape and vining peas. Linseed is another newer crop now grown. There are very few animals to be found in the landscape. Dutch elm disease brought the biggest change to the village scene. When the elms were cut down many hedges went as well and the picture of a shady lane through the village disappeared. However, new trees were planted and are growing and so are the hedges.

If the landscape has changed, so have the people. During the 19th century the large families and local industries resulted in a population of over 400, the majority of whom worked on the farms or in the oyster industry or were in service in the larger houses. Today, most of the inhabitants travel outside to work. There are more retired people and not so many of the old families still live in the village. Green Belt and conservation zones have limited the number of new houses and the population is under 300.

Peldon 🦢

Peldon is a pretty, sprawling village with parish boundaries running down to the marshes and creeks of the river Blackwater estuary. There was a church at Peldon, or Peltenduna as mentioned in the Domesday Book, in 1086.

The present Norman building has a nave dating back to the 12th century with the tower being added at the end of the 14th century. The church of St Mary the Virgin stands on the hill overlooking the surrounding countryside.

In 1086 there were two manors in Peldon, and it is clear that the Saxon freemen were dispossessed by William the Conqueror's Norman men who had come over to England with him. The most grasping of these was William's brother-in-law, Odo, the Bishop of Bayeux who received much land in Kent and vast estates in Essex, including land at Peldon. In 1282, Walter de Peltindone conveyed the manor to the De Neville family, who in the 12th and 13th centuries were the chief foresters of the King. Later in 1545, King Henry VIII granted the manor to Sir Thomas (later Lord) Darcy and Peldon remained in the Darcy family until 1647 when it was acquired by Mr Thomas Reynolds, who became Mayor of Colchester in 1654.

The Peldon Rose, standing at the edge of the Roman road, the Strood, to Mersea, is a famous old smugglers' inn and is now a popular spot for tourists and local people alike. Peldon was close to the centre of the earthquake that shook this part of the country on 22nd April 1884. Much damage was done to the church and local houses.

Various investigations have been made into the famous Red Hills discovered in the parish and it is commonly believed that these had the dual purpose of being not only early salt workings, but also sites for pottery making.

Pleshey

Pleshey is the only Essex village which has the distinction of a mention of some substance in Shakespeare. In *Richard II* the Duchess of Gloucester says to her brother-in-law, John of Gaunt:

'With all good speed at Plashy visit me,
Alack, and what shall good old York see there
But empty lodgings and unfurnish'd walls,
Unpeopled offices, untrodden stones?
And what cheer there for welcome but my groans?'

This is an allusion to what had happened shortly before the time covered by the play. Events at Pleshey were headline news in 1397, when Thomas, Duke of Gloucester and youngest son of King Edward III, was seized forcibly at Pleshey Castle, his residence, and carried off to Calais, where he was put to death on the orders of the royal governor. All this, it was well known, was done at the behest of the young king, Richard II, Thomas's nephew.

Pleshey was probably built by the Earls of Essex in the early part of the

12th century and remained one of their principal castles and residences for many generations.

There had been a church built for the villagers inside the town moat, but Thomas replaced this by a grander foundation which he built and endowed just outside the earthworks. Residences were built nearby for the college of priests.

As a collegiate foundation the church and its endownments fell to the crown when the chantries were suppressed in 1546. In the 18th century the Bishop of London and the Tufnell family, by now lords of the manor, rebuilt part of the church, but a full restoration had to wait until 1868 when Frederick Chancellor of Chelmsford fully rebuilt the church.

Pleshey is probably best known now, at least among Anglican church-goers, as the home of the Diocesan Retreat House. This is next door to the church.

A different, but also well-known, institution in the village is Mr Clements' smithy. He is well-known over a large part of Essex as a specialist in the production of decorative ironwork.

A fine new Village Hall has been erected near the church. It was opened in November 1988, fittingly enough by HRH the Duke of Gloucester. Fortunately in the course of his visit to the village he was at no risk of the foul play meted out to his predecessor in that title nearly 600 years ago.

In 1991 Pleshey won, not for the first time, the top award for 'very small villages' in the County Linen 'Best-Kept Village' competition. This was a most well-deserved award for a village that is not only historic and beautiful, but whose strong corporate loyalty ensures that it is always lovingly cared for.

Purfleet

Local legend has it that Purfleet received its name in 1588 when England was threatened by the Spanish Armada. Local children are usually told one or other of the tales relating to this at their mother's knee.

In 1588 Queen Elizabeth I had to take steps to defend her country. On her way from London to review her troops at Tilbury, the Royal barge was caught in a severe thunderstorm causing her to take shelter on the north side of the Thames, near a village. The Queen is reputed to have landed and climbed the beacon hill – a very steep hill overlooking the river. From its summit she looked towards Tilbury, and, seeing her fleet tossed by the storm, exclaimed 'Oh, my poor fleet!'.

The other story is similar but the ending changes. The Queen, apparently, had a predilection for wearing high heeled shoes, and after climbing to the top of the beacon hill she is purported to have wailed 'Oh my poor feet!'. Purfleet then, according to these stories is a corruption of 'poor fleet' or 'poor feet'!

These stories, although they add colour and romance to an otherwise rather drab place, are of course complete fabrication. It is known from documentary evidence that around the 1300s the village was called Pourtfleet, although there were many variations in the method of spelling. It appears that the name is derived from two Saxon words – 'port' meaning a haven and 'fleet', an arm of the sea, or bay.

The fortunes of Purfleet have since come and gone, first with a military garrison and then with riverside industrial developments like the Thames Board Mills and the various petroleum sites. Nowadays Purfleet is becoming engulfed by the spread of people who are constantly searching for somewhere to live which is within easy commuting distance from London.

With the closure of the London docks and the development of the docks at Tilbury, Purfleet no longer sees naval and merchant shipping plying up the Thames to London, as was once a common sight. Purfleet will be on the map again when the new Thames Bridge is completed in 1991, but instead of the romantic sight of ocean vessels gliding along the river, there will be a stream of petrol-driven monsters rushing between Essex and Kent along a four lane motorway a couple of hundred feet above the water.

Purleigh 🍃

Purleigh is first mentioned in a Saxon will of AD 998 but, like most parishes, no detailed information is available until 1086, when it appears in Domesday Book. Purleigh was then a typical rural community consisting of eight manors in the ownership of four Normans. Substantial areas of woodland are recorded, as well as pasture and arable land and the usual assortment of cattle, sheep, pigs, horses and goats. The population consisted of 35 families of villeins and borders, with ten slaves working on the lord's farms. Purleigh does have the distinction of being one of the few places where a priest is mentioned in 1086.

During the following two centuries either prosperity, or population pressure, or both, caused large areas of woodland to be grubbed up to create new farms, usually up to 20 to 30 acres in size. A few of these farms still bear the name of the former wood (eg Birchwood Farm), or that of an early owner (eg Scotts Farm) and some of their small, irregular shaped fields still survive at Cock Clarks. This expansion appears to have ceased by the early 14th century, and had stopped entirely by the latter 14th century when the plagues had reduced the population so drastically. Of the woodland that remained in the early 14th century, some was used by the manorial lords for their personal income (eg Kent's wood) whilst other areas, where the parishioners had established rights of grazing, gradually deteriorated into the scrub-covered commons of the 16th and 17th centuries (typified by the name 'Furzey common' behind Purleigh Lodge).

During the reign of Elizabeth I, Purleigh's population again began to increase, but the remaining woodland was too valuable to be cleared for homesteads. Consequently new cottages were built on the commons at Cock Clarks, Howe Green and Farther Howe Green. The amount of land allocated to these cottages was too small (half to two acres) to sustain the occupier by farming alone, although they usually had grazing rights on the remaining commons. Consequently, many of these new cottagers resorted to other trades to make a living. During the late 16th and 17th centuries tailors, blacksmiths, butchers, potters, ploughwrights, sawyers, bricklayers, carpenters and bakers proliferated, many of whom also used their homes as alehouses (often illegally) in order to supplement their income.

Towards the end of the 17th century the population again declined, farms became amalgamated and redundant farmhouses and buildings, as well as cottages, were abandoned and demolished. The population level rose again however during the late 18th century, and stayed high for the next 100 years; in fact the 1,213 people recorded in the 1841 census was not surpassed until 1981. This time however, the rising population coincided with a high level of prosperity in arable farming. Consequently many of the newcomers were employed on the farms, although again many new trades appeared in the parish. As well as those mentioned earlier, there were brickmakers, plumbers, glaziers, shoemakers, millers, harness-makers, carriers, hawkers and a surveyor. By now the commons had virtually disappeared (the remaining areas being almost entirely enclosed by 1801) and the high value of arable land meant much of the woodland was cleared to enlarge existing farms rather than to create new holdings. The only remaining areas available for cottage sites were the

167

wide roadside verges, hence the landscape of Purleigh today is one of dispersed farmsteads, small hamlets and frequent roadside cottages.

It is from the last phase of expansion that many of a parish's traditional assets survive in Purleigh. A church has obviously been here since the Middle Ages, but the earliest Nonconformist chapel did not arrive until the 1850s (now Chapel Cottage at Howe Green). A redundant cottage has been used as the poor-house since around 1700, but a purpose built workhouse was provided in 1740 (now the Queen's Head at Rudley Green). In 1769 the rector, Samuel Horsmanden, left an endowment to provide for the education of Purleigh's children, which took effect in 1800 on the death of his wife. Shortly after this the then rector, John Eveleigh, financed the building of a schoolmaster's house and school room (now Eveleigh House). Another rector, Edward Hawkins, financed the establishment of a second school in 1842, Hawkins House at Cock Clarks. By the 1770s a grocer's shop with adjoining bakery had been built on Purleigh Hill, which, although no longer a shop still retains its original bow window. Purleigh's principal bakery further down the hill was converted in the 1830s, functioned until modern times and is still called 'the Steam Bakery'. Valley Stores on the opposite side of the hill had been functioning as a shop since at least the 18th century.

Ramsden Bellhouse
& Ramsden Heath

Ramsden Bellhouse and Ramsden Heath are now two separate villages, but until the first part of the 20th century they were one village, which stretched from Stock in the north to Nevendon in the south. The village was centred around the crossroads, where today the war memorial stands in Ramsden Heath, but confusingly it was known as Ramsden Bellhouse. Here were the blacksmith's and the wheelwright's shops, while not far off were the mill, the parish workhouse, the bakehouse and later the school and the shops. The name Ramsden Heath applied only to an area of heathland to the north of the village.

About 1910 Homesteads Ltd bought Ramsden Bellhouse Farm and built an estate centred around St Mary's church about a mile from the old village. This became known as Ramsden Bellhouse, and gradually the old village became Ramsden Heath.

There are no great national events in the history of this Essex village.

Pre-history, the present Ransden Bellhouse was probably underwater, being part of the course of the river Thames, before one of the Ice Ages re-routed it to its present course. This accounts for its heavy London clay in the lower areas, while the Heath has a lighter, more sandy soil. The evidence of a Roman Ramsden is small, but certainly they would have known and come through the area as Roman remains have been found in nearby Wickford, Billericay and Downham. An empty Roman coffin was found in the southern part of Ramsden, in Stoney Hills field on Woolshots Farm.

The name, Ramsden Bellhouse, is probably derived from Ravensdene meaning 'Little Wooded Valley of the Ravens'. Early records tell us that it belonged to Godwin and three freemen before 1066, but in 1086 the Domesday Book says it was in the Hundred of Barstable, and belonged to the Bishop of London and Robert Gernon. Bellhouse was added in about 1200 when the lands were given to Richard de Belhus.

St Mary's church porch rafters date from the 14th century, whilst the rest of the porch, the wooden tower, the font and the nave roof are 15th century. The church chest is dated about 1480. The rectory was probably sited near Pump Hill but was demolished in 1734. Thomas Cox, the rector of Stock, was presented with the living of Ramsden Bellhouse, and from then until 1967 the two parishes shared their rector. The Congregational church at Ramsden Heath and the Peculiar's chapel (now gone) were built in the 19th century. St John's, sometimes called the Tin, or Iron Church, dates from 1901 and Ramsden Bellhouse Baptist church was built in 1927.

The parish workhouse, which was near Mill Lane, was sold about 1837 while the post mill, from which Mill Lane takes its name, came to a dramatic end. On 22nd November 1873, at about mid-day, while working, the mill blew down with Mr Richard Hamilton, the miller still inside. Fortunately he escaped with only bruises, being between two beams, but it was the end of the mill. A year previously in 1872, the church school was opened almost opposite the mill, and educated the local children for some 50 to 60 years. It was later converted into two houses, called somewhat wittily 'Eton' and 'Harrow', but has now made way for modern development.

The railway divides the village now into 'up the Heath' to the north and 'down the Bellhouse' to the south. The first passenger Great Eastern train went through on 1st January 1889. A station was promised, but never happened. It is interesting to note that in the census of 1841, Ramsden Bellhouse with 462 residents had more people than Wickford with 445 residents. It can only be that the coming of the railway station to Wickford turned it into today's little town. Perhaps we are fortunate the station wasn't built in Ramsden, for in spite of extensive building in both villages, we proudly believe that we still live in the country.

Rayleigh 🐚

A market has been held in Rayleigh for more than 800 years, its first mention being in 1181. Queen Elizabeth I hunted in the surrounding forests and stayed at Rayleigh Lodge in The Chase, about a mile from the town centre.

The tree-lined High Street is unusually wide and is dominated at its upper end by the imposing 14th century Holy Trinity parish church, its massive square tower carrying a peal of eight bells. The Tudor porch has a bench on each side, so that in times past vagrants or poor parishioners could shelter for the night. The porch was also used by one curate as a school for six poor boys. At the edge of the churchyard is the old parish room. This was originally the church school, but it has now been restored and is used as a restaurant.

During the Second World War a macabre murder took place outside the parish church. Following a family feud, a young soldier fixed an anti-tank mine under the seat of his disabled father's wheelchair. Father was wheeled out by his nurse for an airing. She pushed him to the top of London Hill and sat down by the church to rest for a few minutes. Father felt uncomfortable – the wheelchair didn't feel right – he fidgeted to adjust his position and blew himself to smithereens. The nurse, amazingly, was unharmed.

Close by the town centre is Rayleigh Mount, an historical site owned by the National Trust. After the Norman invasion of 1066, a wooden castle was built here on a man-made mound, and if visitors climb the paths to the top of the mount, they'll be rewarded with fine views across the Crouch valley. At the foot of the Mount, ducks have taken up residence on the remaining moat, and here on summer evenings the Southend Shakespeare Company present open-air performances prior to performing at Stratford-upon-Avon.

Just off the High Street is a well restored windmill housing a tiny museum open to the public on Saturday mornings from April to September, and to remind residents of Rayleigh's agricultural past, an old millstone is embedded in the garden in front of Mill Hall, which is Rayleigh's modern public hall.

Halfway down the High Street is the memorial to the Protestant Martyrs who were burned at the stake in 1555, in the reign of Queen Mary, for refusing to convert to Roman Catholicism. The memorial incorporates a drinking fountain, no longer in use. The nearby village pump is well preserved as is the horse trough.

On Crown Hill is the tiny octagonal and thatched Dutch Cottage. Although the date of 1621 is displayed, experts believe it was not built until around 1740. This must surely be one of the most unusual council houses in Britain! It has one living room downstairs and one bedroom upstairs, but nevertheless the census of 1861 tells us that it housed the Bright family of father, mother and six children plus Mr Newman the lodger. Its visitors book has entries from all over the world, including one from a Bright great-great-grandchild, and an entry from a great-great-granddaughter of the lodger.

When the cottage was being renovated, between tenants, some genuine Dutch 'Delft' tiles were discovered around a fireplace and forming a hearth. Some were made about 1630 and they are on display at the Mill Hall's coffee bar. It is thought that the tiles were put into the cottage a good while after they were made. The public may visit the Dutch Cottage by prior arrangement with Rochford Council.

There is an interesting mix of old and new in the High Street. The buildings at No 9 and 11, occupied now by a restaurant and a delicatessen, date back to the 17th and 16th century respectively. Next to them, the three-storey Kingsleigh House was built in the 1790s on the site of a bull-baiting inn. Cottages in Church Street are from the 1600s or earlier, and Barrington Cottages by the market place are probably of 18th century origin. The old Gas Board showroom near the Martyrs Memorial is 16th century or even earlier, although the charming shopfront is 20th century in 18th century style! In 1990 this re-opened as a gentlemen's outfitters. The Crown pub is 17th century with later additions, and the Baptist church, further along in the High Road, was built in 1798. Most of these old buildings, so full of character, have been expensively and lovingly restored in recent years, unlike the 1960s and 1970s when the trend was towards demolition. Mixed in with these are modern supermarkets, banks, shops, surgeries, offices etc. The Rayleigh Civic Society recently erected a fingerpost and an attractive town sign and these add to the considerable charm of Rayleigh town centre.

In June of each year, the town centre is closed to traffic, barriers and grandstand seats are erected and a big event in the British cycling calendar takes place. This is the Rayleigh Town Centre Cycle Races, and more than a hundred helmeted cyclists race around the one-way system, competing for money prizes and trophies.

Ridgewell ✌️

Ridgewell owes its name to its first settler Riddes, not as many think to the existence of the 'well on the ridge' – even though there *is* a well on the ridge! The Roman road from Colchester to Cambridge passes through the village by means of the Causeway, from which you descend to the river Stour, the highest point on the river. It was here that river and road came together and the Romans made a military camp. In the field on the left as you enter the village from Colchester are the remains of a Roman villa, marked today by a single oak tree. A spring of fresh water used to form a stream – now piped – which flowed down to the river Colne through Ashley Meadows. The first house on the left still shows its moat and is one of several moated houses on the hillside between the Stour and Colne.

In the early days it was a place of some importance with its own Trade Guild. The Guild for many centuries had its own Trade Chapel on the north side of the church. Records show that this was demolished at the Bishop's direction in the 17th century. The church, dedicated to St Laurence, in whose honour a fair was held every 9th August, was largely rebuilt in the Perpendicular style. Part of the north wall is of Norman origin and probably owes its preservation to the existence of the Trade Chapel alongside. You can still see the entrance in the strange shape of the east wall of the north aisle. In the tower are five bells, two of which are dated about 1350 and must have come from the older Norman church. The glory of the church is in its roof, despite the destruction in Cromwellian days of the carved angels that carried it (some of the angel wings still remain). The carrying bier is probably England's oldest, dated to the 14th century, as too is the base of the rood screen. Discerning eyes can find a 14th century graffitist's prayer scratched on the pillar near to the steps of the rood screen.

The chapel stands at the north end of the village green. The present building is the third on the site. The first dated from the third quarter of the 17th century and obeyed the 'Five Mile Act'. Round the green itself are many listed houses.

This was at one time a self supporting village, but now suffers from the usual malaise of village life – the closure of village shops in favour of supermarkets. Before the First World War there was Dutty's for groceries and haberdashery, a newsagent's, Nimble's which sold everything ('Nimble' Barnard and his van was known in all the local villages and Blossom, the horse, when not pulling, like his master grazed wherever he could), a butcher, baker, shoemaker, coal merchant, blacksmith, hurdlemaker, wheelwright, carpenter/joiner and painter, not to mention three millers and a milliner.

The village had nicknames for everyone. One old inhabitant can remember Busky, Dordy, Bluey, Hutly, Turk, Suggy, Squd, Ticker, Tot, Fingy, Porky and Chinaman (at one time a churchwarden)! If only we knew how they came by them.

One vicar is remembered for his eccentricities. He walked everywhere and never had his shoes laced up; when offered a lift in a horse and cart he always said 'No, no, I'm in a hurry!'. 'Grubby' was another character. Winter and summer his shirt was open to the waist and his trousers held up by hope and binding string. He never missed Sunday at church, not perhaps dressed in the height of fashion, but always clean and cheerful.

There was at one time a Tuesday market in the village but it must have been discontinued in the 19th century. What did survive until the First World War was the Whit Tuesday Fair and the traditional dinner that day – roast beef followed by plum pudding.

There has been a great change in the village in regard to agriculture. All the small farms have gone, where the farmer and his family worked hard but were happy enough, and the farmhouses sold. In most cases the name 'Farm' has been dropped but two, Hunts Farm and Wash Farm, have retained their name despite having no land. Farm buildings too, unfortunately, have been pulled down. Wash Farm still has its c1880 (now listed) pump and there are another two in the village which are preserved.

Rowhedge 🦢

The village of Rowhedge, part of East Donyland, lies three miles south of Colchester. It was compactly built in Victorian times, when the men were kept busy with fishing in the winter and sailing the big yachts in the summer. Fishermen always kept an eye out for ships being wrecked on the treacherous sands, outside the river Colne. Often carried shoulder high through Harwich after rescuing a shipwrecked crew, they would go hurrying back to the wreck to salvage as much of the cargo as they could, officially to be handed to the Receiver of Wrecks, but often it was easier to bring it straight home! Many of the houses had a cellar or smugglers hole, which were used to hide the hard-won goods, until they could be sold.

Visitors entering the village are attracted by the unusual shape of the octagonal church of St Lawrence. The 150th anniversary of the church was celebrated in 1988, during which year parishioners worked and donated new kneelers. Being worked in tapestry with a red background to many different designs, the kneelers give a welcoming warmth to the well-kept atmosphere in the church.

During the 1920s the village children used the marshland as their playground and the lads used a farm field for football and cricket. However, a group of hard working villagers formed a committee and raised enough money to purchase a farm field in the centre of the village. This was made into a splendid recreation ground with a pavilion, and trees were planted in an avenue each being a living memorial to a village man who was killed during the First World War. Sadly 18 of these trees were destroyed in the 1987 hurricane but all have now been replaced and are flourishing The pavilion still stands, used by the football teams. The village has also recently officially opened a large village hall.

Rowhedge's High Street is in fact the lowest and the oldest street, following the line of the river Colne. Many of the old cottages have been demolished, public houses have been converted to houses, the shipyards have also been demolished awaiting 'development', but the atmosphere of a 'fishing village' still lingers, perhaps because Rowhedge has never been 'fashionable'. The waterfront has always been the focal point of the village and there are two pleasant public open spaces. At the turn of the century these were busy quays, where tons of sprats, coal etc were off-loaded from boats. Masts and spars lay on trestles, while the boats were being overhauled, the whole area being packed with fishing smacks.

Repairs must have been continuous. Every year at the end of the summer the men came back from sailing the big yachts and a Regatta Day would be arranged. The wealthy yacht owners supplied fireworks for evening entertainment. The tradition of a Regatta was revived in 1962 and continued for 25 years, being replaced by a summer fete in the last few years. On Regatta Day the village street is closed to traffic and is packed with people.

Some years ago a local steam enthusiast bought a steam coaster named *Victual*, which had been built at Rowhedge, with two more, in 1945 for the Admiralty. After more than 20 years hard work in Portsmouth docks carrying supplies to Admiralty ships, she lay rusting. Volunteers dug a berth for the 84 ft boat by hand, and she was floated into this permanent berth in April 1973. She was ready for her first trip under steam in July 1974. She steamed to Greenwich in 1975 to see the start of the Tall Ships Race and again in 1977 to join the Regatta which celebrated the Queen's Silver Jubilee. All of these trips were fuelled by driftwood. She is still being well cared for in Holland.

In the heyday of the large racing yachts many men from the village crewed and sailed for rich and famous people, including the King's yacht *Britannia*. This is evident when walking round the village, especially up Church Hill, where the older cottages have names of famous yachts. Several sail lofts still survive, and many of them have a yacht mast doing duty as a pole for the humble washing line.

The village helped the war effort in both world wars, making uniforms in the clothing factory and building and repairing ships in the shipyards, both industries now discontinued. We are still hard at work at Rowhedge however, there is usually at least one boat at the wharf, with its enormous storage facilities, and the attendant cranes, forklift trucks and lorries are kept busy. A large concrete block manufacturer, several car repair firms, two garages, engineering works, many builders and similar small firms, including printing, keep many employed. Several shops have also survived in this village. These include a greengrocer, butcher, Co-operative supermarket, post office cum general store, four public houses which serve good food, and an attractive little flower shop.

On the Fingringhoe edge of Rowhedge stands the largest house, East Donyland Hall. The lovely grounds are opened sometimes for a church fete.

There are some good walks around the village, through Donyland Woods, along the sea wall towards the Hythe at Colchester and along the Roman River walk which eventually leads to Olivers Orchards at

Stanway. Battleswick Farm lies on the north side of the village, now well known by PYO enthusiasts who come when the soft fruit is ready, and spend a happy day. When they have picked the fruit they require, they are welcome to enjoy a picnic while watching the Highland cattle and the rare Jacob sheep.

Roydon 🦢

Roydon is situated on the edge of the Green Belt west of Harlow. The station is a mere 100 yards from the Hertfordshire border.

Not far from the station, opposite a well kept village hall, stands the 13th century parish church of St Peter ad Vincula. There are Roman tiles in the walls and the roof timbers inside have been dated to before 1250. The first incumbent in about 1190 was one William the Chaplain, who witnessed a document at Natteswell in 1198. The church has six hatchments, armorial bearings which by custom were placed on a deceased person's house and after the funeral hung in the parish church. The goblets in the Butler arms are an allusion to the family name, whereas the hogs' heads in the Booth arms have reference to the family business of gin distilling. There are several interesting wall monuments, one of which records Thomas Lord who 'drowned in a rivulet in the sight of his friends in the view of his house in the 72nd year of his age October 31 1771.' The Colte Chapel, the original chancel and choir until reorientation in 1969, behind the rood screen, has brasses of the Colte family. One brass records the death of an ancestor of Dean Swift.

Near the church, by the side of a 15th century cottage, are the stocks and a small wooden padlocked shed which served as the lock-up in the 19th century.

The manor house of Roydon Hall was demolished in 1864 but in 1531 it was acquired by Henry VIII for Anne Boleyn in exchange for Bromhill Priory in Norfolk. In 1538 Henry was at Roydon Hall with his infant son Edward by Jane Seymour, and the child was presented to the people of Roydon who were apparently delighted and trooped down to see the baby Prince.

Halfway down the High Street is a very big, old chestnut tree, which is quite a landmark and looks most impressive in any season. There are four public houses concentrated in about 300 yards of the High Street. Years ago, when horses and carts were a common sight in the village, a big galvanized iron horse trough stood at the T junction at the top of

Roydon Church with 15th century village stocks

the High Street. Young men used to collect there on warm summer evenings, talking and watching the passing show.

In those days the High Street had several shops. A double-fronted draper's shop sold everything from pins to dresses; this later became the Co-op but that too has gone and the building pulled down. Across the road was Hickling's, a big grocer's shop, and there was another grocer's called Brown's further down the High Street. There was a village blacksmith's, which ended up as a wool shop, and two butchers, one of which had a slaughterhouse at the back where they used to kill the pigs. One of these shops belonged to a Mr Hill. Once Mr Hill was very ill and the farmer from the Temple Farm, old Mr Abbey, brought a load of hay in his horse and cart, and spread it on the road in front of Mr Hill's house so that the noise outside did not worry him. The village policeman made him take it all up again, an act considered very brave as many were in awe of Mr Abbey, but of course it could have been very dangerous to traffic.

The river Stort runs through the end of the village, and there are many fishermen in the season. It is lovely and peaceful along the banks of the river. One way there is a lock, through which in days gone by barges and longboats would be raised and lowered. Now there are only pleasure boats on the river. Going the other way, the river passes an old mill.

The Roydon Society has watched over conservation and improvement in Roydon since 1968 with care for the history and character of the area. Revenue from Christmas cards each year is devoted to an extensive tree planting scheme, and many thousands of daffodil bulbs have been planted under the aegis of the society. It has also been instrumental in preventing a four-lane motorway splitting the village.

Saffron Walden 🦐

Waldena, as mentioned in the Domesday Book, was to become known as Chipping Walden when the market moved there from the neighbouring village of Newport in 1141, 'Chipping' meaning market. It flourished in the Middle Ages as a centre for the wool and weaving industry, due to the very successful rearing of sheep in the surrounding area.

The name Saffron Walden was derived following the mass cultivation in the area of the saffron crocus, which was used extensively for medicinal and culinary purposes, and also for dyeing. The Borough Arms depicts three saffron crocuses surrounded by four towers, gateway and portcullis. This idea originated from 1549 when Edward VI granted a new charter to the town from which a new seal was struck.

When it was discovered that local soil produced excellent barley for malt making, and supplies of saffron were being imported from Southern Europe in quantity, malting became the key industry, which eventually finished with the last maltings closing in the 1950s.

Quakers were prevalent here in the 19th century, providing the town with many fine buildings as a result of their great business acumen and their code of ethics. The most outstanding benefactors were the Gibson family, who were responsible for the Friends' School and teacher training college, now Bell Language School, the beautiful Bridge End Gardens, the town hall, museum, general hospital (now sadly council offices), the town library and separate schools for girls and boys. They helped to introduce the railway line and get the local streets paved. Quite incredible achievements for one family.

The town boasts many buildings of great historical interest, some dating back to the 13th century, including the parish church of St Mary the Virgin. This magnificent building is on the scale of a cathedral, dominating the skyline from all directions.

For many years the common was the cricket field for the town and playing field for the boys British school. It has a very fine and rare earthen maze, one of the best in Europe. This has throughout many years attracted old and young alike to walk the brick paths, measuring nearly a mile, or should the prize be good enough, to run. Rumour has it that in the past young men occasionally competed for a girl, or sometimes for a pot of ale. It is situated on the east side of the common, with The Slade, for many years known as the King's Ditch along the south. The town runs parallel to the west, and until the 1960s there was a Carmelite convent to the north. One can also see the castle ruins from here. In the

178

1930s and 40s and probably for many years before, washing belonging to people from nearby cottages who had no gardens, could be seen strung between the trees.

The Battle Ditches which can be found off what is known locally as the Gibson Estate, was once a Saxon burial ground, and to this day bones are still occasionally unearthed here.

Saffron Walden was one of the first towns in the country to have a swimming pool, which was in use until 1981, and of course, like many small towns, for a long time boasted two cinemas, sadly both gone.

On the western outskirts of the town is the magnificent Audley End house, which contains a suite of rooms designed by Robert Adam. The river Cam flows through grounds landscaped by Capability Brown, and the whole is set in a large estate, part of which is parkland open to the public. The house is owned by English Heritage and the estate by Lord Braybrooke.

The northern end of the town now boasts delightfully renovated cottages in Castle Street, but in the 1930s and 1940s it was infamous for its decadence and unlawful behaviour. Many times two policemen could be seen heading in that direction, the only place in the town where they would never venture solo. This was probably due in part to the large number of pubs to be found there, almost all of which are now gone.

Tuesday has been market day in the town for many years, but there are now only the stalls in the Square to make the day. Gone are the mooing cows, squealing pigs, clucking chickens and twitchy nosed rabbits, and spring is not the same without the lambs to visit in their pens.

The population of the town is currently approximately 15,000 and can no longer claim to be a really close community, but it still has families whose ancestors were an integral part of the town for generations. The town at local level is governed by Uttlesford Council which derives its name from the local river Uttle.

There are numerous thriving amateur societies encompassing all the arts, and a leisure centre named after the Member of Parliament who served the town for many years and who is buried in the local churchyard, R A Butler. One of the local primary schools is also named after him.

It was a Walden man, Henry Winstanley, who built the first Eddystone lighthouse in 1696. Charles II was the first to recognise his talents when he worked at Audley End Palace as it was then called. A portrait of Winstanley still hangs in the town hall.

In August 1955 Field Marshall Viscount Montgomery of Alamein visited the town to open the Anglo-American war memorial and playing fields which are attached to Bridge End Gardens. Saffron Walden holds a festival every third year and a Shakespearian play is invariably performed in the Gardens, which lend their atmosphere.

St Lawrence Bay 🐚

Ramsey Wick, Steeple Stone, The Stone, St Lawrence Bay – not many places in south-east Essex could have boasted four names, all acceptable to the Post Office!

The map published by Colonel Colby in 1840 shows Ramsey Island surrounded by Ramsey Marsh with just one building, Wick Farm, in the centre of the island. One lane leads directly from the B1021 in and out of the island and this has not changed today; the lane now named Main Road leads directly to the Blackwater estuary past the site of Wick Farm which was, until recently, a very attractive thatched farmhouse. Alas it is no more, being another casualty of the developers and the modern times.

So in 1840 we have a back-of-beyond island with all the charm of deepest Essex. 'Island', of course, is an academic word as the only time it could be called an island was at high tide and then a small bridge crossed a dyke called The Wade. Thus it remained until the 1890s when with the coming of the railway to Southminster six miles away, the Dengie Peninsula began to open up. People would put their cycles on the train in London and explore. For Ramsey Wick this was birth and at this time Mr Winterbon and Mr Cauldwell began to develop the Oyster Cottages, a small row of wooden two up two down fishermen's residences and by 1902 there were eight standing in their own ground behind the sea wall.

By 1903 Riverview Guest House was built and in those early years Burnham-on-Crouch was becoming a yachting centre and so yachtsmen began to explore the estuaries and creeks of Essex. Two families from London, the Huttons from Regent Street and the Haywards from Berkeley Square, admired Ramsey Wick from the water, 'especially as one could get a cup of tea at the Riverview'. They decided to rent one of the newly built fishermen's cottages whilst exploring the area and eventually bought some land to the west of Ramsey Wick which they named

180

Scarlets. Mr Hayward, a builder, had put up three identical country houses on the site by 1910. Scarlets, being out of the parish of St Lawrence and in the parish of Steeple, caused the first name change to Steeple Stone.

After the First World War the Bebbington family sold building plots. This began the development with sheds, garages and tents. The population between the wars rose in summer to 1,200 and in the winter dropped to perhaps 30. With no main drainage or electricity many acquaintances were made at five am in the morning whilst burying the previous day's effluent!

Tinnocks estate was developed by Mr Winterbon, a private estate facing the Blackwater and to this day it is still run by the trustees. By 1938 Steeple Stone was being referred to as 'The Stone', probably due to the fact that the Ramsey Wick part had almost joined up with the Steeple/Scarlets part and at the outbreak of the Second World War in 1939 quite a village atmosphere had grown up.

There are many rumours and stories of how the name 'Stone' came to be used. One tale is that the Saxons used the island before the battle of Maldon in AD 991 to stock up with stones and boulders on the island for their ammunition. Another story is that the same aggregate was used for ballast for the shipping using Maldon, which until the late 19th century was quite a port, with added shipbuilding taking place in Heybridge.

Riverview was to see a number of changes over the years after 1948. It gained its licence by becoming the Stone Yacht Club although precious little yachting was carried on from its portals. In that year the returning soldiers, sailors and airmen began to see that there was something in this boating lark and so from within the Riverview was born Stone Sailing Club. Wick Farm by this time had also regained its licence as the St Lawrence Bay Yacht and Country Club.

In 1953 the great East Coast Flood did not bypass The Stone. The sea wall was breached in two places on that fateful night and the island decimated at its lowest points. Breezey Point took the full force of the wind and tide and the cottage at this point lifted and turned completely upside down. A great deal of damage was caused but thankfully no lives were lost, but it took many years before the damp and smell left properties flooded that night.

The only change on the landscape of any importance since 1830 must be the Bradwell nuclear power station, which dominates the view three miles to the east of the village.

Written records of St Lawrence's church begin in the 12th century, though most of the present church dates from the rebuilding of 1877. The site is one of the high points of Essex with a view of 25 miles. It is used regularly for worship and it was kept open every day until 1988 when there was some vandalism and an unsuccessful arson attempt. The church is surrounded by mostly arable farmland. There are several nature, conservation and birdwatching reserves in the area, and it has five footpaths radiating from it, the 'St Peter's Way' long distance walk.

In July 1988 a week of events was organised by the PCC to coincide with the erection of an Armada beacon on St Lawrence Hill, 50 metres from the church. A truly wonderful evening saw over 500 people witness the lighting of the beacon, which is still there today with a commemorative plaque.

The Blackwater estuary has changed from a fishing and oyster environment to a water-sports area over the years, but valiant efforts are being made to balance the environmental benefits of this attractive and convenient area. New oyster beds have been laid and fishing is developing but this will only succeed with the co-operation of residents and visitors alike.

The development from sleepy hamlet to full-blown village was inevitable. Electricity came to The Stone during the war and with main drainage in 1975 this made The Stone think in terms of 'St Lawrence Bay'. With the advent of the caravan sites and the inevitable expansion of the modern plot land, St Lawrence Bay has become an organised conurbation, with as many holiday people as residents. The crunch on the stones and the whispers at five am are long gone. That's of course if you've got main drainage.

St Osyth ☙

This waterside village has great charm and is just eleven miles from Colchester. Despite some development of recent years the village can boast an unusually wide variety of scenery. The hills are not bold, nor the valleys deep but it is sufficiently clothed with many attractive tracts of woodland, waterside and countryside deserving to be explored by public footpaths.

The village is enhanced by the imposing Priory and Gatehouse, St Clere's Hall (a rare example of a 14th century aisled hall) and many other listed old buildings. There are a number of 14th and 15th century timber-framed cottages with weather-boarded elevations and pantiled roofs. The owners of these cottages have maintained their character by retaining inglenooks, low ceilings, oak beams and braces.

Fronting the Priory is a large green known as 'The Bury' (bury being a derivation of the word 'burgh' and the site of the original village). Mill Street leads from the Bury downhill to St Osyth Creek and a small quay. In days of yore many sailing barges carried a variety of cargoes from this quay and returned with coal and loads of London 'muck' for the fields. This small area was the scene of smuggling as intensive as that of Cornwall or Kent in the 16th century. These pirates, without doubt, were assisted by the locals. The quay is now a flourishing boatyard and the Dam is a popular venue for water-skiers and other water-sport enthusiasts.

Until a few years ago the only transport available in the village was horses and carts, ponies and traps and penny-farthing bicycles! Much more comfort today with an hourly bus service to Colchester via Wivenhoe and every 15 minutes a small bus to Clacton 'which reaches parts of the village the other buses cannot reach'.

For several years the village has won the award for the 'Tidiest Village in Essex', mainly due to the efforts of two gentlemen who seem to spend their lives wielding rakes, hoes and shovels. Who would not be charmed by Church Square, always attractive but never more so than from early spring to late autumn when the flowers in the surrounding cottages' plant boxes are in full bloom.

St Osyth has a long uncrowded beach, one section of which, away from the main activities, has been reserved for naturists. The large recreation ground, beyond which you can glimpse the sea, is kept in immaculate condition and boasts a fair-sized sports pavilion, picnic tables, tennis courts, football and cricket pitches and a well equipped fenced playground for the tiny tots. The annual traditional Strawberry Fair and carnival brings much animation to an already bright village.

St Osyth Priory is the most well-known and the most impressive feature of the village – it has a fascinating history and much remains to be admired. During the Civil War a Puritan mob attacked the Priory ransacking the house and gatehouse, inflicting considerable damage. The incumbent at the time, Lady Rivers, fled for her life to Long Melford.

In its long history the Priory has had many distinguished visitors. Queen Elizabeth I visited the Priory in 1561 but on the first night there was a terrific thunderstorm and Elizabeth hurriedly departed for London the very next day. But she did return 18 years later. In the 1920s and

1930s the late Queen Mary, Arthur, Duke of Connaught and many others of the Royal family were entertained at the Priory by General Kincaid-Smith, the owner at that time. There are various trees planted around the gardens to commemorate their visits.

The original priory church of St Osyth was actually in the priory grounds and was replaced in the 12th century by a stone Norman church on the present site of the parish church of St Peter and St Paul, which dates mainly from the 16th century when the nave and aisles were rebuilt in brick with a hammerbeam roof.

About 300 years ago St Osyth village was notorious on account of the number of witches reputed to dwell there. There is a book in the British Museum, published in the year 1582, which contains a report of evidence given by Brian D'Arcy JP against a number of women who were suspected of witchcraft. During the Civil War (reported in a volume dated 1645) the Justice of the Peace for the County of East Essex found time to conduct a witch-hunt in the country east of Colchester. Twenty-two women are mentioned in this volume and were indicted for witchcraft. Many of them confessed to possessing 'imps' and to evil doings by witchcraft, possibly in the hope that by confessing they would be pardoned. One, Ursula Kemp, never confessed, but strongly defended herself, able to read and write. Her trial was held at St Clere's Hall.

Sewards End 🌿

Like so many East Anglian villages, Sewards End has changed almost beyond recognition during the past 60 years. What was once a selfsufficient farming community, with its own cottage industries and craftsmen, now is almost entirely residential.

There are several interesting buildings along the first stretch of main road – Hopwoods, a Tudor farmhouse; the Green Dragon, now the only pub in the village but formerly, and appropriately, the Butchers Arms, since it was also the local abattoir; Campions, reputedly the oldest house in the village and famed for its wall paintings, some of which are in Saffron Walden museum; Gaytons, a half-timbered Elizabethan farmhouse; and Everards. Although much renovated and extended, this dates back to the 14th century, and was the first privately owned yeoman farmhouse in the village.

Nearby is the church, which in fact is neither a church nor owned by the Church authorities. It is the chapel of ease, built in 1847 by a wealthy local farmer, Thomas Gayton.

Until the Education Act of 1947, the chapel was also the village school for many years, not only used by the village children but also those from Saffron Walden workhouse, or the 'Grubby', as it was called. Some of the senior residents can still recall the children in their grey workhouse uniforms being marched along the main road, which then was little more than a wide cart track. On occasions, as many as 90 children squeezed into the tiny chapel school, to be taught by just two teachers and the headmaster.

Up to 1915, Sewards End also had its own windmill, a site now occupied by three modern, neo-Georgian houses. The last miller, George Jarvis, also ran the bakery, and such was the poverty at that time, he knew if he did not get the money immediately, he would never get it. Being a generous man, he frequently did not get paid, either for bread or the use of his ovens at the week-end to cook the villagers' meat.

Near the first corner in the main road, although not visible from the road, is The Towers, a magnificently foolish edifice built during the 19th century by William Gayton, the brother of chapel-builder, Thomas. Also on the first corner is another tower – the water tower, built in 1905. This may not seem important to those who are used to unlimited water gushing from their taps, but in those days finding water during the summer could be a real problem for the people of the village. The bucket brigade had to set out early each morning, working their way from pond to pond. Often their search ended at a spring-fed pond at the western edge of the village, followed by a half-mile trudge home.

The green lane running in front of the water tower was the King's Highway, certainly up to 1400, and probably much later. The present main road to Radwinter was just a cart-track to monastery lands, which lay beyond the village at a site called Keburdhey. This is still marked by Kibberdy Cottages, the last two cottages in the village. Seeing the thousands of acres of fertile farmland, it is perhaps worth mentioning that from 1130 it took the monks over 40 years to clear their 60 acres of forest, and then they complained that the land was so poor it was fit only to grow 'weeds and sour thistle'!

In Redgate Lane stand a group of historic houses. The oldest is Swain's Farm, which still bears the name of the original medieval landholder, Sir Walter de Swayne (1292), and it is probable that part of the house dates back to that time. Later, it had strong Quaker connections and at the back of the house there lies an old Quaker burial ground. Next door stands Sewards End Farm, originally Fibe's Tenement, a comparative youngster of a house but nonetheless much older than its Victorian facade would suggest. These days, Victorian ideas of 'restoration' would be considered pure vandalism! Brewery Cottage, one end of which is the old oast-house, Birbecks and the Old Fox complete the group. The Fox was the village's second public house, but is now two private residences. A few years ago, when one came onto the market, the estate agent's blurb described it as 'an older style semi-detached'. It is, indeed. It was built in 1560!

Sheering 🏵

Even before Roman times there was a settlement in Sheering. This was discovered and confirmed when, in 1989, plans were submitted for the building of a meeting room in the field next to the church. An archeological survey was required before any disturbance was made to the site. Here were found small pits containing pottery, bones and worked flints, suggesting that the village was settled in the church area even in pre-Christian and prehistoric times.

The Domesday Survey came in due course to Sheering. The Book mentions that there were two Manors. Sheering Hall, an ancient site with earthworks, was granted by William Conqueror to his nephew Peter de Valognes and the manor of Cowicks or Quickbury to William de Warren, his uncle. Sheering was distinguished in owning a mule, the only other mule being in a village in Norfolk.

Round about 1160 AD the Fitzwalter family had the patronage and began building a church, the Norman tower of which still stands. Later, Robert Fitzwalter Marshall of the Magna Carta Barons (1215 AD) was represented in sculpture, his head and that of his wife Lady Gunnara can be seen beside the main door. The church also has a 14th century stained glass East window which glows beautifully in red, blue and yellow colours.

There are a few lovely old houses, listed buildings tucked away, timber framed 16th and 17th century, pargetted, wattled-and-daubed, weather-boarded. There are no really large houses.

In 1816 the rector, Francis Tutté, gave £100 in trust to teach twelve poor girls of Sheering to read, spell and sew. By 1827 the school was a National Sunday and Day School with fifteen boys and thirtyfive girls. The present attractive, London-stock brick building, was begun in 1851 enlarged in 1874 with a school house and outside conveniences, and finally modernised and further enlarged in 1966. The school began to receive government finance in 1880. It is interesting that girls were first to receive formal education. In later years the trust was altered by the Board of Education to provide prizes for girls in sewing and scripture. The early boy pupils took their penny a week for their schooling and were sent home if they went to school without it. Children took time off to help with the Harvest and often left school when ten years old.

In Victorian times the Glyn family occupied the Manor of Sheering Hall. They took an active part in village life and have two family memorial stained glass windows in the church. Elinor Glyn is famous for her steamy romantic novels.

The old village of Sheering has acquired a lusty offspring. Lower Sheering is about a mile away nestling the border between Sheering and Sawbridgeworth – between Essex and Hertfordshire. This growth began with the advent of the railway. A small industrial area grew using the River Stort and the Great Eastern Railway, later to become the green-liveried steam London and North Eastern. Here thrived the Joinery Works using timber coming by river barge; the Maltings specialising in malt and codliver oil, delicious stuff like toffee, also making special malt in a separate kiln fired using bundles of faggot twigs for very special Scotch whisky malt.

These industries have all closed down. The Maltings are converted into unusual flats and workshops, the Joinery Works site now attractive with houses and flats bordering the River Stort. With the railway began the development of houses for commuters. These days there is a greater population in Lower Sheering than in the old village. The M11 motor-way separates the two parts of the Parish.

Before the second world war the inhabitants were mainly agricultural workers, (always called labourers in the Parish Register), or wood-workers in the Joinery Works and maltsters at the Maltings.

Since the war there has been a gradual infilling of houses and small estates. The coming of the M11 motorway has illuminated the night sky with regulation street lights. The motorway is a continuous roar of traffic, the planes from Stansted mysteriously fly over (Sheering is not officially in the flight path). The Street succumbs to the hazards and fumes of the 'internal' combustion engine and no longer is heard the night cry of the fox and the owl.

The changes have had a big impact on what was a quiet agricultural community. It has seen its village built-up, tidied up, the common verges rounded-up and enclosed with walls, fences and the dreaded Leylandii. It has seen its established rights and usuages eroded. Village children are priced out of the housing market and move elsewhere. Surprisingly Sheering is still an attractive community.

In spite of the lingering regrets about the changing lifestyle there are positive assets. A modern village hall, a thriving playgroup, various clubs, bowling, karate, bridge – the WI and a hard-working Parents Association.

Sheering still, by the skin of its teeth, has a school, a shop and a post-office.

Shenfield 🐚

No longer a village, not quite a town, Shenfield's first mention was in the Domesday Book. It is still a pleasant place to live with long avenues of decent houses and plenty of trees and delightful gardens. Originally Shenfield was a small hamlet, between Brentwood in the west and Mountnessing village in the east.

The church of St Mary the Virgin, circa 1600, was the focal point, on a slight rise. A small but beautiful church, its most interesting feature is the timber arcade of six bays and four centred arches. Each column is hewn out of a great oak tree. The wooden arcade was fashioned in the style of stone pillars, with attached columns. Heavier timber is the sub-structure of the bell tower, with eight posts grouped in pairs and big braces to hold the cross beams. The aisle roof is thought to be 500 years old. Pride of Shenfield is the shingle spire, specially tall and thin with a golden cockerel on top. In the tower are six bells, the oldest first cast in 1626. Every Thursday evening, especially if you live to the east of the church, the bell-ringers can be heard at practice.

South of the church is Shenfield Place, a brick house of 1690, formerly a home of the well-known Courage family. Across from this building is the church school house of 1865. A stone and brick building of Victorian design, its clock in the tower can still be heard striking as it first did at four pm Saturday 28th October 1893.

To the south of the Chelmsford Road at the junction with the Hutton Road, an ancient hostelry still stands, namely the Green Dragon. This public house has no foundations, as buildings of today have, but was built directly onto Essex clay. It lost a tall chimney in the hurricane of 1987. One can imagine the stage coaches stopping here for refreshment, their drivers blowing a horn for the turnpike a few yards down the road, where the Tollbar Cottage still stands today. Fixed to the wall in wrought iron is the date 1700. This was the first turnpike on the Great Essex Road, leading to Chelmsford and Colchester. Much later the coming of the first railway gradually killed the stage coach traffic and the use of toll-gates. Opposite the Tollbar Cottage stands the Eagle and Child public house, built in 1936 on the site of a much older hostelry named the Bird and Baby.

The decisive moment for Shenfield was the arrival of the railway in 1840. In the 1900s it was still a country railway and the sight of the steam trains puffing along would have been a sight worth watching. By 1921 the Great Eastern was swallowed up by the London and North Eastern Railway. With business flourishing, in 1932 the line was quadrupled and a new wider bridge put in place over the Hutton Road. A new station was built in stone and red brick, but the stationmaster's house was demolished to make way for it and alas the garden beside the house also disappeared.

So it continued to serve Shenfield through two world wars until its next milestone with the introduction of the electric train service in 1949, bringing a faster cleaner service to the growing numbers of people who had found this pleasant spot, just half hour or so from London.

To the east of the Broadway under the bridge is Mount Avenue, leading to a very select area of unmade roads and large houses set among the trees. In 1961 a library was built where once was a cornfield, at the junction of Friars Avenue and the Hutton road. The Broadway with its array of banks, estate agents, hairdressers, several butcher's shops and two supermarkets, albeit small compared with those in larger towns, serves the population very well and provides for all immediate needs.

It is still a pleasant place to live, although it seems that every inch of ground is being used to build on. There are still green and open spaces, such as the Courage playing fields between the Chelmsford Road and the church, with a superb view across to the white-sailed windmill at Mountnessing, the houses over in Hutton, and at night the flashing car lights on the new motorway.

Shoeburyness 🌿

Shoeburyness is a somewhat divided place from the geographical point of view as the Garrison lies between 'Shoebury Village' and 'Cambridge Town', the latter deriving its name from the public house named after the Duke of Cambridge.

In the middle of the 19th century there was very little here apart from a few farmhouses, hardly any of which still exist. In 1851 the total population of the parish was approximately 151. The area, like so many parts of the South and East Coasts, was probably one in which a lot of smuggling took place, the marshes and hidden creeks lending themselves very well to such activities.

It was of course, the coming of the RA Garrison and School of Gunnery that very gradually led to the development of the area. The coast curves quite sharply at Shoebury and the Army took over quite a bit of the coastal area together with some inland ground to form the Garrison and some years later the War Department took over the land further east which forms the New Ranges, the only part now in constant use.

The Garrison came in the middle of the 19th century and Shoebury began to grow. Houses were built at the Garrison end of the High Street and Rampart Street. Shops began to open and then more roads leading off the High Street, but even then it was not completely built up until the 1920s and 1930s. Cambridge Town began a little later than the first part of the Village High Street. Residents are used to the firing of the extremely loud and heavy guns. The soldiers were always an integral part of the area and many with their families remained in the town after retiring from the army. The splendid horses belonging to the Garrison were a sight some older residents still remember. They could be heard clattering down the High Street early in the morning. Harry Wheatcroft, the famous rose grower, lived at North Shoebury, and you can guess where the good manure came from; several local people were always to be found at the ready with bucket and shovel!

In the years between the wars, Shoebury was quite well known as a holiday resort The beaches are good and safe for bathing, and it has always been a source of enjoyment to walk out on the mud at low tide, provided of course one is sensible enough to learn how quickly the tide comes in. Sailboarding and water-skiing are now often to be seen.

In the latter part of the 19th century and up until the Second World

War, Thames barges used to carry refuse from London which was used in the local brickworks. The barges were then reloaded with bricks and taken to London and other parts of the country. Children used to love to watch the barges being unloaded.

Across the land from the beach to the brickfields (now nonexistent) were two narrow gauge railways used to draw the refuse and bricks, at first pulled by horses, later by a small engine. Both lines crossed the High Street, but there was no level crossing. Up until the 1930s there was a blacksmith's forge on the beach, just above the sands – another great source of local entertainment.

The main sources of employment over the past years were the brickworks, Garrison and railways, as well as farming. One local resident remembers how she and her brothers used to watch the men working in the brickfields. First they would see the clay (marm) and sand put in a grinding wheel, and then see it come out the front and be moulded and cut into shape. Then the bricks were stacked criss-cross to dry. She now wonders how much money the brickworks lost by the spoilt bricks caused by curious little fingers being poked in to see if the bricks were dry.

There are a number of historic and fine buildings in the area. St Andrew's at South Shoebury is a Norman church started in the 1100s, and the timber porch which is said to be the finest example in Essex was added to it in 1400. St Mary's at North Shoebury is a 13th century church. Other listed buildings include South Shoebury Hall, where the manorial courts used to be held. It is a medieval timber-framed house dating from the mid 15th century. Suttons, which is part of the New Ranges, is a 17th century manor house. At the corner of Elm Road and Wakering Road is the Redhouse, built in 1673 and said to have been the lodge to the manor house. In North Shoebury there is New Farm, a timber-framed house dating from the 18th century. Kent's Moat House was built in the 19th century with a moat round three sides. Parson's Barn, which is now a public house, was created from a 16th century barn. The former post office and adjoining cottage (alas now derelict) was also 16th century and just along Poynters Lane is North Shoebury House, a most attractive 18th century house built of red brick.

There are also a number of listed buildings in the Garrison, including the splendid church and clock tower, the Commandant's House and the Officers Mess to name a few. Historians have discovered evidence dating back to Roman, Danish and Saxon times and in Southend Museum are several artefacts found in the Shoebury area to corroborate this.

South Benfleet 🦋

The attraction of the Benfleet area for the Saxons was the creek with adjoining woods. Here was plenty of water, good access and timber for fuel and boats. For many centuries the timber from Benfleet woods was loaded at a wharf in Church Creek, next to the Hoy and Helmet, on to sailing boats and sent to boatbuilders at Leigh, other places on the Thames and even abroad.

In AD 893 there was a vital battle of Benfleet, Danes had established a fortified settlement at Benfleet and King Alfred's army, led by his son Edward, came out from London in that year, storming the camp, defeating the Danes and setting fire to their boats in the creek. It is likely a small wooden church was erected on the site of the battle. Over the centuries this has been rebuilt and developed to become the present St Mary's church. The history of the church shows existing sections having been built in the 12th, 13th, 14th and 15th centuries.

The church was originally connected with Barking Abbey. In 1067 King William granted Benfleet to Westminster Abbey. In 1540 when, under Henry VIII, Barking Abbey was destroyed, the manor and church of Benfleet was granted to the Dean and Chapter of Westminster who to this day retain the right to appoint the vicar.

Adjoining the church a prestigious building was erected in 1380 which later became the Anchor public house. Recent finds have established the date of the building and have uncovered medieval windows.

In 1970 when the Canvey Road was being built from Sadlers Farm roundabout on the A13 across Benfleet creek, Roman remains were found showing that there was a Roman settlement on the Benfleet side of the creek in the 1st and 2nd centuries.

In the 16th and 17th centuries the sea which came up to the foot of the hills at Hadleigh Castle also enabled boats to sail up Benfleet creek past St Mary's church and along the back of the Anchor. Another creek allowed fishing boats to sail to Hopes Green which was at the site of the present junior school. For this reason the main early settlement at Benfleet was around the church with a small hamlet of fishermen's cottages at Hopes Green.

Benfleet developed with the coming of the railway from London in 1855. Cheap travel gave good access to the City and many commuters came to live in the area. Housing estates developed after the First World War and the period after the second war saw a rapid expansion to the present population, estimated in 1991 at 15,000 for South Benfleet.

Original access over the creek to Canvey Island was by ferry, at a cost of one penny, or by stepping stones when the tide was out. A swing bridge was provided in 1961 and further traffic improvements came when the railway level crossing gates were by passed by building a road under the station.

Although Benfleet is extensively developed, much of the atmosphere and old building around the church remain. The area between School Lane, the church and the station has been declared a conservation area by the local authority.

South Hanningfield 🌿

At the time of the First World War the village consisted of the school, the Windmill public house, the post office and general store, the blacksmith's forge and the parish church of St Peter. 'Bearmains', the big house, was lived in by Mr and Mrs Gray, employing many servants and gardeners etc, and there was a scattering of cottages mainly occupied by the farm workers and their families. Later on Mr and Mrs Walter Hills took up residence and their grandson Mr Norman Gardner still takes an active interest in the village as chairman of the flower show and churchwarden.

The Church of England school had two classrooms, the large room built in 1874 and the small room in 1912, and two teachers. The headteacher taught the children from eight to 14 years old and the younger ones from five to eight years were taught by a Miss K Bright, who worked there all her life and was respected by a good many families. It was heated by an open fire which was usually the standing point for the teachers to keep their backs warm.

There was no power or light and the only supply of water was obtained from various springs supplying wells in gardens or at the side of the road. Everyone had a kitchen stove indoors and this provided heat for cooking and warmth for all, and a paraffin oil lamp standing on the table for all to see after dark. Meals were very simple, mostly rabbits cooked in stews or baked in pies, caught by the men on the farms, eggs from a few chickens kept in backyards, half or a whole pig's head duly made into lovely brawn, bread and cheese and onions consumed in large quantities in the home and at work in the fields. For Sunday a joint of beef was the treat of the week, perhaps with a fruit tart and home-made beer. All vegetables were grown in the workers' gardens, helped out with some potatoes and swedes grown on the farms.

The Windmill public house was very different to what it is today. It was a small country pub with a tap room, the floor of which was covered in sawdust, and it was run by a Mr Tom Hunt and his sister Peg, together with a housekeeper Mrs Aspin. All three were very deaf but managed to keep the locals happy, especially in wintertime with a large fire in the tap room which had seats built in the side of the fireplace. The post office and general stores were run by the Clarence family. You could always purchase lovely hand-cut bacon and cheese, and all perishable goods were kept in a back room with a brick floor, slate shelves and no heat. The blacksmith's forge was run by the two Smith brothers who were kept busy with the farm horses. When anyone wanted the doctor to call from Wickford, a white flag was placed on the smithy's wall and the doctor on his motor-bike used to call there to see where he was wanted (there were no phones in the village until the 1930s). The smith was popular with the children, making iron hoops to fit the size of the child.

When motorised vehicles began to come on the scene the church choir hired one to take its members by charabanc to the seaside once a year, mostly to Clacton, Felixstowe, Walton or Margate. The maximum speed of these was 15 mph, so they left early in the morning, arriving home late at night, causing much worry and concern to their families. Gradually things began to improve. Buses began to get more frequent, lads brought motor-bikes, taking the girls on the pillion, water and electricity were laid on and generally life improved until war broke out again in 1939.

On the whole the village escaped lightly. The end of the war was greeted with a huge bonfire and social evening in the village hall and things seemed to be settling down until a huge reservoir was planned and built on many acres of farmland. Completed in 1954, it completely altered the face of the village. New houses were built and a new road linking West to South Hanningfield. The school was demolished and the Windmill public house was rebuilt.

South Weald 🐾

South Weald is less than two miles from Brentwood but a world away from its busy High Street. The church is large for such a small village and stands proudly on top of the hill. The Saxons settled here and the place is mentioned in the Domesday Book.

St Peter's is the mother church of the neighbourhood and until the middle of the 19th century, Brentwood, with its chapel, came under the jurisdiction of South Weald. The present church dates from about 1150, although the south door, with its chevron ornamentation, is the sole remaining Norman feature. The present memorial chapel at the end of the south aisle was originally Weald Hall Chapel. Within it are commemorated former holders of the manor of South Weald. Sir Antony Browne, the founder of Brentwood School, Erasmus Smith and the Tower family are all represented. The latter were the local squires from 1752 onwards.

The Tower family graves are situated in an enclosed area in the north-west of the churchyard and a private gate from the park gave the family access. Opposite the church tower is the door through which the squire, his family and servants came from Weald Hall to worship. The house, a fine Tudor mansion, stood nearby in the park until 1950, when it was demolished, having fallen into disrepair after standing empty for four years.

Opposite the church is the Tower Arms, a splendid example of early 18th century architecture. Above the entrance are the initials ALAA and the date 1704. The house was originally called Jewells. In earlier times, the village public house was on the west side of the church and was known as the Spread Eagle until about 1878, when it was renamed the Tower Arms. The licence had been transferred to the present house by 1921.

Following the road to the right outside the lychgate, there are two entrances to Weald Country Park. Between them, on the right, is a house now known as Queen Mary's chapel. In the 16th century, Weald Hall was surrounded by a series of walled courts and gardens and included this garden house, built in the same style as Weald Hall. There is a tradition that Queen Mary worshipped there secretly before her accession, but there is no contemporary evidence in support.

Enter the park at the second of the two entrances and you will be near to the visitors' centre with information and literature about Weald Hall and Weald Park. The Park was formed as a deer park in the 12th century, when the monks of Waltham Abbey held the manor. Deer were kept here until 1944, when troops were assembling for the invasion of France and the fences were breached to enable vehicles to enter. The deer escaped. A herd is at present being re-established. With its lakes, the park presents a fine vista and is well worth a visit. On the eastern side of the park, bordering Sandpit Lane, is part of South Weald Fort. This is an Iron Age fortification and has been excavated recently.

Returning to the village, take the right turn into Wigley Bush Lane. It appeared thus on Chapman and Andre's map of Essex in 1777 and was revived in the 1970s, after a period when the name was Vicarage Lane. On the left hand side of the road is Luptons, an early 18th century house which was inhabited by Edward Ind in 1848. He was a partner in the Ind Coope brewery at Romford. His partner, Octavius Coope MP lived at Rochetts, the entrance to which is opposite Queen Mary's chapel. It was largely destroyed by fire in 1975. Opposite Luptons is Wealdcote, a 16th century building, to which was added a 17th century extension. Further down on the right hand side is the school, built between 1957 and 1968 to replace the original building which stood opposite the present church car park and is now demolished. On the left hand side are the almshouses. Ten of these, together with a chapel, were designed by S S Teulon and built in 1854. They were originally established in 1567, through benefactions in the will of Sir Antony Browne. Two additional almshouses were added in 1966. Continuing towards Brentwood, the present vicarage, dating from about 1926, is on the right and succeeded on the left by Weald Hall. The name is misleading, as the original Weald Hall was always in Weald Park. The house dates from 1825 and was built as his vicarage by Charles Belli, whose munificence restored the church and built the school in the village.

After crossing the bypass, Brook Street is reached at the junction with the main road. This was probably the route of the Roman road from London to Chelmsford and Maldon. The Nags Head, built in the 18th century, gives its name to the lane opposite. It was so called in 1777.

Turning left towards Brentwood, Stone House is encountered on the left after about 200 yards. An unusual sight, it was built about 100 years ago of random brick, stone and flint. Adjoining the house is a row of early 18th century cottages, succeeded in turn by the Bull, probably another 18th century house. At the traffic lights, Spital Lane commemorates the leper hospital which stood on the corner from the 12th to 16th centuries.

Two of Brook Street's oldest buildings are reached within 200 yards. On the left is the Golden Fleece, a large 15th century building which is now a restaurant. The remains of the original hammerbeam hall roof are clearly visible from the vestibule of the dining room. Almost opposite is the Moat House Hotel. It had been known as 'The Place' in 1514, but was completely rebuilt in the 17th century.

South Woodham Ferrers ✑

The County Council, as promoter of this the newest of Essex's new towns, has adopted slogans devised to attract new house owners: 'It's the place to be' being a particularly well used example. The Council, with some justification, could have adopted the slogan 'The town where nothing is as old as it seems'.

Asda's weatherboarded clocktower cupola, built in 1978, dominates an area which took on the title of 'Queen Elizabeth II Square' in commemoration of the Queen's visit to the town in 1981. Whilst in the square, turn with your back to the superstore and you will see across the square, past the bandstand, a three-storey classical building which in another age might have been the town hall but today is a bank built, not in the 19th century, but also in 1978.

The historical theme of new building in the town is not confined to the town centre. Wander out to some of the town's housing areas and you will find old weatherboarded cottages, 18th century Dutch gabled housing, bow-fronted Georgian villas and Victorian artisan cottages, every one of them products of the building boom of the 1980s. Whether or not the new town planners intended there to be such a strong historical bias in the design of the town is not clear but what is clear is that unlike earlier new towns that gave the very term 'new town' a bad name, South Woodham Ferrers has tried to learn the lessons of the past. Building forms, building materials and the informal groupings of the buildings themselves reflect the character of the county's older settlements. It is an approach which has drawn scorn from some architectural writers who have labelled it 'pastiche' and 'film set architecture' but it has obviously found a place in the hearts of the many residents, who, for a number of years in the mid 1980s, were moving into the town at a rate of more than ten families a week.

However, anyone who concludes that there is little of real history to observe in the town would be wrong. The railway might be a good

South Woodham Ferrers

198

starting point. During the second half of the 19th century there were a number of proposals to extend the growing railway network into this corner of Essex. One scheme, promoted by Eastern Counties Railway in 1856, envisaged a route between Pitsea and Maldon that would have crossed the river Crouch with what was apparently a combined road/rail bridge at the end of what is now Marsh Farm Road, to the south of today's town.

It was perhaps typical of the bold Victorian enterprises of the time that when the railway finally reached Woodham, then a quiet rural backwater, in 1889 it was not just in the form of a simple railway halt. Woodham Ferrers station, initially called Woodham Fen presumably because it was so far removed from Woodham Ferrers itself, was constructed as a sizeable junction where the Southminster and Maldon lines met. It had a network of lines criss-crossing between two platforms, a goods yard, a coal yard, cattle pens, turntable and weighbridge. The line was built through a thinly populated area and it was clear that, initially at least, much of the traffic would be generated by the farms and smallholdings in the vicinity of the new line.

Within a few years of the lines opening the Victorian entrepreneurs' hopes began to be realised. Two of South Woodham's principal farms, Champions and Eyotts, were laid out with a grid-iron pattern of roads, with hundreds of plots of land offered for sale at the turn of the century. One acre plots could be acquired for £20 and single building plots occasionally dipped below the £5 mark at auctions on the Eyotts estate on the western side of the town.

In South Woodham Ferrers (then more usually referred to as South Woodham Ferris) the break up of these farms led to a haphazard growth of houses, smallholdings, nurseries, weekend cottages and holiday homes. The buildings were mainly one-off structures, often timber-framed with weatherboarding or asbestos sheet covering. Although the new town development swept away many of these 'scattered, substandard dwellings' (as the County Council then described them), in some of the older streets around the station a number of these old buildings still survive.

Elsewhere in the town it is still possible to trace the remains of some of the old plotland tracks where hedgerows and tree-lines have been retained as property boundaries and footpath routes. Alexandra Road, York Road, Louise Road and Top Barn Lane are names from that now distant era which still rekindle happy memories for some of South Woodham's older residents.

At every stage in the town's growth there has been a perhaps understandable opposition and the 1890s were no exception. In 1898 for example there was considerable dissension in the parish as to the rights and wrongs of dwellings that were being built on the plotland estates. Newcomers at that time were described rather unkindly as 'squatters who would be more at home in the Australian Bush or American Outbacks'.

However, such opposition did not stop the growth of the area and by the early 1930s the village could boast five churches, a school, a Women's Institute hall and a smallholders' hall which were all indicative of a growing and active population.

Whilst some consolidation of the central area around the station continued in post-war years and new estates were built in the 1960s, the large outlying areas of plotland development presented insurmountable problems of access and land ownership for potential developers. As demand for new housing increased in the early 1970s, a new town on land purchased by the County Council became the next logical step in the life of South Woodham Ferrers.

Southend-on-Sea

Southend-on-Sea's main claim to fame is for its pier – the longest p ier in the world. The original pier was constructed in 1830 following an Act of Parliament, and was extended in 1846 to one and a third miles in length, with a wide landing stage for pleasure boats. The pier served not

Southend Pier

only holiday-makers. In the Second World War thousands of troops travelled on its electric railway to board their warships. Royalty also made the journey along the pier to join their yachts.

The name Southend originated from the South End of the old village of Prittlewell. One writer described the early development as 'an earthly paradise' and added 'I doubt not but that South End will be the rage.' Southend became fashionable when Royalty visited Royal Terrace, so-named after Princess Caroline stayed there in 1804.

A number of well-known writers lived in the area. Among them, Warwick Deeping, who lived and wrote at Prospect House at the bottom of Southend High Street. The building stood until the 1980s when alas, in spite of protests from local historical societies, it was demolished to make way for a modern shopping centre.

Benjamin Disraeli, who was a novelist as well as a politician, described Southend and district as 'the Essex Riviera'. It is indeed true that the cliff gardens are very attractive, and well laid out. The colour of the first spring flowers are a delight to the eye.

In contrast, the busy and popular area east of the pier is known as the Golden Mile. This is because a 'river of gold' flowed in here from the pockets of visitors who travelled by rail and road. Road travel was greatly improved when the Southend Arterial Road, the A127, was completed in 1925. This 100 ft wide dual carriageway was the forerunner of today's motorways. It was, in fact, more than 20 years ahead of its time.

Southend is well-known for its autumn illuminations. These proved a major attraction in the years immediately following the Second World

War. The blackout-weary public flocked in their tens of thousands, from all parts of Britain, to marvel at the extensive sea-front spectacle.

The annual carnival, held in August, also attracts huge crowds who line the route from Leigh-on-Sea to Southchurch. The parade claims to be the longest in Britain.

Leigh-on-Sea, part of the Borough of Southend, is still largely unspoiled. Fishing boats ply daily out to sea, and their catch is cooked and sold to hungry visitors in the little waterside cafes and olde-worlde pubs. These are favourite haunts of artists and photographers.

Southend has plenty of leisure and sporting activities, golf courses, swimming pools and leisure centres. It is also very fortunate to have a little Edwardian gem of a theatre, complete with its ornate decor of that era. The Palace Theatre, Westcliff, opened in 1912, and was given to the town by its last owner, Mrs Gertrude Mouillot. The Cliffs Pavilion is a popular venue for a wide variety of activities, from musical shows to films, ballet, and exhibitions of all kinds.

For many years the Kursaal amusement centre was a major feature on the sea-front scene. Visitors headed here for scenic railway thrills, and other delights. Originally called the Luna Park and Palace, it was built in 1902 at a cost of £250,000. In its early days, entry to the complex was one penny, and this allowed admission free to the gallery of the Kursaal cinema. The cinema closed in 1940, and much of the area has since been redeveloped.

The Clifftown Parade area of Southend, overlooking the cliff gardens, is largely a conservation area and so still retains houses of character and elegance, plus the pretty Clifftown Garden with fountains, pond, and seats around it. This faces on to the new replica Victorian bandstand, which has been built to the identical design of the original, and was opened by the mayor in 1990. All kinds of entertainment take place here from spring to late autumn, including an annual art exhibition by local artists.

In the 1970s Southend also became a centre for commerce, and huge office blocks replaced the elegant houses in Victoria Avenue. A new civic centre and police headquarters were built, and officially opened by the Queen Mother.

A large new library was also built and incorporates lecture halls, a cafeteria, and space for regular art and photographic exhibitions. The original old library is now a museum.

Southminster 🐚

Southminster is situated in the Dengie Peninsula, between the rivers Crouch and Blackwater with the North Sea to the east.

It dates from around AD 640 when the village grew up around the parish church of St Leonard. The sea came up as far as Pandole Wood, an ancient wood with a small earthwork, and wool merchants came from across the North Sea up to Southminster. Two Dutchmen were employed to advise on reclaiming the land, and the remains of two sea walls can be seen. The sea is now four miles away, across peaceful marshes, full of wildlife, with a view over to Foulness Island, and in summer yachts from Burnham-on-Crouch can be seen coming from the Crouch to the North Sea. Access to the sea wall is not now available, but it can be reached by walking the sea wall from Burnham to Bradwell.

St Leonard's church is of Saxon origin and is situated in the centre of the village. The south doorway being of Norman origin, many Roman bricks were used in building this part of the church. In 1450 the church was rebuilt in Perpendicular style. It has historical connections with Nelson, his chaplain being Dr Alexanda Scott, who was with him when he died and was also later a vicar of Southminster. Relics in the shape of a chart table, bookcase, chest commode and a fireplace were brought from the *Victory* and can be seen in the parish church today.

A good rail service to London's Liverpool Street is now electrified. The railway was opened on 1st June 1889, and centenary celebrations were organised by the Parish Council in 1989. The trains run every hour, and half hourly during rush hour. There are also buses to Maldon and Chelmsford.

Southminster has a fine King George V Playing Fields, well maintained by the Parish Council. Football, cricket, bowls, tennis and hockey are played. Once a year on the second Saturday in July, there is a Grand Flower Show, with exhibits in horticulture, flower arranging, cookery and handicrafts, showing in three large marquees. The show is known for its high standards. Entertainment is provided with Nicholls Fair and fireworks to round off the day.

Southminster has changed in that it was once a farming community. In the 1930s pea-picking was the chief way of earning extra money by the majority of the residents, supplemented by gypsies or travellers who came in brightly coloured caravans to stay in Battlesmoor, a small field on the northern outskirts of the village. Some of these people have now settled in the village and bought their own homes. The coming of the nuclear power station to Bradwell-on-Sea in the 1960s made a lot of difference in bringing work to members of the village. A large estate was built to house the workers who came from the North of England. Southminster still has a few farms, but the majority of residents now commute to London or Southend, or work in the light industrial factories.

The old school, a fine big building, was replaced by two new schools: St Leonard's junior school and the county infants school. Southminster has a good variety of shops, something for everyone including restaurants and pubs! It also has a medical centre with three doctors, a good post office and a chemist. Being rural, it has many walks and is noted for its fresh air. A busy village with much going on, many younger members are working hard to raise money for a swimming pool for the school.

Springfield 🌿

It has been said that the history of England is made up of the combined history of all the village churches and churchyards throughout the country. Springfield is proud to have played its part in that history, and hopefully will continue to do so for many years to come. Heroes of the battle of Waterloo lie in our churchyard. For more than 300 years the church bells have spoken of joy, or of sadness, on many great occasions, and have also joined in more local celebrations. On Tuesday 11th September 1990, for 44 minutes the evening air echoed across the village green and surrounding areas as the ringers rang 1,260 changes in a quarter peal of ten methods doubles to celebrate 75 years of the WI!

Although the village has been incorporated into the neighbouring town of Chelmsford, and virtually swamped by modern development, traces of the old village can still be seen. It is to be hoped that old inns like the Endeavour and the Tulip, and the cottages surrounding them, will stay with us for many more years and maintain the village identity. Stage coaches no longer change horses at the Plough Inn, but the car park there serves as assembly point for parties boarding more modern transport going to places far beyond the reach of the old system.

The old village school, founded by the church in 1812, became totally inadequate for the demands placed upon it, and has been replaced by a new interdenominational establishment, which it is hoped will carry on the educational tradition. Other schools have also been added to cater for the population explosion, and are already developing their own history.

Many new societies and associations have been founded in the Springfield area to serve the residents, whilst other older groups have developed to meet the revised needs of the area, thus continuing the traditions established over many centuries.

Stambourne 🦢

This rural village, first recorded in the Domesday Book, lies 50 miles to the north-east of London along the Roding road, 13 miles past Great Dunmow. Almost on the Suffolk border, it is ten miles from both Braintree and Sudbury. It has retained its sense of isolation by its being distant from any large centre or main route. It never had a railway station and the three now nearest to it are each some 20 miles away. The name, from the Anglo-Saxon roots 'stan' and 'burn' for stony brook, probably derives from the two large flat stepping stones in the rivulet below the church.

It is a street village on the H-plan. Its centre was devoid of substantial dwellings, other than two of the three manor houses and the old rectory, until after the Second World War. There are some 100 houses, of which about 30 are 17th century, though much altered; only eight are still thatched. The Hall and the Red Lion inn have still much Elizabethan oak construction. The inn was Moone Hall and housed the courts. The third manor, Grevill's, is now represented by a cottage, completely rebuilt when its moat was filled in, on the Yeldham road; it still has some massive old beams. The population of about 300 is well down on its Victorian peak of 577 at the 1871 census, but the three dozen horses are the highest number for decades – though only one of them is a carthorse and it is retired.

This remains mainly a farming village though only about a dozen men now work the machines. Many hedges have been destroyed, for there are no sheep and few cattle, but the field boundaries and names are much the same as at the 1837 Tithe survey. The livery stables and a transport company are the only other commerce. One only of the two inns still thrives and a part-time post office is the only survivor of the seven shops and two blacksmiths previously recorded. Amateur groups include the Stambourne Players, the Singers and a flourishing Canine Academy which both draw on neighbouring villages, and a recently revived Archery Club which meets on Sunday mornings in conformity with the Act of Henry VIII. The school closed in 1952 and like the benefice is now combined with Toppesfield. The schoolhouse is the village hall.

The finest monument is the impressive squat Norman tower of the church. It is mainly of local flint with Saxon traces and Roman bricks and was built soon after the Conquest, probably about 1085. The greatest treasure is the medieval stained glass in the east window with its complete heraldic pedigree of the MacWilliams. Sadly only two of their portraits survive in it, that of the donor's father Henry and of his mother, Elizabeth Hartishorn. There are also four painted portraits on the surviving left hand panels of the pre-Reformation part of the much restored screen – Sts George, Denys and Edmund and that of King Henry VI (1422–71), known as the Saint of Lancaster. The four right hand panels in St Andrew's, Great Yeldham are similarly painted but no connection has been traced. Recently the north chapel and the tower have been restored, the latter being refloored with ancient gravestones removed from the churchyard many years ago.

This was a Nonconformist area from well before the Civil War. The Rev Henry Havers BA, rector 1651–1662, formally founded the Stambourne Meeting when he was ejected under the Bartholomew Act. He left the village only for short periods and was preaching regularly here until his death in 1707. He was buried by the rector in the Anglican churchyard for the first chapel was not built until 1716/17 on a 'Parcell of the Wast' granted to his son, also Henry, in 1710. A third Henry continued the Presbyterian Ministry making a total family pastorate of 86 years. Clopton Havers MD, son of the first Henry, was the village's most famous resident. His name is known to every medical student from his description of the Haversian canals in bone and he was elected an early Fellow of the Royal Society during the presidency of Samuel Pepys. The present Congregational chapel dates from 1969 and is the third on the site.

There are two memorials to the First World War; a cross in the churchyard and a plaque on the wall of the chapel. Interestingly, the names on them differ since many of the Congregational members came from nearby Birdbrook.

Stambridge 🐚

There has always been a mill at Stambridge, dating back to Domesday times. Three hundred years on, the original mill was replaced and a tide mill was working there at the end of the 18th century.

In 1814 Rochford windmill was removed from its site south of Rochford village to Little Stambridge in its entirety. Further improvements were made during the 1840s by William Rankin, and a new wharf was constructed to accommodate vessels up to 120 tons. In 1868 Alfred and Hugh Rankin purchased the mill house, water mill and windmill, which was advertised as 'A Superior Water Corn Mill' of four floors, driven by six pairs of stones. It had a flour mill, bolter and dwelling house with an adjoining counting house. Ten years later this mill was burned down but was later replaced with a five storey building, steam driven with rollers instead of stones. The old tide mill was still standing at this time. The milling and agricultural business continued to flourish and was eventually sold to ABC Foods Ltd.

Originally there was a small settlement near the mill known as Winters Corner, with a row of clapboard cottages (now demolished), and a successful brewery which it is thought later became a factory. Later still this building became a private country dwelling house, passing into the possession of A M & H Rankin in 1936. During the Second World War this house, now known as 'The Old Brewery' was used as a hostel for the Women's Land Army, and after the war, during Mr Donald Tanton's residency, the name was changed to 'Winters'. Mr and Mrs Tanton would hold grand Christmas parties for the children of Stambridge school and church.

Nearby stands Rose Cottage now 400 years old, in perfect condition, privately owned and occupied. The cottage has very low ceilings with ancient beams, retaining its character and charm with a typical English country garden. Another old country house in this area is Broomhills. Although unoccupied at the present, with its future undecided, it was at one time the hub of Stambridge life.

There is still a small beach area near Stambridge mill which can be approached by public footpath from Mill Lane, skirting Rankin's cricket pitch, still widely used, passing in front of Broomhills, then down a lane to the river bank. It is a favourite spot for local people at weekends and school holidays, where families can picnic whilst children play. Although these days the younger generation may prefer more sophisticated pur-

207

suits, this area remains a quiet oasis approached only by foot. At the appropriate season of the year, sea lavender blooms in profusion giving an ethereal beauty at sunrise and sunset.

Whilst nearby areas such as Canewdon can lay claim to witches, Paglesham to smugglers etc, this area remains largely an agricultural and farming community of considerable interest with many social activities. Development is probably inhibited by the fact that it is Green Belt and bounded by the river Roach. It is possible to walk a considerable distance along the sea wall, which has great views for miles around.

Stanford Rivers ✤

Approaching the village from the south-east along the London road, one sees scattered cottages, several farmhouses and a lovely view on the right over the Roding valley. Waylett's, Mitchell's, Tracey's and Murrells are all 15th, 16th, 17th and early 18th century farmhouses, of timber and plaster construction, bricked in later. Close to each other on the right, are the Woodman and White Bear inns.

On the right again, as one enters Little End is Stanford Rivers House, 17th century with a 15th century core. The exterior imitation half-timbering was inserted during this century. Considerable interior altera-tions have taken place over the years. There are two water wells, one outside and the other inside. On the first floor landing is an old priest hole. It was the home for 40 years of Isaac Taylor the second, who was the son of the famous dissenting preacher Isaac Taylor, minister at the Congregational church in Ongar from 1811 to 1829. Isaac was himself a famous artist, engraver and author, and is buried in St Margaret's churchyard.

The road to Toot Hill is flanked on both sides by farmland, and there are distant views of old farmhouses, and the spire of St Margaret's church stabbing the sky from its nest of mature trees. St Margaret's was built around 1150, and has been in the gift of the Duchy of Lancaster since 1557. It is a Norman-style church with a 15th century bay roof. It has several rows of ancient oak pews, and there is a gallery at the west end of the nave that incorporates nine carved traceries from the former chancel screen, and the Arms of the House of Lancaster.

'Noel Gay', born Reginald M Armitage and the composer of *The Lambeth Walk* and *Run, Rabbit Run*, popular songs from musical comedies of the 1930s, is buried in the churchyard, and there are still people who can remember the influx of showbusiness personalities attending his funeral in 1954.

Stanford Rivers Hall is an early 19th century building on the site of the baronial hall that in the 11th century had been in the estate of Earl Eustace of Boulogne. Its garden abutts the churchyard.

Continuing towards Toot Hill, the road now becomes School Road . .. very confusing for outside visitors and delivery men. The change reflects a time when the village school occupied a site on the left side of the road. An old Victorian drinking fountain is all that remains of the school. The site is now used by travelling people.

Stewart's and Blake Farm are two more of the farmhouses of the parish. Both are 18th century buildings on the site of older houses. Bugle Cottage, standing near the small surviving fragment of village green, is an amalgamation of three 17th century cottages with possibly some medieval features.

In his manuscript history of the parish, the Rev H Tattum, mid 19th century rector of St Margaret's church, wrote:

'It is sometimes possible to see St Paul's and the hills of Kent from Toot Hill.'

A somewhat doubtful claim, but at over 300 ft, Toot Hill is certainly the highest part of the parish. Strung out along the Epping Road, it has several interesting houses, notably Does Farm, a 16th century farmhouse with a cruciform chimney stack with five polygonal shafts.

Opposite the Green Man, which occupies a central position in the hamlet, is a lane leading to Clatterford End. The village hall stands just off the start of the lane that then winds through farmland and high hedges to reach the Drill House, an old inn on the north-eastern edge of the parish. It then joins Mutton Row, a lovely old lane that returns after a mile of winding through farmland to St Margaret's church. On its journey it passes Newhouse Farm, and its fine old farmhouse, with its three 18th century wig cupboards and profusion of old oak beams. Clark's Farm occupies high ground on the left side of the lane on the site of one of the few Essex buildings mentioned in the Domesday Book.

On the western border of the parish the Central Line stations of North Weald and Blakehall fringe Ongar Park Wood. An old Roman road to Dunmow has been traced across this area, and legend has it that a ghostly legion can sometimes be seen marching through! Closer to our time, Blake Hall station gained some fleeting notoriety when John Betjeman, the late Poet Laureate, said that he would love to retire to it as its stationmaster!

Stansted Mountfitchet 🐿️

The village of Stansted Mountfitchet is first recorded as a Saxon earthworks which became a Norman castle of motte and bailey construction, and took its name from the Norman family who became its overlords. It was first recorded in the Domesday Book under the Roman name of Stansteda. The restored Saxon castle is now used as a tourist attraction, and for educational visits by children from all over Essex. The original centre of Stansted is now known as Lower Street, and was the shopping area in medieval times. Many fine Tudor buildings remain.

Ascending Church Hill to the east, leads to St Mary's church, a fine Norman building standing on a Roman site; it contains many outstanding features from the 13th, 14th and 17th centuries, together with rich furnishings and carved monuments. The most imposing is the statue of Sir Thomas Middleton; made of marble and 20ft high, it was erected after his death in 1631.

Behind the church is Stansted Hall, rebuilt in 1875 in the style of a folly with interesting architectural features. Occupied by the Findlay family for many years, it is now used as the Arthur Findlay College for the Advancement of Physical Science.

In Cambridge Road, a large building on the right, now being converted, was originally 'Green's Stores', which provided all the necessary commodities for the local population. These ranged from ladies corsets, hats, household linen and groceries (you could watch the sugar being weighed and packed into blue paper bags, and see the apprentices being taught to use the wooden 'pats' to shape the butter), to shoes, candles and menswear. The bacon and cheeses were stored in the large cellars below the shop. These were intriguing to walk through, and at one end there was a small counter with a window at pavement level, where the grocery manager used to grind the coffee in an antiquated machine, by turning the very large handle. The Store employed a large number of people, and it was seldom that people went further afield for their shopping.

From this Store, all the local villages used to be served, not only with groceries but any other goods that might be required. At first it was delivered by horse-drawn vans, then later motorised. The vans would visit each village in turn on a weekly basis. This was about the only contact a good number of these people had, outside their own village. It was part of everyone's life for many years. The light four-wheeled carts

210

were drawn by high stepping ponies, and the rattle of the iron-clad wheels as they returned at the end of the day through the archway on the right, is not to be forgotten. The stables at the rear are gone, and the shop is now converted into units.

Further along the Cambridge Road, many of the old village houses are in the process of modernisation. Here on the green are comfortable iron seats where one can rest and contemplate. Standing back on the left is Hargrave Hall, which was part of the Stansted Hall estate. It has since served its time as a hostel, convalescent home, orphanage, and a home for handicapped children.

To the south can be seen the old windmill, built in 1787 with bakehouse and malthouse. The latter was destroyed by fire, but the floodlit windmill, recently restored, is visited by many thousands of visitors each year, and is now listed as an ancient monument. A Roman Catholic church stands on the site of the miller's villa. Nearby is the Old Bell inn on Silver Street, once a famous coaching inn and hostelry. It continues to serve as a modern hotel and restaurant, but is still reputed to be haunted.

Still in Silver Street can be seen a metal sign marking the original southern parish boundary, and depicting the Norman Mountfitchet Arms. A similar one marks the northern boundary.

Following Silver Street past many old cottages and stately houses, alas now converted into modern units, we pass Blyth Dairy, which took its name from the 1st Baron Blyth of Stansted Mountfitchet in 1850, who was responsible for much of the restoration work to the windmill and its nearby buildings. We now reach the crossroads and fountain. Here a resident remembers an iron milestone cover, which protected the old milestone against passing wagon wheels.

Stansted is probably more famous in recent years as London's Third Airport, opened by Her Majesty Queen Elizabeth in March 1991. In 1940 it originated as one of the longest runways in Great Britain, for the forward use of heavy bombers. After the war it was brought into use as a commercial airport, in the main, for cargo. An interesting museum and display can be seen at the airport, depicting these scenes. It is currently the most advanced design for an airport terminal, incorporating a direct rail link to London and Cambridge, and direct slip road access to the M11 London-Cambridge motorway, together with moving walkways from concourse to aircraft for speedy passenger use.

When the Great Cambridge Railway was built in the 19th century, linking Cambridge with London via Stansted, its impact destroyed much

211

of the close-knit rural atmosphere. Today with its nearby motorway and airport, it may not be long before Stansted Mountfitchet loses its village status for ever.

Stebbing

The village of Stebbing is said to owe its name to the Saxon tribe of Stybba. The great earth mound which they fortified still exists and, today in spring, is splendid with daffodils.

Doubtless in those times it had its odd characters, but there have also been a few from the last hundred years or so. One such was a local farmer who, driving his pony and trap from the village, asked his passenger if he had ever before been thrown out of such a vehicle as his. The passenger was a chapel minister who had that day preached locally. His reply was 'No'. 'Dammit then, you shall be', said the farmer. The horse's head was immediately pulled sharp left. It made an effort to jump the ditch. The trap did not and out went the reverend. He was picked up, brushed down and transported home. It is said that, at some time later, the farmer caused the death of his own sister by insisting on driving through a swollen river ford.

Another character, less outwardly respectable than the farmer, was of gypsy stock. On summer evenings he would be at the main roadside holding up a rabbit or hare. The motorists who stopped for one were asked half a crown and there would be an immediate offer to put the rabbit in the car boot. Many boots were opened and slammed but few rabbits went inside.

1946 was the year that the national press descended in force on the village. The Brigadier's daughter, pretty and talented, married a gypsy, a pleasant, uncomplicated and charming fellow. Many years after, when she died, Arthur left the house and lived in the shed.

Before the Second World War, whist drives and concert parties were always a feature. The Stebbing Players put on classics and the 'Stebbing-oes' comedy revue. One Stone Age scene was disrupted when a character came on stage and put his bare foot on a drawing pin. Nowadays the famous 'Stebbing Elizabethan Fayre' is held every four years and attracts thousands of people. The main concern of the Stebbing Society is the preservation of the desirable features and character of the village. It also arranges concerts, orchestral and choral of very high quality, in the beautiful 14th century church with its rare stone screen. The acoustics complement the music.

Henry de Vere Stacpoole lived by the church and wrote a number of successful novels including the famous *The Blue Lagoon*. His little workroom is still there, attached to the house. He could quite often be seen in the street, practising golf swings with his walking-stick; there was little danger from traffic. Mr H G Wells, who lived at Little Easton, was an occasional visitor.

Stebbing, though small, had its war-time quota of bombs. A thatched barn was burned to the ground and a time-bomb demolished some houses where now is the bowling green. The Tudor Parsonage Farm was used by the RASC and an American airbase for fighter-bombers was built on farmland on the village outskirts. One runway is still used for private flying. After the war, the village gradually settled back into normality, the RASC and the Naafi left Parsonage Farm and the US Air Force left Andrews Field. Members of the Forces were demobbed and returned home to Stebbing, though sadly some did not.

Sometime after 1950 new people began to move into the village when several new estates were built. Stebbing is a place where a newcomer is not regarded as an intruder and most residents who stay become involved in one or many of the social and sporting activities within the village, although few are employed here.

So far, Stebbing has escaped wholesale development and in 1986, thanks to the efforts of the Stebbing Society, successfully defeated a plan to extract gravel from a large area on the edge of the village, but with the expansion of Stansted Airport some extra housing is inevitable. However, whatever may happen, Stebbing is still a very pleasant place in which to live.

Stisted

Stisted is situated just outside Braintree in north Essex; a typical village of its type with its church, church school and village shop and a couple of hundred houses representing a wide spectrum of society. Some locals still remain here but there has been an influx of newcomers in recent years which has altered the face of the village to a certain extent.

However, just over 100 years ago in 1881 records show an interesting picture of the village and its structure. There were 174 houses, ten of them unoccupied, containing a population of 381 males and 364 females.

It was almost self sufficient and for many there will have been no need to go into Braintree for necessities. It had a miller to grind the corn (no baker, as housewives made their own bread and cakes in those days), a wheelwright, two blacksmiths, a grocer, a butcher, a publican, a postmistress, a cooper, six boot and shoe makers, a builder, two painters, a bricklayer and two carpenters. The innkeeper was also a blacksmith and a beerhouse keeper. No undertaker, this service was probably provided by the builder as often happens even to this day. No greengrocer either, as much of the fresh produce was grown on the allotments or large vegetable gardens. Travelling salesmen and pedlars would also provide many of the miscellaneous household items which might be needed.

A study of male occupations shows that no less than 84 heads of households were agricultural labourers with 77 of their sons engaged in the same work, a huge figure for what is a small village. Next in numbers came 14 full-time farmers with a few combining farming and another operation. This was then followed by eight gardeners.

The social structure of the village also throws up some fascinating insights. At the top were the occupants of the 'big house', Stisted Hall, where resided Paul Onley, 87 and his wife Jane, 63 and their daughter Maria, 23 as well as two grandchildren. At Stisted Hall as well as the family, no less than twelve servants lived – a governess, a butler, two footmen, a groom, a housekeeper, six assorted maids as well as a ladies maid. At the lodge leading into the estate lived a woodsman and his wife registered as a lodgekeeper, and probably most of the eight gardeners were employed on the estate, as well as a shepherd and two gamekeepers.

At the rectory lived the Rev Charles Tarver, his wife Sarah and a niece, Katherine Tarver with a staff of three servants. The rector also farmed 155 acres employing seven men and two boys.

The schoolmaster, William Rutherford, lived alone in the school. There was also a schoolmistress and a pupil teacher who lived at home. John Cooper, the miller employed three men and he no doubt had frequent contact with Samuel Rayner, a corn merchant who lived at Vine Cottage. There was also a thatcher whose son worked with him, and an organist. The police constable's son was listed as being a railway clerk which must have provided some difficulty in getting to and from Braintree.

Very few of the married women had occupations outside the home and those that did were recorded as laundresses (two), tailoress, charwoman, dressmaker, nurse and one strawplaiter. Most of these tasks could have been carried out at home so probably very few actually worked elsewhere. Apart from these few the large families of the time would have prevented housewives from finding time outside the home to earn something to alleviate their conditions. Five, six and seven children was common enough at this time. Consider the case of Robert, 47, and his wife Hannah Weaver, 41, who already had ten children living at home ranging from 20 years down to eleven months. Returns show that it was not unusual for women to be bearing children into their mid and late forties.

Before leaving this brief review of the people of Stisted it is worth dwelling on the last entry on the census forms. All places seem to have their odd man out who doesn't fit into the normal categories. So what do we make of 67 year old William, shown as being a general labourer, ie odd job man always willing to earn a few bob. Often very well known to the local PC, gamekeepers and local magistrate and on very familiar terms with the publican. His place of abode was given as the 'hay-loft' so we may be sure that William was right at the bottom of the social ladder.

Stondon Massey 🐝

Stondon Massey, two miles south-east of Chipping Ongar, is a very small rural parish. It has a pub, the Bricklayers Arms, a shop and post office. About 700 people live there and the parish consists only of 1,127 acres lying partly in the Roding valley. The village had a brief moment of publicity in 1986 when part of a Stansted-bound plane fell into one of its fields.

Entering the village over Hallsford Bridge from the direction of Chipping Ongar, the road begins its gentle ascent past Little Myles, one of Stondon's 15 listed buildings, to the top of the gravelly Church Hill that gives the village its Saxon name; stone-dun meaning stony hill. The name 'de Marcy' (Massey) was added after the Conquest by a Norman family who held land in the area. The very hill that gave Stondon its name was recently under threat, for beneath its gravel layer lies London clay which can be made into aggregate. A simple country brickfield, near Hallsford Bridge on the edge of the parish, has gradually, over the past few decades, been turned into a substantial industrial complex producing 'Leca'.

The London clay is first excavated and 'minced', then baked in a huge rotating kiln. The heated clay expands into Lightweight Expanded Clay Aggregate, hence the name Leca, which is then sent by road to other factories where it has various uses, the main one being the construction of lightweight building blocks. In 1989 the large company who now own the factory, submitted plans to extend their clay excavations and rubbish tipping by a further 88 acres right into the heart of Stondon Massey itself. After a three week public inquiry in February 1990, the decision by the Secretary of State for the Environment accorded with the views of the local population; that the requirement for Leca did not warrant the detrimental impact on the environment and local residents. The lovely view from Church Hill over Green Belt land, which is also designated as a special landscape area, thankfully has been saved for the enjoyment of future generations.

From the top of this hill, overlooking the river Roding valley and Stondon's oldest manor house, Stondon Hall, stands the small church of St Peter and St Paul built around 1100. The Norman builders who erected the church managed to incorporate in their construction some thin Roman tiles. A band of these tiles, in the typical zig-zag pattern of the Normans, can be seen embedded in the mortar at eaves height on the west wall. Other Roman relics have also been found in the area. Half a Roman coin was found on nearby farmland a few years ago, and, in 1886, when a shallow gravel pit was opened to the north-east of the church, some workmen discovered seven grey clay urns in an oblong trench eight ft long and two ft wide about a foot below the surface.

The lidless urns, containing a powdery ash substance, lay in a row at the bottom of the reddish coloured trench. Unfortunately, instead of gently trying to raise one or two urns intact, the workmen who found them impatiently broke them up with their picks to see what was underneath. The rector of that time, the Rev Reeve, who recorded this in his history of Stondon Massey in 1900, took two surviving fragments of the urns to the British Museum, and was told that they probably came from Roman burial urns. The British Museum authorities also suggested that from the twisted irregular curve of one of the pieces it appeared that the urns might have been crudely and hurriedly made, perhaps on the spot. Although their origins will never be known for sure, we should perhaps be grateful that at least the finding of the burial urns so close to the church was carefully recorded.

In Elizabethan times, William Byrd, composer of some of our most beautiful religious music, lived at Stondon Place for over 30 years until his death in 1623. In 1717, 78 years after William Byrd's death, Stondon Place was completely rebuilt. Unfortunately this building was destroyed by fire in 1877, after which the present Georgian-style house was built.

It was at Stondon Place in 1841 that Stondon's ghost decided to make his presence felt once more.

Jordan's ghost, as it was known locally, had been freely walking in Stondon since the rather difficult burial of Mr Jordan, churchwarden and medical man in 1754. Tradition has it that after Mr Jordan's funeral, at which eleven clergy assisted, the sexton peered into the Jordan vault to make sure that all was well. To his horror, he found it was not! For there, outside the coffin, lay the still and motionless corpse of Mr Jordan. Eventually the unfortunate remains were securely chained down. Such an unusual burial was, perhaps, bound to provide a ghost, although Rev Reeve who recorded this story explains that it was not uncommon practice in those days of body-snatching to chain down coffins. Wild tales inevitably were soon rife in the district. Jordan's ghost had been seen by terrified passers-by 'hovering' in the churchyard; a man reported that he had encountered it on his way back from having his scythe sharpened in Ongar. As he tried to raise his scythe to decapitate the apparition, his arm remained 'poised in the air paralysed'. Stories of the ghost abounded well into the 1800s.

However, no more has been heard of the ghost since 1845 when he was last seen flitting near Stondon's whipping post on the small grass triangle at the junction of Chivers Road. The whipping post, with its irons now sadly missing, still exists, but of Jordan's ghost nothing more remains. Or does it?

Tendring ⚜

The village of Tendring is a scattered one, set in an agricultural area of arable farms to the east of the historic town of Colchester.

The parish church of St Edmund, named after Edmund, king of East Anglia who was martyred at Framlingham in AD 870, stands in what was the centre of the village. It is an impressive building standing in a prominent position and surrounded by beautiful rural countryside. The church itself is built of rubble and stone in the transition style from Early English to Decorated, though it is possible that some sort of church was in existence prior to the days of St Edmund. The walls have been covered with plaster, and the dressings are of limestone. The roofs are tiled. Recently a large sum of money was required to retile the roof and replace some of the timbers.

The school has always had a close association with the church and quite often the Chairman of Managers has been the rector of the time, the most recent being the late Rev M P McCready MA, who died in October 1945. He was also Platoon Commander in the Home Guard and the training meetings were often held at the rectory, although they usually ended at the Crown where all, including the rector, enjoyed a pint (or two).

The old Crown is now Crown House and a private dwelling. It was built about 1600 as a small coaching inn on the road from Thorpe-le-Soken to Ipswich. It is believed that the inner walls were so built to hide smuggled goods. As one might expect, this is a listed building.

Just across the road from the pub stood the blacksmith's shop and forge, where Charlie Marven shod horses from the surrounding farms, repaired and sharpened harrows and carried out repairs of all kinds. He also had the job of gravedigger across the road in the churchyard and it was said by some that when he saw any newcomers to the village he would make a mental note for future use.

Horses were of course the main source of power on the farms in those days and one well known local character tells of the time when he and the governor were carting muck with two horses and tumbrils and using a trace horse in the field, which was on a steep slope. When he arrived with his load in the field he found the governor's tumbril, load and horse had turned completely upside-down on the hillside, the horse with its feet in the air and unable to move. The trace horse was just standing patiently with the trace chains crossed, and when released simply trotted off home, leaving the two men to disentangle the other horse. Those who used horses for this job in their youth will be well able to picture the scene, but what a pity that no camera was available at the time.

The stone spire of the church was built in 1877 through the generosity of John Cardinall, lord of the manor and owner of a large part of the parish. The Tendring Hall estate was sold by auction on 25th June 1910, in 41 lots situated in the parishes of Tendring, Weeley and Thorpe-le-Soken and four lots at Great Clacton, in all 984 acres.

The present Hall was built on the site of an earlier house that was used as a hunting lodge by King Stephen. The gardens, laid out by the famous landscape gardener Percy Cain in the late 1920s, have as their centrepiece a magnificent Cedar of Lebanon which is about 600 years old, close by two lakes and flanked by a really wonderful display of rhododendrons, azaleas, other shrubs and trees. Over the years these gardens have been open to the public, by kind permission of the owners and in aid of charity, on one or two days and are well worth a visit if the opportunity arises. Sometimes the annual flower festival in the church is held on the same weekend, and as the two sites are only about 300 yards apart, it contributes to a very enjoyable afternoon.

In 1863 it was proposed that a railway should be built from Mistley to Thorpe-le-Soken and thence to Walton-on-the-Naze, passing through the parishes of Tendring and Kirby-le-Soken. It was to be called the 'Mistley, Thorpe and Walton Railway' and, although work was commenced, the project was abandoned some six years later. Sections of an embankment can still be seen today in Tendring parish.

Terling 🐚

Early man wandered up the river Ter, found very good springs here and settled. By 1066 there were two water mills, and slowly the village grew around the river. It is only a little winding river of 13 miles, but the banks are beautiful, especially in summer.

Villages, like human beings, are individuals, no two are alike and Terling is a village of outstanding beauty. It is seven miles from Chelmsford and if approached from Hatfield Peverel along a tree-lined country road where the cows graze on either side in the meadows, you will feel a sense of peace and tranquillity and find it difficult to realise you have come only three miles from the busy A12 road.

This peace and beauty enhances the rustic architecture to perfection. It is rare today to find a village so carefully maintained, particularly the preservation of the original features of the houses and cottages, many of which date from the 16th century.

This was a time of prosperity and progress when the Church Green boasted a brewery and a malting house, which must have added to the gaiety of the annual fair and helped the trade of the thriving market, both of which took place on the green. Today there are houses only on the south side of the green, some very early examples, with small windows and low roofs.

Tudor House standing on the east end of the green is a wonderful example of 16th century domestic architecture, with exposed timbers, two cross-gables and a large west chimney stack decorated with a blank stepped gable. Here, there is the original plaque required when insurance was introduced.

Terling is fortunate in having four pleasant greens, two on the east side of the river and two on the west. On Flacks Green a large attractive house called New House was built in 1726. It is surrounded by a beech hedge and a fine old brick wall. Inside the house is a beautiful Jacobean fireplace, thought to be the only relic of the Old Palace which stood in grounds behind the church.

On the site of the Old Palace now stands Terling Place, a fine late Georgian country house built between 1771–1780. The garden is full of lovely trees and shrubs which have been planted through the years and is carpeted with snowdrops, spring bulbs and dwarf cyclamen.

Some people in the village, now in their late eighties and who were born here, have such vivid memories of days gone by. Some memories of happy days and some of hardship and toil. One lady, a member of the WI for many years, remembers that before the First World War when King Edward VII was on the throne, nearly every child in the village attended Sunday school. Each child looked forward to the one outing during the summer, the wonderful Sunday school treat. Girls would be dressed in their best serge frocks, spotless white pinafores, long black stockings and shining black lace-up boots. The boys would be looking as smart as their mothers could make them!

For some children, however, life was hard. An old man remembers that he was twelve years old on Maundy Thursday, the day he left school, and on Easter Monday he became a farm worker and was sent into a 20 acre field, alone, scaring rooks off the growing corn and at other times picking up stones. For him, the day was long and the work hard.

An old man who died recently in his 97th year, had been a gamekeeper all his life as his father before him. He worked side by side with nature, out in the fields and woods and his knowledge of birds, wild life of all sorts, trees and plants was endless. When he retired he moved to a small bungalow near the ford and here he tended his garden with loving care. He grew flowers, large vegetables and good fruit and when the Harvest Thanksgiving Service was held in the parish church each year in September, he filled his wheelbarrow with the best produce from his garden, pushed it down the hill and across the meadows to the church. Here he filled the space in front of the door of the south porch with the fruits of his labours, arranging it all so lovingly in thanksgiving to God. A window in the church which has recently been restored bears his name, together with a pheasant engraved in the glass, in memory of a true countryman.

From the churchyard there is a splendid view across the valley of the river, up to the cricket field and beyond. There are many sporting activities in the village and the cricket club has a delightful setting for its pitch and a thatched roof to its pavilion. The Cricket Club was founded about 1881 as during that year records show that 'As a cricket match was being held in the village, there would be no scripture lesson that afternoon and school dismissed at two pm'.

One of the interesting features of Terling is its smock mill, now restored and turned into a very attractive residence. Up until 1950 the mill ground the corn from the farms and gleanings from the cottagers but this came to a sad end when by a tragic accident the miller's coat became entangled in the machinery and he was killed. In the mid 1930s the mill was used in a film called *Oh! Mr Porter* starring Will Hay. The camera crews spent a fortnight here on location, the people in the village, especially the children, being most amused by their antics.

Thaxted

It is September in the year of Our Lord 1578 and Thaxted is in a festive mood. The cobbled streets have been cleansed of sewage and litter, the medieval timber-framed houses have been smartened and decorated and people are wearing their Sunday clothes. Queen Elizabeth I is on her way to Horham Hall, the home of Sir John Cutte, lord of the manor of Horham, and will pass through the town.

The Queen had been staying at Long Melford Hall and was on her way back to London from her summer progress. Every summer the court would leave the heat and smell of London to find some measure of safety from the plague by travelling the countryside. This was not the Queen's first visit to Thaxted. Lord Burghley suggests in a letter 'from the court at Horam' that she had stayed there in 1571, but the visit of 1578 is recorded in the Acts of the Privy Council, which sat in Thaxted.

First the cart teams would be seen arriving in the town, about 400 of them, amounting to some 2,400 horses, carrying her baggage. The movables included large amounts of furniture, canopied beds and mattresses, chairs, carpets, mirrors and silver warming pans and many chests containing up to 40 gowns in each, and numerous other changes of clothes. On her visit to Kenilworth in 1575 it is recorded that during her stay she wore more than 50 changes of clothes.

Then would come the retinue of over 400 people. Lords of the court followed by trumpeters, soldiers and huntsmen; members of parliament in long red coats with rabbit fur lining; two courtiers, one carrying the Queen's mantle and the other her hat. There was the chancellor of the

Thaxted windmill and almshouses

realm, the vice chancellor – the beautiful Sir Christopher Hatton; the treasurer and the secretary – Mr Wilson; the Earls of Warwick and Leicester. Then came the Queen's horse led by a gentleman, the trapping, saddle and bridle were gold and covered in pearls and precious stones. Now came the Queen, perhaps in a carrying chair – a half canopied bed – covered with gold and silver. She wore a red velvet mantle lined with ermine and a crown on her head. Or she may have been in a coach, a heavy wooden body lashed with leather straps to the unsprung axle, luxuriously fitted with canopies and cushions.

Along Newbiggen Street the procession would have come, past the Guildhall of the Guild of St John the Baptist which housed the newly formed grammar school. Down the hill, past the church where the bells would be pealing out a welcome and into the market square. There the 2,000 strong population of Thaxted, and probably many from the outlying villages would have assembled to greet her. On the steps of the Cutlers Guildhall would be the mayor and local gentry to present a formal welcome and perhaps to offer a gift. The boys from the grammar school would make a speech in Latin. In the background the rest of the population cheered, thrusting forward their children for the Queen to touch, or to give her nosegays.

The procession would leave the town travelling down Park Street, past the newly built Park Farm surrounded by walls made from stones taken from the dissolved Tilty Abbey, and along the three miles to Horham Hall.

The house that Queen Elizabeth would have seen was much larger than it is today. 'Horam Haule, a very sumptuous house. A goodly pond or lake by it and faire parkes there about', wrote Leland in the early 1500s. The house is one of the finest examples of a red brick Elizabethan manor house. The bricks are laid in English bond with diagonals of patterns of blue bricks and in the middle a towering oriel window. Two flanking wings ran down to the moat linked by a gatehouse across the entrance, but these had been demolished by the 18th century to make the house a more manageable size. The tower could have been built by Sir John Cutte so that the Queen could watch hawking in the park.

The court stayed there for nine days. Two privy council meetings were held and she received the envoy of the Duke of Anjou, who was seeking her hand in marriage. On Sunday she and the court would have attended church, perhaps in the magnificent parish church in Thaxted which has altered little over the centuries.

The court would have eaten a huge variety of meats, chickens and 22 different species of birds, fine white bread, tarts, jellies of many kinds and innumerable quantities of very sweet and highly spiced puddings that so delighted the Elizabethan palate.

It is rumoured that her visit ruined her host financially and in 1599 John Cutte was forced to sell the house.

The house still stands on the road between Broxted and Thaxted. It is privately owned, but in the summer is occasionally open to the public. If you go you will be able to see the room Queen Elizabeth slept in, but not her bed as she brought that with her.

Theydon Bois 🍃

Theydon, once a mere hamlet in a forest clearing, has always had close associations with the neighbouring forest, once the Forest of Waltham, now known as Epping Forest. The name is probably of Saxon origin – 'Thugn Dun' or Thane's Hill, the domain of a Saxon thane. After the

Norman Conquest the manor was divided into three – Theydon Bois, Theydon Garnon and Theydon Mount. All three manors appear in the Domesday Book.

In 1305, possibly following hospitality received during a tour of Essex, Edward I granted a charter to Hugh Gernoun, of the manor of Theydon Garnon, to hold a weekly fair and market, and for he and his heirs to 'have warren in all their demesne lands of the said manor' for ever. The market was never held, but the fair was abolished in 1872 because it was frequented by rowdy elements. A replica of the charter hangs in Theydon Bois village hall, but the original is held by the Essex Record Office.

The original parish church of Theydon Bois stood about one mile south of the centre of the village, and next to the original manor, Theydon Hall. The Hall was in earlier times known as Gaunts House because John of Gaunt, son of Edward III and father of Henry IV, lived there. The name is also perpetuated in Gaunts Wood and Gaunt Cottage. The present Hall is early 18th century. Another historic house within the parish is Parsonage Farm, where it is believed clergy from St Bartholomew's in Smithfield in the City of London, to whom the parish church was gifted in the 13th century, would stay overnight when attending the church.

The old 13th century church was demolished in 1843 and replaced by a new church more central to the village, at a cost of £2,231. This church was consecrated in 1844, but because of poor construction and weakened foundations it was pulled down in 1850 and the present church built (at a cost of £1,574!). The church stands in a delightful setting surrounded by forest land.

One of the oldest buildings in the village is the Bull Inn, which has probably been an inn for about 300 years, although a much more ancient building stood on the site, called the 'Tylehouse'. This building was located close to a gate into the forest, known as Theydon Green Gate. Another of the village's four inns is the Sixteen String Jack, named after a notorious highwayman of the early 18th century, called Jack Rann. His title arises from his appearance in the dock at the Old Bailey with 16 coloured ribbons tied at the knees of his breeches.

In the 19th century the lords of the manor were a family called Hall-Dare. They planted the avenue of 62 oak trees across the green, many of which still stand, despite suffering severe damage in the gales of October 1987. The manorial rights were purchased by Mr Gerald Buxton, of Birch Hall, in 1900. Birch Hall, recently demolished for redevelopment, was built in 1892 near the site of a far more ancient building. An earlier occupant of the old Birch Hall was Edward Elrington, chief butler to Edward VI, Mary and Elizabeth I.

A building which stands in front of the churchyard of St Mary's parish church was the original village school, built in 1840. This building was enlarged and extended over several years, but ceased to function as a school in 1959 when the present primary school in Orchard Drive was opened. The old building is now occupied by the College of Preceptors, a body concerned with the training and qualification of teachers. Another educational establishment in Theydon Bois is Wansfell College, a residential college which holds a wide variety of adult courses in all fields.

There is little doubt that the present situation of Theydon Bois owes much to the preservation of Epping Forest, dedicated in 1882 by Queen Victoria for 'public recreation and enjoyment'. This extremely attractive village, with about 4,500 inhabitants, plays host to many visitors in the summer, driving out to enjoy picnicking on the expansive green, still officially part of the Forest and the responsibility of the Epping Forest Conservators. Modern development has inevitably crept in, but the local Parish Council and the Rural Preservation Society do their best to ensure that the rural aspect of Theydon Bois, less than 20 miles from the centre of London, is jealously guarded, surrounded as it is by the Green Belt and large areas of farmland.

Tillingham ❧

Tillingham is in the Dengie Hundred and lies on the edge of the Essex marshland. It is the oldest manor held by the Dean and Chapter of St Paul's. In early Saxon times King Ethelbert of Kent gave this manor to St Paul's, who have owned land in the village ever since, a fact recorded in the Guinness Book of Records. The many white weatherboarded houses are an attractive feature of the village.

Parts of the parish church of St Nicholas are Norman, the chancel and sanctuary 13th century. In 1708 the church was rebuilt through a rate levy on the population. It was again restored in 1807, and the tower partly rebuilt in 1888 after being struck by lightning. There is also a Congregational church and a Peculiar People's chapel. The former Baptist and Primitive Methodist chapels have been converted into dwelling houses.

The village school was built in 1868. It came to the end as an all age school in 1958 when children over eleven years of age were transferred to St Peter's school in Burnham.

An important feature is the village green, once an acre in size, now divided by diagonal roads and known as The Square. It has been the venue for many events and seen many changes. Here cricket was played, water fetched from the pump and fights took place frequently. A petition from the villagers resulted in the closure of the Cock Inn; later it became the doctor's surgery, where you could also get a tooth pulled out in an emergency.

Once the green was the site for visiting pedlar's fairs, the celebrations of the Silver Jubilee and the Coronation, Nativity plays and village festivals. It was the meeting place of the local Hunt, and during one very severe winter when it was blowing a gale from the east, the Square was full of geese blown in from the North Sea. Shops surrounded the Square; two general stores which sold just about everything, a sweet shop and newsagent's. Now all that remains is the Fox and Hounds public house and a weekly visit from the mobile vans – the library, butcher, fishmonger and fish and chips.

Toppesfield & Gainsford End ஜ

When William the Conqueror had the Domesday survey made there were about 70 people living in this parish; in its heyday, according to the 1841 census, there were 1,071 populating the village. Now there are about 500 inhabitants living in just over 200 dwellings. Almost all of the working population commutes to work in London or towns within easy reach. Few of the inhabitants work on the 3,200 acres of productive agricultural land. The village has the appearance of having been built in about the last 60 years, as surprisingly few of the old timbered houses have survived; those that have are splendid examples of houses built about the 16th century.

There is a multiplicity of organisations serving the varied interests of the population, such as the annual flower show, the Garden Society, the Good Companions, the Women's Institute, the playgroup, the toddlers group, and such like. All of these organisations are able to function efficiently because the village has a particularly good village hall, purpose built in 1961. There is also a village school serving 79 pupils, with a staff of four full time teachers and two part time. The school was built in 1856 and opened in 1857. Some of the pupils are recruited from adjoining villages.

The religious life of the village is well provided for with the availability of a church and a chapel. There is evidence that in the middle of the 18th century there was a strong movement of nonconformism. According to a report by the Toppesfield parson to the Bishop in 1766, the majority of the village population supported the nonconformists and few attended the church. There is clear evidence which dates a chapel as having been built between 1813 and 1830 and that building is still in existence, known as the schoolroom. The present chapel was built in 1881.

Toppesfield has not always been a peaceful village. In 1612 there was a witch-hunt in the village. One Alice Batty, a spinster, was brought before the court and charged with bewitching three people. However, she managed to convince the court of her innocence and she was discharged. In 1775 Samuel Norfolk became infatuated with a maid of the house and as a consequence he drowned his wife in the farm pond. He was found guilty of murder and hanged.

In 1551 the rector here was the Rev Thomas Donnell, who married when the restrictions on clergy marrying were removed after the ousting of the Roman Catholic church by Henry VIII. However, with the advent of Queen Mary to the throne there was a renewal of the restrictions. As a result Thomas Donnell fled to Frankfurt to avoid being burned at the stake, as happened to many of his colleagues. In due course he returned to Toppesfield.

In the first half of the 19th century there was sporadic outbursts of setting fire to farm ricks. Substantially this was due to the unrest created by there being such poverty around the countryside, and no doubt sometimes to settle grudges. In 1835 a Toppesfield man was charged at Chelmsford Assizes with setting fire to ricks belonging to a Mr Daire. He was found guilty and hanged before a crowd of about 1,200.

The past is not without its humour as is exemplified by an article which appeared in the *Gentleman's Magazine* for 1794:

'February, 1794, at Sible Hedingham, County Essex, Francis Chatter, by his own desire, he was carried to Toppesfield in a hearse, followed by five carts, by his own relations to the Green Man (a house he formerly frequented) and placed on trestles in the middle of the parlour; the attendants stood round and spent a guinea (the coffin serving as a table) and after several of the relations, in the joy and loyalty of their hearts, had sung God Save the King, he was interred in the churchyard.'

Twinstead 🦢

Twinstead is an attractive little village which can be found four and a half miles north of Halstead on the Essex – Suffolk border. The main part of the village and hamlet lies just off the A131 Halstead – Sudbury road.

The Church of St John the Evangelist is a small red brick building dating back to 1859. On the west wall is fixed a large board containing the following:

"ISAAC WYNCOLL, of Twinstead in the County of Essex Esqr. by his will dated the 1st of March 1681, amongst other things Declares his mind and will to be as Followeth uits; Item my will is, that Such person or persons as for the time being shall enjoy the premises meaning Twinstead Hall, or receive and take the rents and profits thereof shall yearly and every year for ever, Cause to be killed upon the premises at Christmas time in every year, one good bull in good plight and case to be killed upon the premises, and give out all thereof Except the hide, with assistance and derection of the Church wardens and overseers of the poor for the time being of Twinstead aforesaid and the poor people of the sverall parishes of Great Henny, Pebmarsh, Lamarsh and Alphamston, in the Said County of Essex."

This Isaac Wyncoll Charity (or Bull Money) is now administered by the Charity Commission. Instead of a bull being killed, a small sum of money is distributed to the needy at Christmas.

There has never been a shop in the village and with little transport, people in the past were very grateful to old 'Niddles Howard' and his donkey cart. He could neither read nor write, but with various notes and shopping lists tucked into his many pockets, he would shop in Halstead, Sudbury or Earls Colne – always returning with the correct goods and change.

The post came by way of Sudbury, the postman either walked or cycled, starting his delivery in Ballingdon, then on to Henny Street and across the fields to Twinstead, he also brought the newspapers with him. He stayed in the village all day, cooking himself a meal in his small hut on the village green and repairing people's shoes, returning to Sudbury with the afternoon post.

In 1916, a Wagonette took people to Halstead and Sudbury, once a week. Mr Charles Nott had the first car in the village, a Sudebaker in about 1917. Doctor Hinks had the second car, a Hillman convertible in 1927. Today most people in the village own a car, but while there is no bus service, there is a Country Car taking villagers to Halstead and Sudbury once a week.

In 1820, there were 202 people living in the village, the total population is 150, but the number of children under 15 years has decreased greatly, perhaps a worrying feature of the village. The homes are of many, varied styles ranging from small cottages to the large Manor House and Hall. The erstwhile pub, now a private house, not only brewed and sold beer but also supplied the village with pork. In 1830 about one hundred and forty years before Ballington Hall was moved further up the hill in Sudbury, Roses a charming old house which is now a Riding School, was moved on logs pulled by horses, to a better position near the road, where it still stands.

At one time long shallow pits were cut out of the village green, these were then filled with broken chalk brought in from Sudbury and mixed with water, and when dried out, the chalk was cut up and sold for the whitening of houses and other buildings, if cow dung was added preparing this for use it would enable the mixture to stick and also last much longer, without, strangely enough, discolouring it.

The village hall today, found near the Church, used to be the school from 1860–1907. On its closure, the children had to walk to Wickham St Paul's, Pebmarsh or Great Henny, sometimes bowling their hoops to help them on their way and in the summer, stopping to pick the wild fruits in the hedgerows. Unfortunately on wet days, they had to sit in their extremely damp clothes all day. The hall is used for many functions still today, including the annual Guy Fawkes celebrations and a very successful Fuchsia Festival, which brings many people to the village, plus many more social functions.

Wildlife has changed. No longer do we hear partridges; there used to be two or three coveys in every stubble field, with six to ten pairs of hares racing after each other in the Spring. The colonies of rooks – many hundreds would fly in black clouds across the sky, they were nicknamed 'The Doctors'. A well known recipe was breast of rook soaked in milk, also rook pie. It could be said that no house garden was without its trees, apple, greengage, plum, sloe, walnut, cob and hazelnut. Most families kept a pig and it was quite an event in the village when the animal was to be slaughtered by a well known character, Mr Russia Binks, who lived locally.

Ugley

Ugley – call it just plain 'Ugly', not 'Ewjley' as some 'foreigners' do to pronounce it politely!

The varied topography and delightful views from the low hills of the north-west Essex upland encourage groups of ramblers, with companions from neighbouring villages, to explore the delights not just of Ugley but of all the adjoining parishes. The parish makes a long finger near the Herts/Essex border north of Stansted, so that the church is some two miles from the southern hamlet of Ugley Green.

The parish registers date from 1559 to 1812 and the patrons were for many years the Governors of Christ's Hospital, who built a 'new house' in 1722 (now the Old Vicarage). The church is still used, loved and cared for by the parishioners some of whom can recall the flower services of their childhood when the vicar received huge bunches of wild and garden flowers at the altar. These were afterwards taken five miles to hospital – on foot of course. In 1930, the Rev Dr Stewart came to Ugley after being a missionary amoung the Eskimos for 33 years. He could often be found wearing his snow-shoes in and around the vicarage!

The school has gone, joined with the next village, but the school house still stands on the green and, opposite, the village pump where the boys swung over the railings to annoy the 'keeper'.

People who were here during the Second World War saw, and felt, bombs dropping all around the village hall causing much damage; the sky full of planes towing gliders on their way to Arnhem; doodle bugs passing over; and watched Americans collect gravel from the local pit (still active) to build Stansted airport. People expect to be troubled by the extra noise from the enlarged Stansted one and a half miles away. But Ugley is in the 'sound shadow' of the runway and can watch 'silent' planes who scream their way out over Bishop's Stortford or throttle down from Thaxted.

Neither saints nor witches figure in Ugley history, but who would think that from a village of just 400 souls (unchanged in size since 1901) Ugley women could produce such personalities as two Suffragettes, the first and only woman to do the Cresta Run (her injuries led to a ban on women participants!), a young woman international parachutist, and no less than a Deputy Lieutenant of Essex?

But the 'salt of the earth', those born and bred here, who have put their whole working life into the village and who may never travel far from it – they are the ones who keep Ugley beautiful.

Waltham Abbey gatehouse

Waltham Abbey 🦡

In the years immediately before the Second World War the town was much smaller, with a population of about 6,000. Highbridge Street was almost a separate 'village' – it possessed, in addition to the town hall, a county court, a solicitor's offices, a number of fairly large houses (mostly owned by the Government and occupied by officials of the Royal Gunpowder Factory), several public houses, many cottages and shops of all kinds. There were two butcher's shops, two baker's with the delicious smell of hot bread in Mrs Panter's shop, two excellent grocer's with a greengrocer's, several sweet shops, a newsagent's, a fish shop, a pawn-broker's, an estate agent's, a cooked-meat shop (or what we should now call a delicatessen) and an outfitter's owned by a family called Macbeth. This last was a fascinating place occupying three adjacent premises and

231

one went up and down steps between the departments, dodging between racks of garments.

There were two schools – the council school in Quaker Lane and the Leverton School in Paradise Road – and here the majority of the children of the town began their formal education. At Quaker Lane the boys, girls and infants schools were separate, each with its own headteacher, and unless one was fortunate to win a scholarship to a grammar school, the age of 14 saw the end of one's schooldays.

There were very few factories in the town, most local employment being provided by the Royal Gunpowder Factory or its neighbour, the Royal Small Arms Factory at Enfield Lock, or the nurseries which flourished in the Lea valley producing vast quantities of tomatoes and cucumbers.

The town market was held on a Tuesday, as was the cattle market in Romeland, and both could be relied upon to provide plenty of interest and fun. How many people remember the 'Banana King' who sold his fruit from a lorry in the centre of the Market Square – 'A shilling, elevenpence, tenpence, ninepence – who wan' 'im?' – and someone would acquire a large bunch of bananas for a relatively small sum. There were stalls selling biscuits by the pound, and sweet stalls where toffee and humbugs were sometimes made on the spot – not as hygienic, perhaps, as modern wrapped sweets, but they did taste good. The cattle market was always a busy scene with pigs, sheep, calves and lambs in the pens and bullocks tethered to a stout rail which ran along the edge of the pavement to the west of Romeland: in fact, folk who lived there were quite accustomed to opening their front door and finding themselves face to face with a startled bullock! Many of the sheep and cattle were driven to the market from the railway station at Waltham Cross and on one occasion a young steer galloped into a small sweet-shop, the floor of which was down two steps from the pavement outside: it's hard to say which was more frightened, the animal or the owner of the shop.

The May and September fairs were eagerly awaited and provided children with three days of excitement, from the arrival of the wagons and the 'set up' on Thursday to the final (and best) evening on Saturday. By Sunday morning most of the wagons would have gone, the 'pull down' taking place during Saturday night so that the fair would be away from the vicinity of the church by Sunday morning. Stalls were set up in Highbridge Street, from the corner of Romeland to the front of the church (where there was usually some large amusement such as Chair-o-planes or a switchback), and almost blocked Church Street. Fortunately, there was much less traffic then and a good deal of it was horse-drawn, so nobody seemed to mind. Some of the generators which provided power and light for the various amusements used to stand between the old Cock Hotel and the Vicarage, in the cul-de-sac which was then dignified by the name of Park Lane (there was an enamel sign to this effect on the corner of the Cock Hotel).

The sounding of the fire-siren was another excitement, at least for the children. In those days, the fire engine and the Red Cross ambulance were housed at the town hall (or, rather, in part of the same building) and when the siren sounded the volunteer firemen would leave their various jobs and make for the town hall at top speed, some on foot, some on bicycles, and all carrying their helmets and tunics. It was considered almost obligatory for any children who happened to be about to run behind the fire engine to see as much of the action as possible.

There were many ceremonies in the town in the course of a year, notably Empire Day celebrations and the Armistice Day parades. The Lord Lieutenant in his plumed hat would appear on these occasions, together with other notabilities. Funerals were a source of great interest to the children particularly if the hearse and carriages were horse-drawn, the horses being black, of course, and decked with black plumes on their heads. One hearse was so impressive with a great deal of silver about it that it was generally known as 'the cakestand'. Children would line up to watch the arrival and departure of the cortege but they were always very respectful and the boys never failed to remove their caps.

Walton-on-the-Naze 🐚

It seems that all the seaside resorts in Essex have developed as Siamese-twin type communities, where the most affluent residents have at some time established their own enclave a mile or two away along the beach from an original settlement. Certainly this has been the case with Walton-on-the-Naze and Frinton-on-Sea. Visitors today would be hard put to say where the boundary divides Frinton from Walton, and this truly reflects the current cosmopolitan nature of the joint population.

However, it is not long since there existed a fierce pride of identity on both sides of the border which led to many unfair comparisons, indicating that Walton was somewhat inferior to her neighbour. The Waltonians countered such aspersions by claiming that Frinton was a modern upstart when compared to their town's history. There is justification

Walton-on-the-Naze

for such pride of ancestry. Walton was home to some of the earliest men in Britain judging from archaeological finds of flint implements and butchered animal remains recovered from the Naze. Even today holidaymakers may be lucky enough to find flint arrowheads, as they search for prehistoric sharks' teeth or seashells at the base of the Naze cliffs, although no one has unearthed a Bronze Age burial or bones of mammoth and reindeer for some time.

Walton probably supported a community in Roman times; it is thought the septaria used in building Colchester's walls came from Walton and Dovercourt cliffs. The name Walton-le-Soken is Saxon in origin, being the 'ton' (place) of the 'Walsh' – the old folk, the indigenous Celtic race displaced by the Germanic and later Scandinavian invaders. The Soken villages were an estate, referred to as Eadwulfsness in the Domesday survey, which was not subject to the local authority of St Osyth Priory, but took its orders directly from the Bishop of London at St Paul's Abbey. Thus residents of Walton, Kirby and Thorpe could boast of rights and privileges not shared by the rest of the Tendring Hundred. The name was changed to Walton-on-the-Naze to suit the expansion in the 19th century.

Many reviews of Walton have described it as a small fishing community, but it is unlikely that fishing ever formed a major part of its industry; although, as now, it probably always supported a few professional and a great many part time fishermen hooping for lobsters and long lining for cod, together with seasonal trips for sprats and herring. Its main employment would have been agricultural and its market and fair attracted visitors from far afield. Four other sources of income succeeded one another to boost local trade. In the 17th century the collecting of septaria, lumps of calcined limestone, from the beach and trawled from the seabed to make Roman cement for building, was a regular occupation. When Kentish Portland Cement quarries made this unprofitable, the beachcombers turned to copperas, petrified twigs, used in tanning and ink manufacture for additional income; this continued until the middle of the 19th century, by which time tourism was well established.

Then came Warner's iron foundry which employed the town's labour force until 1921 when it closed as a result of industrial action; it reopened just before the Second World War and continued to cast items such as piano frames until it finally closed down ten years ago.

Tourism came to Walton in the wake of the Prince Regent's promotion

235

of sea bathing at Brighton. The 1820s saw the first expansion of Walton as a seaside resort and subsequent development during the rest of the century kept alive the oft repeated description of Walton as 'an up and coming seaside resort' – which in fact never quite made it! Today it is still small and quaint, unlike the extensive sprawl of terraced villas found in most established Victorian resorts.

During the first 50 years as a resort, the visitors were upper class families, who moved in for the summer season, taking over houses and bringing their entire entourage with them. A number of large buildings of good quality were constructed to house these households. They can be seen in an obscure Constable sketch showing Walton seafront with its first diminutive pier in the 1830s and also in a better known painting by Ford Madox Brown, showing the town in the 1850s when several of the Pre-Raphaelite artists came to stay in Station Street.

In 1867 the railway joined Walton to London and this was followed by the 1872 National Bank Holiday Act; together they promoted the arrival of vast numbers of common folk who invaded Walton and entirely changed the pattern of its development. For the last hundred years the town has sought to attract the average working family to come to Walton for its summer holiday, to spend time on the beach, to enjoy the entertainments on the pier and to spend money in the town. Over the years many people have made it their regular annual holiday and have often moved here on retirement, thereby giving a base for succeeding generations to discover the town. Between the wars a number of families became so regular they formed the Walton Summer Visitors Association which organised beach activities, variety shows in the town theatre and mid-winter dinner dances in London.

Peripheral to the promotion of the beach have been the added leisure pursuits of golfing on the Naze, until the club's demise at the outbreak of the Second World War, the water sports of yachting, wild fowling and sea fishing associated with the Backwaters, and generally using the town as a base for walking, bird watching and touring this interesting part of East Anglia.

Weeley 🐝

Weeley is on the railway line from Colchester to Walton. It has its own railway station, which was built when the line first opened in 1866.

The village is known to many people because of Weeley Hall Wood.

This is one of the largest ancient woodlands in the county. It belongs to the Essex Wildlife Trust and is normally open only to members of the Trust. There is no public right of way across the farmland to the wood. However, during the first weekend of May each year, the Trust opens it to the public, so that they may enjoy the sight of the carpet of bluebells which covers almost half the area of the wood. Deer, foxes, badgers and many small mammals are known to be present. It is not known how old the wood is, but it is at least possible that part of the present wood could have survived from the virgin forest which once covered much of the Tendring peninsula.

The church stands in open farmland near to Weeley Hall Wood, dedicated to St Andrew. Although the main part of the church building is comparatively recent, having been rebuilt in 1881, the tower is thought to have been built in about 1512. For a building nearly 500 years old, it is in remarkably good condition. Its builders obviously intended it to last and the walls of the tower, at ground level, are five ft thick.

The village is proud to have its own church school. The oldest part of the school dates from 1867, but many additions have been made to the original building. The village also has its own village hall. This was built in 1987 and replaced the old hall which had been in use since 1921. The old hall consisted mainly of two old ex-army huts from the First World War.

Near the station is the Weeley Bridge Caravan Park. This has been in existence for about 20 years, and for the last six years it has been owned by Compass Leisure. It comprises mainly residential caravans, but also caters for a small number of tourist caravans. Many people from London find the setting ideal for a quiet holiday away from the pressure and bustle of the town. During the summer residents are provided with all the necessary facilities, including shops, social club etc.

Weeley has for many years been a farming community. In early times it was mainly arable, but today it is more mixed, with cattle, sheep and pigs. The Tendring District Council has its offices in the village. There is also a local fire station, ambulance station and crematorium.

Many people who do not know the village have had dealings with Honey Pot Farm from which Ken Muir supplies his famous strawberry plants, and other garden requisites, all over the country.

Wendens Ambo

Wendens Ambo is one of many little villages surrounding the market town of Saffron Walden in the north-west corner of Essex. Despite its small size, with a population of only about 360 people, it has a very long history. Originally there were two villages, Wenden Magna and Wenden Parva. They were both mentioned in the Domesday Book of 1086, when the population of Great Wenden was given as some 95 people and that of Little Wenden approximately 45 people.

Little Wenden church disappeared before the end of the 17th century. Great Wenden church was extended in the 13th century, when the south aisle was added and the chancel completely rebuilt, no doubt to accommodate the increasing population. A further extension was made early in the 14th century by adding a north aisle, and columns were inserted to support the roof. Further alterations were made in later centuries, but a harmony was kept by using only local materials, polled flints and chalk stone. One interesting feature, however, is the Norman door in the tower which has a round-headed arch of Roman bricks that were taken from the remains of a Roman villa about half a mile to the south-west.

The name, Wenden, came from Saxon times and meant a 'winding valley'. The Saxon settlers must have been attracted to the fertile valley, with a clear stream of water, and protected by the surrounding chalk hills. This was when the two Wenden villages originated. In 1956, when a trench was dug for the foundations of a new house, a complete pot of late Saxon St Neots ware was found, together with two post holes that suggested the wall of a building. Other buildings may come to light if further research is ever undertaken. The Saxon pot, known as 'the crockern', was later donated to the church, where it is on view in a glass case.

Going back further in time, it is known that there was a Bronze Age settlement (6000–3000 BC) in the valley, as flint tools from this era have been found, and also the remains of an Iron Age settlement of the period 300–200 BC that showed the outlines of round houses, drainage gulleys, grain pits and areas for the slaughter of animals. Later more substantial barns appeared, and when the Roman villa was built nearby a roadway was made between. Unfortunately, the site of the Roman villa is now covered by the M11 motorway, built 1977–79, which runs through the west side of the village.

In 1662 the two parishes of Little and Great Wenden were formally

238

united and became Wendens Ambo, 'Ambo' being Latin for 'both'. The vicarage of Little Wenden was retained, together with the church of Great Wenden. The other church and vicarage have since disappeared.

In the early 18th century the prosperity of the Earls of Suffolk declined, and in 1721 it was decided to demolish the greater part of nearby Audley End House, as the cost of upkeep was so enormous. The back of the central court is all that remains of the house today. The Audley End estate was divided in 1753, and the smaller part that included Wendens Ambo went to the Earl of Bristol. He remained until 1810 when his estates in Wenden and elsewhere were sold to the second Lord Braybrooke who, by this time, had already succeeded to the rest of the estate which had been partitioned in 1753. The Audley End estates thus controlled the most important part of Wenden, but not all, as the rest of the parish south of the stream was privately owned.

In 1844/45 a railway line was built from Bishop's Stortford to Cambridge, passing through the east side of Wendens Ambo and the Audley End estates. The local station, built on land purchased from Lord Braybrooke, was appropriately named 'Wenden', but only for three years, as on 1st November 1848 it was changed to 'Audley End'. In the village a row of cottages was specially built near the station for the railway workers. Though the train service was poor at first, this improved when the Eastern Counties Railway was absorbed into the Great Eastern Railway in 1862. Pressure from local interests in Saffron Walden led to the creation of the Saffron Walden Railway Company and the building of a line from Audley End station to Bartlow, passing through the town. During excavations necessitated by the building of a bridge over the river Cam, 16 ft down the workmen found an astonishing quantity of bones, mostly of animals, including a horn from the now extinct Great or Irish Elk, somewhere between 4,000 and 7,000 years old, and also a human skull, probably female, of the same period, thus linking Wendens Ambo to the Stone Age!

The population grew during the first half of the 19th century from around 270 to the highest figure recorded at any time, 421, in 1851, the year of the first census following the arrival of the railway in Wenden. This was due to the influx of railway workers from distant places, and in consequence there were many marriages to local girls. Between 1804 and 1870 some 70 boys from Wenden attended Newport Grammar School, when members of the local Robinson family were trustees of that school. There was no other education for the children, except for the Sunday school which taught reading and writing in addition to religious

239

instruction. A brick building was erected for this purpose on The Croat, an open space near the church, in 1838, and it is still in use today as the village hall. The village did not get a proper school until 1881, when there were a total of 73 pupils. The school survived until after the Second World War, having coped with an influx of evacuees during the latter.

The residents are keen to preserve the rural character of the village, and many objected when some light industries were set up in new buildings near the station and hope that this development will not grow too large. In 1979 a committee of local residents was able to purchase a pig field in the centre of the village near the church from the ninth Lord Braybrooke, as the result of many fund-raising efforts, to be the village green and recreation area for the children. There is also a flourishing cricket club, and many other village organisations, such as the Wendens Ambo Society, and the local Women's Institute.

West & East Horndon

The easiest way to approach West and East Horndon is along the Southend Road from London. After the junction of the M25 the countryside takes on a rural look, with hills rising as high as 100 metres on one's left, covered in trees and here and there arable fields, while on one's right is fenland of London clay. There are several streams running down from these heights into the Mardyke which drains the fens out to the Thames at Purfleet. There was a time when it was planned to make the Mardyke into a canal but it was never brought to fruition.

Originally there were three manors in the area of West Horndon, Tillingham Hall being the one which had most of the land in its borders. In 1066 Alwin, a free woman held it, but by 1086 it had passed to Swain of Essex in the Hundred of Barstable. Following this the Tillingham family held the Hall for several hundred years. It was eventually sold to Sir William Bawd, who conveyed it to Cogglesham Abbey, where it remained until the Dissolution of the Monasteries. It is thought that the Abbey began to restrict the rights of the commons, for there were many proceedings in the manor courts against the ordinary people, supposedly trespassing on the land of the lords. After they acquired the commonland it was mostly left as wild heath and woods, much as we see it today, the later lords of the manor having much pleasure hunting to hounds through it, even as far as Southend.

One cannot miss the church of All Saints standing on rising ground above East Horndon at the junction of the London/Southend road and the Brentwood/Tilbury road. The church is built almost entirely of brick, the present one being the third on the site. The village of Torinduna (Thornhill) referred to in the Domesday survey was around this hill. The Saxon church was built around AD 807, then rebuilt in the Norman style by the Neville family about 1200.

There were two manors in East Horndon, Heron on the north of the church, and Abbots on the south. By the 14th century the Tyrells of Herongate had been gaining influence, and became the patrons of the church. This family demolished most of the Norman church, rebuilding it in the present style. The chancel and south transept are late 15th century. There is a splendid limestone figure of Alice, wife of Sir John Tyrell, flanked by her children, all named. The south and north chapels were built for the interments of the family. Climb the stairs to enter the south gallery – a pleasant living room for the chantry priest in pre-Reformation times, even a Tudor fireplace. Outside this attractive building is a squat tower with distinctive corner turrets, and a stepped parapet.

Two legends persist about the church. One tells of Sir James Tyrell who went to slay a dragon and died. It appears that he had been asked to kill a serpent-type animal, which escaped from a ship in the Thames and roamed the woods round the manor of Herongate and the church, terrifying the people. He managed to slay it, chopping off its head, but he died from his exertions. His son, looking for him, trod on a bone of the animal and, gangrene setting in, he lost his leg. There is a glass window at Heron depicting a one-legged man. The second legend is that Queen Anne Boleyn's head or heart is buried there.

Below, on the south of the church, East Horndon is reduced to the original old road to Herongate, winding up the hill, two restaurants and two houses. Crossing the road bridge to the other side and turning back the way we have come, we find the old road running off towards the Thames, and in its angle is East Horndon Hall, the old manor of Abbots. There is reputed to have been a tunnel from the Hall to the church across the present Southend road.

Thorndon Avenue is a long straight road leading to the heart of the modern village of West Horndon. Half way down is the junior school with playing fields at the back, and opposite is the modern church of St Francis with its lively congregation. If we continue we reach a double-storeyed building, with grass and a car park, which is the village hall, built around 1961. Outside are the shops and a garage. This is the centre of the village. If you wish to find the station built in 1886 on the London

241

to Southend line, pass the new housing estates and the restaurant, reaching the Railway Hotel which was once a coaching inn, and behind is the station, with trains every half hour.

Opposite the station gates is an industrial estate where many people work, not all from the village. This is not the old type of village with sheep and farmworkers but the modern type with commuters catching trains morning and evening, but it is also a quiet place one can retire to, away from the rush of the city.

Wickham Bishops ✣

There can be hardly a field in Wickham Bishops without its own special name. It is not easy to learn much about these names. Some, like Matthew's Etch, Turner's and Collins are derived from the name of some owner or copyholder. Some are descriptive, such as Humpy Meadow, Thorney-hedgepiece, and Heathpiece.

Chalk field near the new rectory, may have been a central dumping ground for chalk fetched by waggons from Maldon quay for use on the farms. Pond field in the Church Road near Heathgate was almost certainly the village Pound.

References to people bearing the names Littlehaze (Likely) and Spark haze (Sparkey) have been found in the 14th century manor court rolls and in these also are recorded many of the field names which are still in use today.

Those who use Handley's Lane will take pleasure in the thought that their ancestors also experienced its peculiar delights for Mr. Grimes' Orchard bore the apt title of Plain Slough.

But who was Loblolly, and who named the Rainbow Field?

Wickham St Paul ✣

The small attractive rural village of Wickham St Paul is situated on the north Essex/Suffolk border, between the two nearby market towns of Halstead (Essex) and Sudbury (Suffolk). It is often misspelled as Wickham St Paul's, and has been described as a 'blink and you'll miss it' kind of place due to its size – in fact it has been known for visitors to bypass it completely!

The village name was derived from its connection with the Dean and

Chapter of St Paul's, dating back to the 11th century. The main and obvious attraction, and pride, is the large village green. This is well cared for and well loved by residents and visitors alike, though the sheep, horses and cows which once grazed it are long gone. Cricket is still played on the green, and it is hoped that football will be resumed again soon, as well as the various fetes that were until recently a regular attraction. Past jubilees and similar events have also been celebrated on the green.

Until a few years ago the village schoolchildren would also have been seen on the green. The children from Wickham and the adjoining village of Twinsland were taught at the village school, which though small in size had great character. Unfortunately character and charm were not enough and now the school is a private house.

Situated just outside the main part of the village is the small but attractive church of All Saints. The earliest part was built in the 12th century, with additions in the 14th and 16th centuries, and it was restored in the 19th century. There is a bell tower and bell ringing practice is held weekly. There is also some pretty stained glass in the main building. The churchyard is kept in good condition and the Parochial Church Council organises a voluntary 'clean-up' annually. The church is used by the community for ventures such as flower festivals and exhibitions, and during the music festivals the church is usually full.

There used to be a shop, which was a boon to villagers. Unfortunately, probably due to the size of the village, it had to close. The shop is much missed, especially during winter months, as it was a general store selling everything from eggs to bootlaces. Anything you needed that was not stocked was 'got in specially'. The shop was also renowned for being the place to go for any gossip – a true village pastime! Since the closure at least one enterprising villager has applied to open a shop, but permission has not been forthcoming. Near the village is a pick-your-own fruit orchard, run by the Spenser family, which is well known locally.

The village hall is close to the green and though comparatively new does not look out of place with the rest of the central village. The post office is also run from there. One of the other favourite places in the village is the public house. Properly titled the Victory Inn, it is known to locals as 'The Ship'.

Wickham St Paul is a farming community, though only three are now proper, working farms. There are still many small cottages and even the modern houses do not look out of place. The broad country accent still remains, as does the image of distinctive country characters. Community spirit is one of the main aspects of village life, and it is certainly alive in Wickham St Paul.

Widdington 🌿

The village of Widdington has been described as 'the biggest cul de sac in Essex'. Situated between Saffron Walden and Stanstead, the road into Widdington really only serves the village. The river Cam flows between Widdington and the main road, the B1383.

It was thought the Romans passed it by, but during a survey on Priors Hall by English Heritage some Roman tiles were found. This find does not prove Priors Hall to be a Roman site as the tiles may have been brought from another area, but English Heritage did establish Priors Hall is Saxon, not Norman as previously thought. Priors Hall is a private house. Priors Hall Barn is definitely Norman, and can be viewed by the public, as the barn is managed by English Heritage.

There are a number of other Halls in the village – Widdington, Thistley, Amberden, Swaynes, Mole, all going back many centuries. Amberden Hall open their garden to the public one Sunday during the summer for the Gardeners Benevolent Society. Many visitors come to see the garden, and enjoy a cream tea organised by the local Women's Institute.

Mole Hall is very old and still has a moat around it. The grounds are a Wild Life Park, where hundreds of visitors come each summer. Many are children from London who delight in the animals and butterflies.

Widdington has plenty of wild life of its own. If you are lucky you may see a pack of deer roaming across the fields, or hares playing and even a fox crossing the road. Owls can be heard at night, and kestrels hover by day. Some landowners have made wild flower meadows, and with the flowers come the butterflies.

The village is surrounded by many footpaths with lovely names: Moon Lane, Jock Lane, Green Croft Lane, Samsons Lane, Beetle Lane, America Brook. The large open fields also have fascinating names: Jingling Baulk, Little Hartley, Big Hartley, Small Pieces, March Field, Four Acres. Two fields are called the Americas as they are supposed to look like America in shape. Many of these field names are mentioned in the court rolls and rentals of Queen Elizabeth I.

Within living memory there were some ten working farms, each farm employing an average of ten workers. Today only two farms are worked with a workforce of five between them. The old farm houses are now private homes, so there are no sad derelict sites. The workers today commute to London or to the towns nearby.

The church of St Mary was reopened in 1873 after much restoration. It is on the original site of the first church built in the 12th century. Although there is only a small congregation it is a much loved church and well cared for, with many items of interest for church historians.

The village hall consists of two halls, one old, one new. The old hall, still called by some residents 'The Hut', was an army hut purchased in 1916 from a site in Debden. The hall is much used by the village as a meeting place for local organisations.

The village school closed in 1965 and the United Reformed chapel in 1990. Both were demolished and houses built on the sites. There are several thriving businesses, a car repair service, an antique shop in a converted barn, televised for the series *Lovejoy*, several builders and decorators, a dressmaker and carpenter, and stained glass windows and lampshades are made in the village. As the traditional skills of the blacksmith, baker etc have gone, so other skills have come to take their place.

Widford

Widford was originally called Wedeford. The Clovil family cleared the forests and built a house at Highlands, the village growing up in this area. One hundred years ago the village had a life of its own. Under the patronage of Arthur Pryor, who lived at 'Hylands' from 1858 to 1904, it received a new church building at St Mary's in 1862, its own school building in 1867 and even a railway station in 1882, although this took the form of a siding for railway coaches reserved especially for visitors and guests at Hylands.

Today Widford is incorporated in the Borough of Chelmsford and has lost some of its character and old buildings, such as the post office and shop, and the only Silent Woman in Essex. The latter was a public house on the old main road opposite the White Horse. The original pub sign showing a picture of a woman with her head cut off is now in the Chelmsford and Essex Museum in Oaklands Park.

There are still two inns left. The old coaching inn, the White Horse, has been reopened recently after standing empty for over a year, and in the village street beside the village hall stands the Sir Evelyn Wood. This is another unique pub sign which pays tribute to the Essex celebrity of that name who was born in the vicarage in Cressing in 1838 and became a great military hero in Victorian times. Large crowds gathered at the Shire Hall, Chelmsford, when he was presented with a Sword of Honour on the 14th October 1879, and again in 1903 when he received the Freedom of the Borough in recognition of his promotion to Field Marshal. He died at Harlow in 1919 at the age of 71 years.

The new Princes Road (until recent the A12) was opened by the Duke of Kent in 1930 near the Chelmsford Wood Street roundabout; this was later joined by another road constructed to bypass the village. This in effect destroyed the rural atmosphere of the village; many of the cottages were pulled down to make way for modern houses.

The village may now be part of the Borough but there is the well known private school with its famous boys choir, to carry on the name, and Widford WI intends to make sure the history of the village is not forgotten.

Witham 🎋

St Nicholas, the parish church of Witham is situated on Chipping Hill which is the oldest part of the town and was built in the 14th century. The church is probably the oldest building and this part was the original town centre. It still retains some of its early character with the green and forge and the river Brain running under the hump backed bridge. In the reign of Queen Elizabeth I cloth manufacturers fled to England from Holland and some settled in Witham. This fact is preserved in the name of the Woolpack Inn not far from the church, and in this area there are still some timber framed and plastered houses. The cloth industry was very important to Witham. The weavers lived mainly in the town and the spinners in the surrounding villages. Several 'clothiers' were very success-ful and one of the most prosperous was Henry Barwell who built 'The Grove' which sadly was finally demolished in 1932. By the early part of the 18th century the cloth industry was on the decline but it did not cease altogether until Essex was cut off from its chief markets in Portugal and Spain during the Napoleonic wars.

After this farming was the main industry and because of the nearness to London, it made food production worthwhile. Prosperity continued and Witham was home to several small industries apart from the large flour mills. There were water mills at Chipping Hill and Guithavon Valley and several breweries and maltings. Again because of its advantageous position coachbuilders and smithies flourished as did also the wheelwrights and saddlers. For the innkeepers it was a very prosperous time. The population of London was growing and the road between the capital and Colchester was improved greatly. In 1717 stage coaches ran from London to Harwich twice weekly but by 1755 there was a daily service. The Spread Eagle, The White Hart and Blue Post were some of the many inns used as stopping places.

Even in the mid 1750s there were a number of retail shops, two lawyers and an estate agent. By this time Witham was considered one of the social centres. Witham Parish government looked after the needy providing money for medical and nursing care and paid funeral expenses.

By the 19th century schools were being set up, drains laid and the town generally modernised. It was in the middle of this century that the gas works and tannery in Mill Lane were built.

The coaching trade began to decline with the advent of the railways, but this proved to be an important factor in Witham's selection as an 'overspill' in 1965. Easy access to the London and east coast ports by road, together with convenient rail link to the metropolis proved once again that the town was in a very strategic position.

Crittalls metal window factory was built in the 1920s providing the town with its first major place of employment. Houses were built to cater for the rising population which reached 9,000. After that no big new development took place until 1965 when Templars Estate was built. The Freebourne's industrial estate was built on land adjacent to the A12 and a wide sphere of factories was built to bring employment to the populace from London and the local inhabitants.

Old local residents have many memories. During the First World War the lists of those killed and missing were posted outside the old Post Office which is where Coopers is today. The Second World War brought bombs on Crittalls when local inhabitants were so amazed that some ladies thought the plane was dropping a string of sausages. One house at least was demolished and the railway line was a prime target. Those who were not in the forces worked in munition factories and the old police station which was situated at the bottom of Guithavon Street was an A.R.P. post. This was manned 24 hours a day, the night shift starting at 10.00 p.m. with four hours on duty and four hours resting which was not always easy as sleeping in a cold prison cell is not exactly conducive to sleep!

Near the Swan public house was the fire station and there was great excitement when the first motor engine was purchased in 1930. Previous to this Witham had a steam fire engine and a horse drawn vehicle both of which were used to quell the fire at the old constitutional club which was in Newland Street in front of the church which is now the United Reform church.

Next to the church was an ironmongers in whose large windows china was displayed. Next to this was a second hand shop which also operated as a pawn brokers, then the post office and a haberdashery where instead of a farthing change one was given a paper of dressmaker's pins or little gold safety pins. There was also a wine and spirit merchant, newsagents, cabinet maker, men's tailor and outfitters, three bakeries and a cycle shop at the corner of Collingwood Road in addition to two others lower down in the town. Many of these shops were typical of the establishment found in many provincial towns and although some still remain many were demolished when the shopping area was expanded in the mid 1960s.

In recent years even the old Co-operative grocery store has closed although there has been one in the town since 1887 (though not on the original site). The International and Home and Colonial survived for many years and the old butter shop opposite Coates at the end of the town existed until the early 1960s.

The national school was in Guithavon Street and was opened in 1842. 100 boy pupils were educated separately from the 100 girls and there were about 90 infants. Until the early 1920s slates were used until pen, pencil and paper came into use. The school was next to All Saints Church where all the pupils attended a service on All Saints Day, the 1st November, and flowers were put on the graves. May Day was always celebrated with a dance round the maypole erected in the playground. Going round one way was always successful but unwinding it when skipping in the opposite direction inevitably finished up in a muddle. Empire Day, the 24th May was also an important date in the school year with Britannia in helmet and full regalia and the children singing 'Land of Hope and Glory'.

Witham has come a long way since it was listed in the Domesday Book of 1086 as having 60 inhabitants, to the town of 25,000 occupants as it is today. Still expanding but plenty of organisations and societies to cater for the young and those of a more interesting age.

Wix 🐟

Wix is a small village on the old road from Colchester to Harwich. It now has about 220 houses and 680 residents. The houses range in age from those of the 16th or 17th centuries to those built within the last few years.

The centre of Wix is fairly compact. It has 2 public houses, The Waggon at Wix at the cross-roads and the White Hart by the War Memorial. There are also 2 shops, one of which houses the Post Office, 2 garages, a school, a Methodist Chapel and the Parish Church of St Mary. The present school was opened in 1931, taking over the education of the children that was previously provided by Church schools. In 1975 the village school at neighbouring Wrabness closed and the children from there are now bussed to Wix. The school roll has shown great variations over the years, and now, in 1991, it stands at 63, with approximately equal numbers from the two villages.

The main business in the village is Anglian Timber. This woodyard was started in 1837 by Edward Paskell and the ownership passed from father to son until it came under the control of Roger Paskell who was a well-known authority on timber and who travelled far and wide to find suitable trees. He was also known to be a helpful source of specialist needs such as the special shovels required for the maltings at Mistley. One noted employee of the firm was a venerable character called William Wilberforce Wake – a highly skilled wheelwright who could saw up a complete trunk of a tree by hand over a sawpit. The trunk was brought into the yard on a 'timber jim' drawn by large cart horses hired from local farmers for that express purpose. The wood was sawn into the necessary shaped timbers to construct a complete farm waggon, including wheels. This man was probably the last wheelwright in Essex capable of doing this.

Across the road from the woodyard was the village forge which supplied the iron bands for the wheels and other iron fitments to complete the carts. Another off-shoot from the wood-yard was an undertaking business as, of course, there was a ready source of wood for the coffins. On the death of Roger in 1980 the woodyard was sold to Anglian Timber and the nature of the business has changed. The firm now mostly deals in soft wood for the construction industry. The undertaking business has moved to Manningtree, but still trades under the name of Paskell and Son.

In the days prior to the Second World War the roads were quiet enough for children to play on, bowling the iron hoops that were made for them at the forge – and this in spite of the fact that the village was on the main road to Harwich. After the war, however, traffic increased to such an extent that the Waggon at the cross-roads was constantly being damaged by the heavy lorries. Everyone was greatly relieved when the by-pass was eventually opened in 1973.

The history of Wix goes back a long way as it was mentioned in the Domesday Book. At that time the land was owned by Edith, queen of Edward the Confessor, and she gave it to Walter the Deacon whose children in turn gave it for the foundation of Priory for Benedictine Nuns. It was suppressed in the time of Henry VIII when he ordered the Dissolution of the Monastries. From then on the church was allowed to deteriorate. It is probable that materials from the Abbey were used to build the Abbey Farmhouse. The church itself was renovated about 1740 and again in 1888. Of the two bells, one hangs in a little turret on the church itself, and this is used to call the faithful to services, while the other, known as the Danyell Bell, is thought to have been made about 1460 by the bell-founder John Danyell and is contained in a bell-cage in the churchyard. Up to about 30 years ago this bell was always tolled for funerals, but now it remains silent.

Woodham Ferrers ✍

Woodham Ferrers, situated some nine miles south-east of Chelmsford, is a linear village along a highway, running from north to south.

The southern end is the bottom of Town Hill, where the village sign is located. This is the junction of Workhouse Lane (or Moss's Lane or Ilgars Lane, so called as it leads to one of the ancient manors of the parish called Ilgars) on the left and Edwins Hall Lane on the right. At the moment the area is known as Happy Valley, which is a bit incongruous as the cottages on the left stand on the site of the old workhouse. Behind is Mill Hill, another misnomer as a mill has never stood upon it, nor is it the burial ground of plague victims as some people think. It would indeed take an incredible amount of bodies to make a hill that big!

Edwins Hall Lane leads, naturally, to Edwins Hall. Originally it was Edwards Manor but was renamed after Edwin Sandys, Archbishop of York 1576–1588, who lived there for a time with his wife Cicelie whose fine memorial is in St Mary's church in the village. Before becoming

Archbishop, Bishop Sandys was a strong supporter of Lady Jane Grey (a member of the Ferrers family), the 'Queen of Nine Days', and was one of the very few of her supporters to escape with his head. Edwin Sandys is buried in Southwell Minster in Nottinghamshire, where he lived while Archbishop. Edwins Hall is a fine moated Tudor house, said to be haunted, and today only about a third of the original dwelling is standing.

Walking up Town Hill, you can see the small spire of St Mary's church and to the left of this a very large Victorian residence which used to be the rectory and is now a home for the elderly called Eastham. The Rev C P Plumptree built this 'new' rectory in the 19th century to house his very large family as the old rectory was too small.

St Mary's church is built on an old Saxon site in the most elevated position in the village. It was built by Robert de Ferrers in the reign of Henry II, using local materials, mainly pebble, ragstone, flint and fragments of brick. In 1703 the tower collapsed and was rebuilt on a smaller scale in 1715, but again by 1774 this was unsafe and so in 1793 a small wooden belfry was built to house the one remaining bell.

At the entrance to the churchyard is the war memorial. This used to be situated near the Bell car park on the opposite side of the road but was moved between the wars to its present site. It has the distinction of listing all those villagers who served in the First World War and not just those who died.

If you walk up the hill past the old cottages and the village shop and post office, on the right is the Bell pub, the only one in the village nowadays. Next door to that is the old post office which closed only a few years ago. Next to Pegram's shop is Forge House, obviously the site of the village smithy, and next to that is the old rectory. This is reputedly haunted by an old lady both in the house and walking towards the church.

The road divides just here, with the older original road to the right, called The Street. Here used to be sited the Eagle pub (where Eagle House now stands) and opposite was the wheelwright's shop. Further along on the right is the Peacock Bakery where, in the evening, wafts the smell of newly baked bread. Woodham Ferrers used to be a small town with a market, and there were probably many shops in this area around The Street.

If you join the main road again, you will pass St Mary's school built in the 1960s to replace an old Victorian one, and Birketts Hall, which is a farm and riding establishment. Farther along on the right is the

251

Congregational church built in 1884 to replace an earlier church in which was housed the village school, opened in 1845. Opposite is a row of timber-framed cottages. The one next to the church car park used to be a beerhouse called the Labourer's Friend and was also at one time a pork butcher's shop. The pigs in the village were all slaughtered here in the backyard.

On the corner of Crows Lane used to stand Wantz Farm, an old clapperboard farmhouse which was demolished in 1965. This whole area is called Woodham Wantz – 'wantz' is an old word meaning crossroads. Set back on the left is Dyers Farm, an old timber-framed house. Here also on the left on the corner of Lodge Road stood the Butcher's Arms, now long gone to be replaced by a new house. Lodge Road used to be a private gated road leading to Woodham Lodge, an interesting timber-framed house with Georgian additions.

The last building of note in the village is Woodham Hall, a farmhouse. This is one of the old manors of Woodham Ferrers and the present house, dated about 1800, replaced a much earlier timber moated dwelling to the east of the present farmhouse. The moat still remains and the foundations of a bridge over the water have also been found.

Index

253

Saffron Walden castle ruins